BEYOND THE QUR'ĀN

BEYOND THE QUR'ĀN

Early Ismāʿīlī Ta'wīl and the Secrets of the Prophets

DAVID HOLLENBERG

THE UNIVERSITY OF SOUTH CAROLINA PRESS

Published by the University of South Carolina Press
Columbia, South Carolina 29208

www.sc.edu/uscpress

Manufactured in the United States of America

24 23 22 21 20 19 18 17 16
10 9 8 7 6 5 4 3 2 1

Library of Congress Cataloging-in-Publication Data
can be found at http://catalog.loc.gov/.

ISBN: 978-1-61117-678-0 (cloth)
ISBN: 978-1-61117-679-7 (ebook)

This book was printed on a recycled paper with
30 percent postconsumer waste content.

CONTENTS

PREFACE

Ismāʿīlism, one of the three major branches of Shīʿism, is best known for *taʾwīl,* an allegorizing scriptural exegesis. Using taʾwīl, Ismāʿīlī missionaries claimed to derive secret, hidden truths behind the Qurʾān's exterior sense. While scholars have long mined Ismāʿīlī taʾwīl as a source for Ismāʿīlī doctrine, surprisingly few articles have been dedicated to the genre and practice with which Ismāʿīlism is closely associated.[1] Focusing on the mission from its rise in the mid-ninth century through the reign of the Fāṭimid Caliph al-Muʿizz li-dīn Allāh (d. 975), this book addresses this lacuna.

The bulk of early Ismāʿīlī taʾwīl that is extant was composed by missionaries during the late ninth and tenth centuries. Taʾwīl was the vehicle through which salvific knowledge was disseminated. According to the sources, this knowledge flowed from God, through the rightly guided Imāms, to the missionaries. This saving knowledge transformed the initiate, binding him to the "call" (*daʿwa*) on behalf of the rightly guided Imām who would rule the world with justice just as it is now beset with tyranny. The daʿwa was both a call on behalf of the Imām and a term for the organization who worked on his behalf. Taʾwīl bound the believers to the daʿwa by training them in an entirely new way of reading (in the broad sense of the word, as "interpreting"). The habits of mind inspired by this rearing bound the believers together and differentiated them from those outside the movement.

Working in small secret groups in conjunction with a larger movement, missionaries at the beginning of the movement in the late ninth century used taʾwīl to sow the mission among the semiliterate populations in agricultural regions such as the Yemeni highlands, the Caspian Sea region in northwest Iran, the Berber mountain territories in North Africa, and the Sawād (agricultural region) of Kufa. Missionaries taught converts that there was a secret sense behind passages of the Qurʾān, ritual, tradition, and *realia.* Read properly, underlying all these objects of interpretation are patterns of *ḥaqāʾiq* (eternal truths), archetypes of reality in its pure, unmediated form. These ḥaqāʾiq are manifest in their purest form in the Fāṭimid mission itself, the hierarchy from the Imām to the missionary, to the new acolyte.

Acquisition of this saving knowledge through taʾwīl entailed, then, more than different interpretations of particular Qurʾānic verses. It was an entirely new mode of interpretation. Through the prism of daʿwa knowledge, the entire world could be viewed in its divinely ordered patterns and forms. In the sources the believer's gradual acquisition of this gnosis is referred to as "rearing" (*tarbiya*).

This notion of being "reared" in knowledge is one of many life-cycle metaphors that recur in taʾwīl. The initiate's taking the oath of allegiance to join the mission is referred to as "birth" (*tawallud*) or "creation" (*fiṭra*). The believer is spiritually "circumcised" when he learns the identity of the Imām of the age. He is "suckled" in this secret knowledge and gradually ascends through the ranks of the mission. Eventually he "learns to speak," that is, he has sufficiently internalized the language of the mission to become a missionary with the capacity to proselytize others. Warnings against transgressing one's proper rank in the daʿwa hierarchy are also expressed in these life-cycle terms. In his treatise *Taʾwīl sūrat al-nisāʾ* (Interpretation of the Qurʾānic Chapter "Women"), Jaʿfar ibn Manṣūr al-Yaman interprets Qurʾān 4:23, a verse in which God prohibits a man from marrying various classes of relatives (mothers, daughters, sisters, and nieces), to refer to missionaries' improper disclosure of knowledge that they are not yet entitled to access or disclose.[2]

The extended life-cycle allegory—from birth, to maturity, to heavenly reward—implies a complete transformation, but one that requires many steps. The saving knowledge on which the acolyte is weaned is disseminated gradually. As we learn from anecdotes within Ismāʿīlī literature, the strategy of revealing and concealing knowledge according to rank was meant to produce a particular affect: the experience of epiphany or anagnorisis, the sense that the veil of ignorance has been lifted.[3] For the Ismāʿīlī believer, it was not acquisition or mastery of the secret knowledge alone that was crucial; it was the awareness of a vast imaginal world of transcendent noumena glimpsed only in fragments, and to which the believer currently had but limited access.[4] A dynamic of concealment—even from the "believers" who had formally joined the movement—was conducive to maintaining the sense of continual anagnorisis, of recognition that one was continually at the beginning of an ever-widening vista.

Taʾwīl's form and style facilitated this experience of epiphany. Ismāʿīlī taʾwīl's two most prominent stylistic techniques are, first, its broad and unconventional range of objects of interpretation, and second, its view of them as components of a small number of schema and themes. Decontextualized and emptied of their original intellectual content, familiar Islamic sources are shown to be apposite to symbols anathema to the Islamic tradition. Thus Islamic material such as verses from the Qurʾān, the testimony of faith in God (*shahāda*), and sayings of the family of the Prophet were shown to have hidden parallels to the Christian cross, the church hierarchy, stories in the Torah not found in other Islamic sources, and doxographies attributed to the ancient Greek luminaries Aristotle, Plato, and Euclid.[5] Through their pairing, the missionaries demonstrated that both familiar and exotic sources alluded to the same hidden schema—the pleroma beyond the material world, and the cyclical hierohistory and mission hierarchy within it. By harmonizing these culturally dissonant sources, the missionaries created a bricolage that incorporated foreign elements and exoticized familiar ones by reducing them to the same underlying schema. Through disclosing the secrets of sources closed to non-Ismāʿīlīs, the missionaries were abe to provide the believers access to knowledge reserved only to the elite (*khāṣṣa*).

Needless to say, this unconventional mode of interpretation made Ismāʿīlism anathema to medieval Muslim scholars. And this may, in fact, have been the point. Sociologists of sectarianism have shown that for sects to thrive, they must create a sense of tension with those outside the sect. Bryan Wilson writes that one crucial trait of sectarian movements is their intentional differentiation from the prevailing patterns of the dominant tradition.[6] Placing the sectarians in a state of tension with the surrounding society raises their sense of commitment and allegiance to the group.[7] For some groups this can take the form of antisocial behavior, distinctive clothing, and the flouting of mores in public—in Islam a phenomenon represented by the dervish groups after the twelfth century.[8] In covert movements sectarians maintain this dynamic through the adoption of materials known to be beyond the pale of acceptability. I suggest that for Ismāʿīlī missionaries, the taʾwīl of aberrant materials such as the Christian cross, the church hierarchy, the Eucharist served this purpose. Embracing such exotic materials as the source of secret knowledge put the members of the sect in tension with those outside the movement and perpetuated their sectarian ethos.

A significant component of taʾwīl entailed the recital of schema of the mission hierarchy and cosmogony. Taʾwīl's penchant for repeating the same schema again and again and its missionary context call for an interpretive approach different from the classical Islamic exegesis of the traditional scholars (ʿulamāʾ). I suggest that taʾwīl was meant to habituate its audience to new habits of mind. Scholars of sectarianism in Second Temple Judaism such as Ilkka Pyysiäinen and Jutta Jokiranta have shown the utility of cognitive models for textual analysis in order to appreciate the organizing principles of mind expressed in literary forms.[9] This theoretical shift from text to mind also informs Tanya Luhrmann's recent ethnography of the Vineyard, a "renewalist" Protestant church in Chicago. She observes that the congregants' internalization of the language of faith and practices of prayer shapes the congregants' understanding of their own experience, as well as the experience itself.[10]

In the study of religion, the implications of what we might call "the cognitive turn" of textual analysis reflected in these studies were anticipated by Ernst Cassirer's philosophy of symbolic forms in the early twentieth century. Because the literary material with which Cassirer was concerned is somewhat similar to taʾwīl, his concepts provide a useful theoretical mooring for taʾwīl's analysis. His reflections on mythical consciousness and literatures that employ secrecy, numerology, and letter symbolism are particularly relevant.[11]

Cassirer wrote that mythical thinking reflects an irreducible cognitive order or modality, a consciousness that departs from what Cassirer calls the "rational" or "scientific" mode.[12] The components of mythical consciousness lie in the structures, principles, and theories of causality that underlie myths. In a mythical consciousness, contiguity in space, congruence in time, comparable sounds or letters of two words, similarity in shape of objects, and correspondence in number of two or more entities may be viewed as potentially causally related. Cassirer calls these combinations "modes of configuration." In his terms the significance of sequences of dyads in taʾwīl—"the two [supernal] roots" (*al-aṣlān*), the sun and the moon, the two lines of the Christian Cross, the earth's ecliptic and equator, the speaker-prophet and his legatee—reflects the principle that numeric congruence implies a causal connection. Thus number equivalence represents a "mode of correspondence," and the number "two" a "symbolic form." Other symbolic forms include water, which signifies special knowledge, and "life and death," which signify "joining or leaving the mission." Collectively the principles underlying taʾwīl's modes of correspondence and the schema that make up its symbolic forms constitute the sect's collective mode of cognition, its consciousness. In the sources their presence represents both an expression of the mission's cognitive mode and a tool for its perpetuation. They teach an awareness of a "second world" mapped on to this one.[13]

Cassirer's theoretical language allows us to move from analyzing literary sources as such to interpreting them as evidence for the structures and principles of the consciousness that generates them. For those initiated into and familiar with this imaginal world, such elements are not merely textual themes and topoi; they are hints to an ultimate reality disclosed in glimpses. A Cassirerian analysis focuses on the logics that underlie causation and apposition. In taʾwīl this takes the form of similarity of the sounds of words, numerological patterns, and similarity in structure of leadership hierarchies. Upon internalizing these modes of configuration, and the particular forms that signal them, the believer has internalized a new way of viewing the world and his place in it.

The function of taʾwīl in early Ismāʿīlism was to bind the community by their adoption of habits of mind that set them against those outside the movement. After delineating the logics and symbols of "daʿwa knowledge," I clarify the schools and sects from which the mission distinguished itself. Previously, scholars have emphasized that Fāṭimid polemics were directed against Sunnī scholars and the companions of the Prophet who were their heroes; my reading of taʾwīl suggests that the Fāṭimid missionaries polemicized against other Shīʿites, particularly renegade Ismāʿīlīs who had refused to accept the Fāṭimid Imāms as legitimate. Further, scholars have assumed that when Ismāʿīlī missionaries interpreted the Torah and Gospels, they intended to convert Jews and Christians to the Ismāʿīlī fold. I show that these interpretations taught the Ismāʿīlī believers that, like the Israelite prophets and their followers, they too could gain access to special, hidden signs through the true Imām of the age. The Ismāʿīlī believers learned that the rightly guided Fāṭimid Imām alone possessed this secret knowledge that was crucial for their salvation.

A final note: In the pages that follow, I consider the ethos of Ismāʿīlism's beginnings, a time when it was sectarian and militant according to discrete definitions of such terms that I discuss in chapter 1. I do not intend to suggest that these traits are defining features of Ismāʿīlism. For most of the past millennium, Ismāʿīlism has not been particularly militant; on the contrary Ismāʿīlism has not infrequently suffered from intolerant strands among other schools of Islam. For the past century, Ismāʿīlism has been a progressive, modernizing Islamic community. My aim is not to label Ismāʿīlism as sectarian, but rather to describe how a certain body of sources and ethos served its first generations.

ACKNOWLEDGMENTS

The completion of this book is due to the help and support of a great many people. I would like to thank Hanan Ahmad, Sean Anthony, Faten Arfaoui, Karen Bauer, Tamima Bayhom-Daou, Cécile Bonmariage, Stephen Burge, Sandra Campbell, Joyce Cheng, Rick Colby, Garrett Davidson, Marilyn Drennan, Ahmed Eshaq, Daniel Falk, Federica Francesconi, Bruce Fudge, Heidi Gese, Deborah Green, Brynn Grossman, Najam Haider, Abbas Hamdani, Russell Harris, Bernard Haykel, Asma Hilali, Shah Hussain, Mary Jaeger, Nadia Jamal, Janika Jordan, Carol Kleinheksel, Julia Kolb, Arzina Lalani, Khadija Lalani, Joseph Lowry, Wilferd Madelung, Toby Mayer, Alnoor Merchant, Yahya Michot, Rana Mikati, Wafi Momin, Shin Nmoto, Jessica Otey, Eileen Otis, Sarah Savant, Karen Schiff, Naushin Shariff, Stephen Shoemaker, Savannah Smith, David Stern, Heather Sweetser, Samer Traboulsi, Mark Unno, Luise Vormittag, Paul Walker, Malcolm Wilson, and Seth Wilson.

Special thanks are owed to Farhad Daftary, Omar Ali-de-Unzaga, and Gurdofarid Miskinzoda. Through their auspices, the Institute of Ismaili Studies offered critical support and office space in London during periods of the manuscript research for this book.

I thank Jim Denton at the University of South Carolina Press for guiding the manuscript through the publication process. The final draft of this book was greatly improved at its final stages by the anonymous readers from USC Press, and also the helpful suggestions of Orkhan Mir-Kasimov and Jessica Otey. Professor Ismail K. Poonawala offered useful criticisms for chapters 2 and 4.

The way I read Arabo-Islamic sources has been greatly influenced by two luminaries in the field of Arabic and Islamic studies, Patricia Crone and Everett Rowson. Patricia entered my graduate career at a critical stage in my intellectual development, and her seminar on Ismāʿīlism and feedback on my early work continues to guide my thinking. Everett Rowson, the foremost Arabist in North America today, is my model for a scholar and professor.

I would also like to thank my family, Ilana Hollenberg, Norman Hollenberg, Deborah Hanson Hollenberg, and Leonard Rubin, for their love and support.

Finally I would like to give a special thanks to my mother, Donna Hollenberg. She read and commented on every page of the manuscript and offered immeasurable support and enthusiasm throughout the writing process. This book is dedicated to her.

ABBREVIATIONS

EI^2 = *Encyclopaedia of Islam.* New Edition. Leiden: E. J. Brill, 1954–2003.
IIS = The Institute of Ismaili Studies, London, U.K.
[. . .] = a lacuna in the manuscript or nonsensible word in the edition.
Ms. = manuscript
v = verso
r = recto

I adopt the conventions of the Library of Congress for the transliteration of Arabic. In the case of two words, I do not elide the initial *ḥamza,* for example in the phrase *fī al-bayt.* In longer phrases or sentences, the elision of the initial *ḥamza* in phrases is rendered as *sallama zayd ʿalā l-ustādh.*

Translations of passages of the Qurʾān are those of Marmaduke Pickthall's except where noted. Pious formulas are removed from the translation.

Competing Islands of Salvation

CHAPTER 1

The Early Ismāʿīlī Mission 870–975

Early Ismāʿīlī taʾwīl was used to explain doctrinal shifts and historical developments of the early Ismāʿīlī mission and Fāṭimid Imāmate. From the vantage point of the daʿwa, the single most important event in Ismāʿīlism's first century was the establishment of the Fāṭimid Imāms as rulers of an imperial state. Some Ismāʿīlī missionaries accepted the Fāṭimids' claims; others rejected them. Disagreements over the status of the Fāṭimid Imāms weighed heavily in taʾwīl.

Most previous histories of Ismāʿīlism during the Fāṭimid period have viewed Ismāʿīlism and the Fāṭimid state as inseparably linked. Thus in his monumental history of the Ismāʿīlīs, Farhad Daftary writes that after founding the Fāṭimid state, the Ismāʿīlī Imām continued to be actively engaged in the mission, and the daʿwa was, from its inception, intended to found such a state.[1] Michael Brett writes that Ismāʿīlī religious rhetoric was meant to align with the needs of an empire; thus the universalistic claims of the Neoplatonic speculative philosophy of al-Sijistānī served the imperial aims of the Fāṭimid Imām.[2] Paula Sanders links Fāṭimid ceremonial and Ismāʿīlī taʾwīl. For example she reads the procession during the Festival of the Fast Breaking (ʿId al-Fiṭr) under the Fāṭimid caliph al-ʿAzīz as enacting the hidden sense of the ritual as interpreted by al-Qāḍī al-Nuʿmān.[3] Bierman argues that Fāṭimid public texts such as writing on mosques and coins represent an attempt to inscribe different levels of meaning for different audiences. Thus the concentric circle design of coins initiated by al-Muʿizz and the Qurʾānic verses on mosques under al-Ḥākim encoded a secret sense to the Ismāʿīlī believers.[4]

My analysis of Ismāʿīlī taʾwīl leads me to draw a strong distinction between dawla rhetoric and daʿwa knowledge—between state and sectarian rhetoric. This is not to say that the Imām was not central to missionaries and believers. Symbolically the Imām was the possessor of the supernal resources from the immaterial world, the earthly link between heaven and earth, the ship who can guide the believer through salvation. However, during the period in question, there is little evidence that the Imām or his state apparatus took an active role in leading the mission. Moreover, pace Brett, Sanders, and Bierman, I find little evidence that the symbolism of state ceremonial and "public texts" such as coinage and architecture had special meanings according to the Ismāʿīlī missionaries, or that the doctrines of Ismāʿīlism were of direct utility for the Fāṭimid state. Fāṭimid state rhetoric and Ismāʿīlī daʿwa symbolism may have both focused on the Imām, but the two were distinct and should be analyzed as such. Missionaries did at times claim that the Imām possessed supernatural charisma, and we know that the Fāṭimid caliphs such as al-Muʿizz corrected the errant views of missionaries from the Iranian dioceses during private sessions of instruction in Ismāʿīlī doctrine (*Majālis al-ḥikma*), but this seems to have been rare. Generally speaking it was the missionaries who led these teaching sessions, not the Imām himself. There is little evidence that the Imām spent a great deal of time setting out either the interior interpretations or exterior laws for the community.

This distinction is important for analysis of Ismāʿīlī taʾwīl, for if it can be established that the Fāṭimid Ismāʿīlī missionaries were primarily concerned with ecclesiastic (rather than state) politics, we are better equipped to recover the intention of their polemics and apologetics.

The centrality of the concept, "daʿwa" in Ismāʿīlism cannot be overstated. In practical terms to join the daʿwa meant to pledge one's loyalty to a religio-political movement that intended to displace the false tyrant from power with the rightly guided Imām descended from the Prophet. To join the mission of God was to be reborn, or, in another common metaphor, to take refuge from the seas of ignorance on an island of salvation. The daʿwa, after all, preceded the formation of the state and survived its passing.

Although in Western scholarly literature daʿwa has become strongly associated with Ismāʿīlism, the Ismāʿīlī missionaries were not the first Muslims to invoke the word, nor even the first Shīʿite sectarians to do so, and a discussion of what daʿwa connoted prior to Ismāʿīlism is a good place to begin.

Daʿwa

In the Qurʾān daʿwa occurs in the nominal form four times, and in verbal forms over two hundred more. It usually connotes "call" or "supplication" and is often paired with "to answer" (*ijāba*). Usually it is God (or God through one of His prophets) who calls on the believer to believe, and the believer is enjoined to answer by praising Him (Qurʾān 17:52). In one passage it is the devil who issues a call; the believer should resist it and choose God's call instead. Sometimes in the Qurʾān the agent and recipient of the call is reversed: When one who has been wronged calls to God, God responds (Qurʾān 27: 62).

Whether the call is issued by God (on humankind to believe) or by downtrodden believers (for God's help), the "call" assumes an ongoing relationship based on support in times of need. Humans are dependent on God, and so they call Him for help; God is humans' master, and so He calls them to worship Him.

A more specific and different sense of the word daʿwa comes in Qurʾān 3:153, at least as it is understood by early exegetes. The verse refers to a "calling out to the believers from behind." This is understood by the second/eighth-century commentator Mujāhid as the Prophet exhorting believers from behind in their battle against the pagans, a "call to arms" issued by God (via His Prophet Muḥammad) to the believers.[5] It is this sense of daʿwa as call to battle that seems to be meant in some early prophetic traditions. "Every Prophet has a daʿwa," whereas the idols have no daʿwa in this world or the next, reports Mālik ibn Anas in *al-Muwaṭṭāʾ*.[6] Thus Moses, too, was said to have erected a daʿwa against Pharaoh.[7]

In early traditions and proto-Sunnī histories of the life of the Prophet and the Islamic conquests, the word daʿwa connotes both a "call to arms" and also a call on pagans to convert before military action.[8] In the *Kitāb al-mubtadaʾ* composed by Muḥammad ibn Isḥāq (d. 150/767), the Prophet's military campaign against the pagan Quraysh is referred to as a daʿwa.[9] But in other traditions set in the context of the Islamic conquests of pagan Arabia, daʿwa refers to the call for pagans to convert to Islam before they would be compelled to do so militarily. The key phrase was "daʿwa before warfare" (*al-daʿwa qabla al-qitāl*), a tradition attributed to the Prophet.[10]

This sense of daʿwa, a call for non-Muslims to convert before being compelled to do so, appears in one of the earliest extant theological epistles, the *Kitāb al-taḥrīsh* (The Book of Provocation) attributed to the early Muʿtazilite Ḍirār ibn ʿAmr (d. c. 200/815).[11] I translate the relevant section in full.

> On Daʿwa
>
> Then a group [*qawm*] came to him [the jurist] and asked: "What is your view of daʿwa? There is a group that claims that daʿwa does not cease until the day of resurrection, and that it is a prescriptive [law] which one must undertake [*farīḍa wājiba*]." So he [the jurist] said: "Guard against them, for they are advocates of innovation and straying [*ahl al-bidaʿ wal-ḍalāl*]."
>
> ʿAbd Allāh ibn ʿUmar said: "the daʿwa of the Prophet, peace be upon him, was attained during his life. It ceases after his death until the day of resurrection. An enemy is not the object of a call, and a call [*duʿa*] is not a necessity." Al-Ḥasan al-Basrī also [holds this view].
>
> The al-Bayhisīya accepted this from him [al-Ḥasan al-Baṣrī], for this agreed with their own caprices [*ahwāʾihim*]. When they appeared, they

> forbade daʿwa and waged war. Because of this tradition, they slaughtered the people indiscriminately—those who had committed crimes, and those who had not.
>
> Then another group came to him [the jurist] and asked: "What is your view about he who claims that daʿwa has ceased—that [now] there is no daʿwa." He said, "be on guard against them, for they are advocates of innovation and straying. Write that the Prophet, peace be upon him, sent ʿAlī ibn Abī Ṭālib secretly and said: "ʿAlī, do not fight them until you have called them and warned them. Verily, this is what I commissioned and this is what I commanded.'
>
> He [the jurist] said, "when a young man was captured from the clans of [pagan] Arabs, and they said, 'O Messenger of God, no one called to us, and your decree [amr] has not reached us!' He said to them: 'Do you swear?' They said, 'By God, your decree has not reached and no one called us to that.' He said, 'leave them on their way until the daʿwa reaches them. Verily, my daʿwa will not cease until the day of resurrection. Protect those seeking protection, repeat the daʿwa.'" Then he (peace be upon him) recited, "this Qurʾān hath been inspired in me, that I may warn therewith you and whomsoever it may reach" [Qurʾān 6:19]. 'Umar ibn al-Khaṭṭāb would not go to battle until he called and recited scripture [*yaqraʾu ʿalayhim kitāban*] to them. Some accepted that and approached him, while others were in opposition [*takhallafū*].[12]

An anonymous jurist (*al-faqīh*) is asked about the views of two groups, one that claims that daʿwa is a legal prescription carried out at all times and another that asks whether daʿwa was limited only to the mission of the Prophet and is proscribed after this time, a view tied to a tradition on the authority of ʿAbd Allāh ibn 'Umar and also attributed to al-Ḥasan al-Baṣrī (d. 110/728), a politically quietist theologian who shunned active engagement with state politics. The jurist explains that the latter view—that daʿwa after the time of the Prophet is proscribed—was used as a pretext for the Kharijite group known as "the Bayhasīya" to attack their enemies without first calling them to the faith. The jurist's own view is that daʿwa is indeed intended to continue. He adduces a tradition that ties this view to the reason for the revelation of a verse of the Qurʾān, which implies that the Qurʾān's reach will extend to the future.

The fact that the topic, daʿwa, merited its own section in the epistle suggests that during the eighth century, it was a topic on which theologians offered considered opinions. Since the anonymous jurist seems to represent Ḍirār b. ʿAmr's own views throughout the epistle, one can conclude that, in modified form, an early view of daʿwa was a call to non-Muslims to convert to Islam.[13] This would become the predominant association of the word in Sunnism that obtains until today. The case within Shīʿism is somewhat different.

Daʿwa in Early Shīʿism

Shīʿites hold that the leader of the Islamic polity must rightfully be a descendent of the Prophet's clan of Hāshim, usually descended from the Prophet's cousin ʿAlī and daughter Fāṭima. For early Shīʿites daʿwa was an abbreviated form of the phrase *daʿwat al-ḥaqq*, literally, "a call to the truth," or, since as the word for truth "*al-ḥaqq*" is one of God's ninety-nine names mentioned in the Qurʾān (Qurʾān 6:62), a "call to God." Furthermore certain second/eighth- and third/ninth-century sources suggest that for early Shīʿites, *daʿwat al-ḥaqq* implied something more specific. It was a call to remove from power the false caliph currently ruling the Islamic lands and to install in his place the true Imām, a descendent of the family of the Prophet. As this figure was charged with both ruling the state and shepherding the faithful to heaven, daʿwa was simultaneously a call for political revolution and a religious mission to save Muslim souls from perdition.

The figure charged with carrying out this mission is called the dāʿī, a word that is usually translated "missionary." The word *dāʿī* is simply the active participle of the word daʿwa (call), thus a "caller." The dāʿī functioned as a religious missionary and a political operative and consultant: in addition to bringing acolytes and conscripts into the politico-religious movement, he explained shifts in the doctrines of the movement to the believers.

An important second/eighth-century Shīʿite group that frequently invoked the term daʿwa was the Zaydīs. They held that the Imām should be the most knowledgeable candidate descended from the Prophet's daughter Fāṭima and cousin ʿAlī who takes up the sword against the false caliph and founds a state. For them daʿwa clearly implied a "call to arms" on behalf of this Imām. According to Zaydī jurists, when Muslims are ruled by an unjust tyrant, joining a just daʿwa is a legal obligation for the community.[14]

Also during the second/eighth century, the term daʿwa was used by Shīʿite groups with radically different doctrines. Like the Zaydīs these sects sought to replace the figure in power whom they believed was a tyrant with a descendant of the Prophet, the rightful political and spiritual leader of the Muslim community. But unlike the Zaydīs, they held that their leader was more than merely the rightful Imām: he was a supernatural figure, a divinely guided savior who would initiate the End of Days. These sects, known by their opponents as *ghulāt* (exaggerators or extremists, that is, those who hold doctrines other Islamic theologians deemed extreme, such as the belief that their Imām has the capacity to communicate with angels or is God incarnate), missionized among the semiliterate communities in agricultural towns and villages on Islam's fringes.

Some of these sects claimed that the Imām is currently in hiding (*ghayba*). He will return (*rajʿa*) at the End of Days, a period marked by natural catastrophes, bloodshed, and miraculous celestial phenomena such as the rising of the sun in the West. He will defeat the enemies of the family of the Prophet and their followers and fill the earth with justice.[15] Others claimed that ʿAlī was Muḥammad's waṣī (legatee), and that the relationship between the Prophet Muḥammad and his waṣī ʿAlī is similar to that between the Prophet Moses and his wāṣī Aaron. The Imām had access to special books and scrolls that he inherited from the Prophet's cousin ʿAlī.[16] Other sects claimed that the Imām receives prophecy, or, more commonly, that he knows scripture's secret sense.

These groups thrived between the first and third centuries. Although Anthony and Bayhom-Daou disagree on the period these early Shīʿite groups thrived, they do agree on the order in which their doctrines developed.[17] The earliest doctrines of Shīʿite sectarians included imminent messianism and eschatology, militancy (engagement in violent struggle or the threat of future such warfare), and *waṣīya* (belief that God provides to every age a Prophet and a legatee).[18] As Bayhom-Daou established, a second phase is marked by gnosticism and esotericism, the belief that a demiurge below the supreme God created both a spiritual, luminous, immaterial world, the pleroma, and this evil material world. The human soul originated in the former higher sphere but fell into the lower world of matter and forgot its origin. Through recourse to secret, higher knowledge brought by a savior to a small elite of followers, the soul may be awakened and gradually rise to its true home. In the Islamic context, the so-called Shīʿite "exaggerators" (*ghulāt*) betrayed such beliefs as the transmigration of souls (*tanāsukh*), spiritual cycles (*adwār*), and that their Imām was an incarnation of the divine light, a prophet, or, according to some, a demiurge-creator.[19] It is likely that both the messianic and esotericist phases took root in the semiliterate agricultural regions in Iraq where such notions had existed for some time. Some of the technical terms of these sects were later adopted by Imāmīs and Ismāʿīlīs over a century later. These terms include the disappearance (*ghayba*) and return (*rajʿa*) of the Imām, inspired interpretation (taʾwīl), and a "speaking Prophet" (*nāṭiq*) and "silent legatee" (*ṣāmit*). How this terminology persisted is uncertain; it could very well be that, as Bayhom-Daou suggests, these sects actually existed later than the sources purport.

In describing these sects, modern scholars have applied the language of these groups' enemies and referred to them as "extremist." This is problematic on several levels.[20] First, such scholars do not explain the criteria for why Imāmī or proto-Sunni scholastics should be accepted as orthodox or normative, and their opponents who hold such views as the supernatural character of the Imām as "extreme." Second, during the second and third Islamic centuries, the doctrines in question, and the status they held, were fluid. The ritual cursing of Abū Bakr and ʿUmar was labeled extreme (*ghuluww*) during the eighth century but became normative for most Shīʿites by the ninth.

To describe early Shīʿite sects, I would suggest that concepts derived from hostile sources should not be adopted as categories to be applied, but as evidence to be considered. The late ninth- and early tenth-century theologians applied the term ghuluww as a trope to establish their doctrines as normative and their opponents as deviant.

Rather than adopt the standards of orthodoxy from a particular moment of Shīʿite history, it is useful to develop terms from outside the tradition to describe Shīʿism's doctrinal landscape. Social scientific studies of sectarianism serve this ends.

Sect in Classical Islam

In the social sciences, research on sects and sectarianism by sociologist of religion Bryan Wilson and historians Stark and Bainbridge have followed lines established in the "church-sect theory" of Max Weber and Ernst Troeltsh. Wilson defines the sect as a voluntary association that holds a well-defined sense of the source of evil in the world and responds to this evil.[21] To explain the genesis of new movements, Stark and Bainbridge posit a reward-cost theory of social exchange based on the degree of a group's social tension with the external society. Those who benefit from the status quo are likely to maintain low-tension associations, whereas those who suffer a high degree of social deprivation gain rewards from joining high-tension associations. Some empirical elements for measuring tension among religious associations include difference, demonstrations of antagonism, the establishment of group norms, and separation.

This "church-sect" paradigm does not square easily with classical Islam. Both Bryan Wilson's and Stark and Bainbridge's models of sectarianism assume a church that occupies the orthodox or dominant mainstream position in society; the sect departs from, and is in conflict with, this church.[22] Since in classical Islam there was neither a central church nor a clearly established "dominant position" that defined belief and praxis, the categories "school" and "sect" are preferable.

A school may be defined as a voluntary association associated with a great scholar of the past and with the works he was known to have composed. Islam's schools of law and theology emerged in the ninth and tenth centuries based on the teachings of eighth-and ninth-century scholars. They emphasized that there had been a direct, scholar-to-scholar aural-written form of transmission, and that the growth of the tradition tends to accrue through commentary (*sharḥ*) on the sources (*uṣūl*) composed by the school's founder. Christopher Melchert shows that a juristic school (*madhhab*) was defined by the presence of a chief scholar, the production of commentaries on standardized epitomes, and the ongoing transmission of knowledge.[23] Insomuch as it could be said to have existed, "orthodoxy" meant simply staying in sufficiently good graces with one's scholarly cohorts to maintain a distinguished reputation during one's life, and for posterity.[24]

A school is characterized by its porous borders, informal membership, and varying levels of commitment among its following. It was common for a single scholar to identify with multiple schools at the same time. Thus a fourth/tenth-century scholar such as the Iraqi-born Muḥammad b. Aḥmad al-Kātib (b. 281/894) could be both a Shāfiʿī and a Shīʿite.[25] When members of a school express their disapproval of the views of scholars from either the same or different schools, they recognize them as legitimate (if wrong). Humble dicta such as "God knows best [who is right]" and "every jurist is correct" (*kull mujtahid ṣaḥīḥ*) reflect an appreciation that human understanding is limited and intellectual work reflects probability, rather than certainty. In short, disagreement was an expectation among the community of scholars who inhabited the schools. This aspect, the capacity for members of schools to relativize their position historically and intellectually, is among the most important features that distinguish a school from a sect.

Borrowing from Wilson and from Stark and Bainbridge above, a sect may be defined as a voluntary association that requires an exclusive commitment from its members. In addition, sects:

- encourage a tense, antagonistic relationship with outsiders;
- encourage a sense of protest against the state or authority;
- agitate against their enemies who are viewed as metaphysically evil;
- apply symbols and technical terminology particular to the sect.

The sectarians alone possess the truth; all others are damned. As the fifth/eleventh-century Ismāʿīlī missionary Aḥmad b. Ibrāhīm al-Naysābūrī put it, one is either in "the mission of truth" or "the mission of Satan"; there was nothing in between.[26] Sectarians are in turn deemed anathema by outside authorities.[27] Wilson and others have suggested that for sectarians, antagonism fulfills an important function. It instills an intense sense of commitment in its members.

Sectarian literature is devoted to maintaining separation from the external world. This is reflected in interpretations of the cosmos and history. Like the movements of the celestial spheres or the relationships between the primary elements of fire, water, earth, and air, the events of history and the actors within them are part of a divinely ordered fabric that the sect's leader alone has the capacity to decode. Rather than viewing events as particular and specific, sectarians view history as a pattern in which the adherents of good—the members of the sect and its heroes—battle the forces of evil.

This separation is also achieved through the development of an argot, an elaborate technical vocabulary particular to the sect. Umayyad and early ʿAbbāsid period Shīʿite sects bristle with technical terms unfamiliar to those outside the sect, such as *taḥdīth* (the capacity to speak to angels), nāṭiq and ṣāmit (speaking Prophet and silent interpreter), and *al-Qāʾim* (the arising redeemer). Such language suggests that a sect constitutes what has been called a "community of discourse," a group whose use of special language sets them apart from outsiders.[28]

Sectarians animate their movement using deeds and images. They view human events of history as a stage in which the cosmic and heavenly worlds meet; God Himself is present in the mission. There is a sense that the world is alive and pregnant with meaning to those with the code to unlock its secrets.[29] Among the early Shīʿites, the Kaysānīya, a sectarian movement on behalf of Muḥammad ibn al-Ḥanafiyya that thrived during the Umayyad period, exemplifies this ethos.

After the Prophet's grandson al-Ḥusayn's martyrdom in 61/680 and subsequent failed attempts by Shīʿite partisans known as the *tawwābūn* (penitents) to avenge his death, the partisans of ʿAlī in Kufa continued to hope for an ʿAlid candidate to rise and topple the Umayyad caliph. Al-Mukhtār ibn Abī ʿUbayd, a Kufan allied to the al-Thaqafī clan, capitalized on these sentiments. He raised a revolt on behalf of ʿAlī's son Muḥammad ibn al-Ḥanafīyya, proclaiming Ibn al-Ḥanafiyya the Mahdī (rightly guided redeemer) and himself as the Mahdī's deputy (*wazīr*). He successfully conquered Kufa and its surroundings, ruling between 66/685 and al-Mukhtār's death in 67/687.[30]

Al-Mukhtār's sect drew heavily from Israelite symbolism. He would declare that just as the Israelites possessed the Ark of the Covenant, "a relic of the family of Moses and the family of Aaron," so too did al-Mukhtār's daʿwa have ʿAlī's throne. Al-Mukhtār's followers would place the throne on a mule with seven men on its right and left and carry it into battle. The power of the throne was remembered as instrumental in defeating ʿUbaydallah b. Ziyād at Bājumayrā in Syria. The sources suggest that al-Mukhtār's throne symbolism bore apocalyptic valence; his allusion to the holy of holies (*al-sakīna*) dwelling in ʿAlī's chair empowered the faithful to fight. In a movement that expressed itself in symbols, images, and battles, ʿAlī's chair led al-Mukhtār's followers to view him, the throne, and, by extension, themselves, as enacting the immanent will of the divine presence.

Al-Mukhtār's movement represents the closest historical example of an ideal type of the sect as we have defined above. The narrative traditions that make up what Henry Corbin first referred to as "hierohistory" represent a paler, secondary, textual version of what groups like the Kaysaniyya experienced firsthand: the perception that God works through human history through His rightly guided Imāms.[31]

Ismāʿīlism, too, began as a millenarian sect, and there is evidence that its followers, too, viewed themselves as agents of the divine through their deeds. As is well known, Ismāʿīlīs shared a number of terms and concepts with earlier

Shīʿite sects.[32] What distinguishes it from the many other Shīʿite sects of early Islam is its substantial and lengthy political success: It was a sect that established an empire that lasted almost three centuries and, with the ʿAbbāsids and Byzantium, served as one of the great powers in the Mediterranean basin.

The Early Ismāʿīlī Daʿwa, c. 860–909

Heinz Halm's *The Empire of the Mahdi* presents the most convincing account of the rise of early Ismāʿīlism and the Fāṭimids to this point, and much of my narrative below borrows from Halm's work. Halm's description of the early mission is based on the correspondence of Fāṭimid and non-Fāṭimid sources. Particularly important in these accounts is a report of a certain Ibn Rizām, a descendant of Muḥammad ibn Ismāʿīl, the hidden Imām around whom the daʿwa rallied. Ibn Rizām possessed intimate knowledge of the movement; it seems likely that he was once an Ismāʿīlī who apostatized and left the fold. His account of the daʿwa was transmitted by the Sharīf Akhū Muḥsin (thrived mid fourth/tenth century), a *sayyid* (descendant of the Prophet) from Kufa. This "Akhū Muḥsin from Ibn Rizām" account is preserved in a number of chronicles.[33] Halm harmonizes these sources with early Fāṭimid accounts, the most important being that of al-Qāḍī al-Nuʿmān's *Iftitāḥ al-daʿwa.*[34] However, the correspondence between diverse non-Fāṭimid reports (al-Qummī, al-Ṭabarī, and al-Masʿūdī) with Fāṭimid sources leaves Halm's reconstruction the most plausible. Unless otherwise indicated, the following paragraphs follow the lines set by Halm, at times supplemented by subsequent research.

The Ismāʿīlī daʿwa first surfaced as a millenarian movement during the middle of the ninth century in a town in Khuzistan (in modern Southwest Iran) called ʿAskar Mukram, a small trade and industrial town known for the production of textiles, sugar refining, bazaars filled with shops, and warehouses.[35] There a figure known as "ʿAbd Allāh the Elder" propagated a secret mission on behalf of a hidden Imām. Prospective acolytes were told that there existed a divinely guided Imām, a descendant of the Prophet through his martyred grandson al-Ḥusayn, who was presently in hiding. Soon he would arise to abrogate the law, reveal the secret sense of all laws, and usher in the End of Days. Upon the advent of the Qāʾim-Mahdī (rightly guided arising one), paradise would be established, those who recognized the redeemer's advent would be rewarded, and opponents of his mission, punished. After they had joined the movement and could be trusted, the acolytes or "believers" were told that this redeemer figure was Muḥammad ibn Ismāʿīl, Jaʿfar al-Ṣādiq's grandson from a different line of his descendants from the Imāms venerated by the Imāmī Shīʿites.

From the vantage point of the ʿAbbāsid caliph and his entourage, a message of an alternative head of the community represented revolutionary sedition; from the perspective of the scholars, reports of the imminent abrogation of the law was antinomian heresy. Thus it was for good reason that ʿAbd Allāh the

Elder and his comrades hid their beliefs and aims. They were, however, discovered by the ʿAbbāsid authorities and forced to flee the region. They landed on the western edge of the Syrian desert steppe, the mountainous region of Jabal al-Summāq. From there, in the town of Salamīya, the Ismāʿīlī missionaries established a base for an ever-expanding network of cells—small secret groups working toward a common aim. By the end of the third/ninth century—that is, in a mere two generations—Ismāʿīlī cells could be found from the Indus River in the east to the Maghreb (North Africa) in the west, and from the Caspian Sea in the north to Yemen in the south. Each of these "islands" (*jazāʾir*), as they were called within the daʿwa, were directed by the leadership in Salamīya—that is, by ʿAbd Allāh the Elder and his retinue and descendants.

It was the missionaries who were charged with expanding the daʿwa. We learn their strategies for proselytization from sources both within and outside Ismāʿīlism. Missionaries were told to focus their efforts in regions in which Shīʿte sympathies were strong. ʿAbd Allāh the Elder is reported to have instructed a new missionary to: "Go to Rayy! In Rayy, Ābeh, Qum, Kāshān, and the province of Ṭabaristān and Māzandarān, all the people are Shīʿites, and loyal to the Shīʿa. They will answer your daʿwa."[36] The ninth-century missionary ʿAlī al-Faḍl was known to look for converts at Shīʿite sanctuaries such as the shrine of al-Ḥusayn at Karbalāʾ.[37] Not only in Shīʿite centers in Iraq, Iran, and Daylam, but also in North Africa and Yemen, the missionaries sought to convert families and clans with Shīʿite sympathies.[38]

There is reason to believe that in the middle of the third/ninth century, Imāmī Shīʿites would have been fertile ground for proselytization. The community had been dealt a traumatic blow when, in 860, the eleventh Imām died without leaving a son to lead the community. This contradicted a central pillar of Imāmism and should be impossible. Since the Imām is the "proof of God" (*ḥujjat Allāh*) on earth without whom the world ceases to exist, it should not have been possible for an Imām to die without leaving a son to succeed him. Imāmī doctrine would come to hold that al-Ḥasan did have a son, a certain Muḥammad who was in "occultation" (*ghayba*) and would return to usher in the End of Days in the future (thus the Twelver-Shīʿites' doctrine until today). But this doctrine took time to gain acceptance, and Ismāʿīlism arose in a period precisely when Imāmism was in transition to Twelver-Shīʿism. According to accounts in sources, the missionaries targeted young men who were spiritually lost and emotionally distraught without a leader of the community to guide them.[39]

The social status and educational backgrounds of both the missionaries and their targets varied. It seems many were from the lower social strata and were likely non- or semiliterate. ʿAbd Allāh al-Akbar's first convert, al-Ḥusayn Al-Aḥwāzī, reportedly worked as a guard for stores of dates. Among al-Aḥwāzī's converts was an ox driver named Ḥamdān; their bond was forged when al-Aḥwāzī came to Ḥamdān's assistance when he lay sick on the road and nursed him back to health. Ibn Ḥawshab, a missionary from near Kufa (and Jaʿfar ibn Manṣūr al-Yaman's father), was a linen weaver (or cloth exporter, or carpenter—depending on which source we choose). Abū Saʿīd ibn Bahrām al-Jannābi was a flour merchant from the Iranian coast. We read that his converts consisted of "little people, butchers, cart-drivers, and the like."[40]

There were also missionaries with scholarly backgrounds. Early in the daʿwa, missionaries infiltrated and converted secretaries in the ʿAbbāsid caliphal court. Some scholars also joined the movement. One, a certain Ghiyāth, debated the ʿulamāʾ of Rayy. In this "island," in particular, Ghiyāth's generations of successors produced an intellectually rich literature meant to convert the philosophically inclined Samanid denizens of court. There the Ismāʿīlī missionaries converted rulers, ministers, generals, and courtesans; Ismāʿlism was a major factor in politics in the Samanids for much of the fourth/tenth century.[41] In Iraq, too, ʿAbdān composed sources that applied a Pythagorean cosmology that reflects knowledge of astronomy.[42] In North Africa Ibn al-Haythām and later al-Qāḍī al-Nuʿmān were from learned Shīʿite families; they drew on their knowledge to lure scholars among Shīʿites, Mālikīs, and Ḥanafīs in al-Qaryawān.

The strategy of the missionaries was as follows. A missionary first attempted to convert kin—his close family and perhaps his clan. After reaching sufficient rank, the dāʿī would be sent to a nearby town to proselytize; this, of course, entailed greater risk. To avoid being discovered by enemies, the missionary would not reside in the town or village in which he was missionizing, but in the adjacent village. He would begin by attempting to convert one or two individuals. If he was successful, they, in turn, would convert their families and then repeat the process, traveling to another site. Thus al-Ḥusayn al-Aḥwāzī converted Ḥamdān Qarmāt, who, in turn, converted his own family. Ḥamdān's brother-in-law, ʿAbdān, expanded the mission and sent missionaries to adjacent districts.[43] The missionary would thus eventually become the head of a network of cells.

The conversion of entire tribes was particularly prized. When two members of the Ḍubayʿa clan of the Rabīʿa tribe joined the daʿwa, the missionary ʿAbdān sent them to convert the Bedouin tribesmen of the districts of Kufa. The Rifāʿī, Yashkur, and other clans were converted. Al-Qāḍī al-Nuʿmān reports that in this way most of the Sawād (agricultural regions) of Kufa joined the daʿwa.[44] The successful conversion of clans in Iraq and Yemen was crucial for gaining momentum for the daʿwa. Most crucially Abū ʿAbd Allāh al-Shīʿī applied his knowledge of tribal culture to convert clans from the powerful Kutāma tribes in North Africa; these peasant soldiers would become the army of the Fāṭimid Imām from the second decade of the tenth century.

How did the missionaries attract prospective converts to the fold? According to conversion accounts, the missionary forged an emotional and intellectual bond with the potential acolyte. This bond was forged by their shared pathos over the plight of the family of the Prophet. He would show the prospective acolyte that his current state of knowledge is inadequate. In Halm's apt description, the missionary would take the potential convert "partly into confidence, while at the same time provoking new questions from him and enticing him with further revelations . . . the technique of the half-suggestion, the meaningful pause and the mysterious silence."[45] He hinted at possessing salvific knowledge and knowing the rightly guided leader; but he would withhold more than he shared.

We read in several sources that the missionaries used written materials (*kutub*) to proselytize. The ninth-century dāʿī al-Jannābī was sent to the Gulf coast to proselytize with a written source (*kutub*). Elsewhere we read that the missionary would teach acolytes from written sources in a secluded corner of mosques.[46] One missionary read from a notebook (*daftar*) where it was known he received divine instructions.[47] Ḥamdan, an illiterate ox driver, grew increasingly curious about the secret wisdom contained in the missionary's written sources (kitāb). He begged the missionary to administer to him the secret "oath of allegiance"—itself, as Heinz Halm has shown, a fixed, secret, written text—so that he might gain access to this knowledge.[48] During the Fatimid period, al-Qāḍī al-Nuʿmān reports that as the lead missionary, he was sent written sources of esoteric knowledge (*kutub ʿilm al-bāṭin*) and instructed to read them to the believers in the Majālis al-ḥikma (sessions of wisdom). After the session believers would come to the front of the hall, and the missionary would stroke the believers' heads with the written source from which he had been reading so that they might derive blessing from the signature of the Imām written at the end of the text.[49]

The discrepancy between frequent mention of "written materials" in a period in which the daʿwa presents itself as targeting semi- or nonliterate classes raises important questions. In the early second/ninth century, paper was not yet widely available, and it was the littérateurs, not the scholars, who occupied the "writerly world" of books.[50] By the end of the ninth century, we have evidence that written sources were available to scholars of al-Qayrawān, and that they at times read these books outside the presence of a teacher. In 285/898 the Ismāʿīlī convert Ibn al-Haytham borrowed a copy of a book on daily religious duties called *Kitāb yawm wa-layla* (The Book of One Day and One Night) from the Imāmī scholar Muḥammad ibn Sallam al-Kūfī. Ibn al-Haytham reports, "He brought me a copy of 'The Book of One Day and One Night' on which [was written] the name 'Ibrahīm ibn Maʿshar'—my neighbor and an associate of mine who used to sit with us. I memorized the text of it entirely."[51]

But while such activities were common in a scholarly center, it is likely that there were few books in the towns and villages in which the daʿwa first established its foothold. Paper was a new technology and expensive, and in any event many who resided in these regions could not read, and we know these people were the target of the missionaries. It is thus likely that written sources were scarce in many sites in which the missionaries were focused.

It could very well be that it is precisely their scarcity that made books a potent tool. In a setting in which this technology was uncommon, reading taʾwīl aloud from written sources would have added to the aura of the secret wisdom the sources held. Ethnographers of nonliterate cultures have written that in such societies, writing and books have been associated with special powers.[52] In addition, by the late third/ninth century, Shīʿites had long held that the Prophet had bequeathed divine revelation in written sources to ʿAlī, and that these works were still in the possession of the family of the Prophet.[53] A written wisdom literature offered special allure.

The mystique of the written word may explain why the oath of allegiance was a *written* source. The believers were told that the oath was identical to the one administered to prophets that God had referred to in the Qur'ān 33:7. When they were administered the oath from a booklet, it might very well have been among the first written sources that many early acolytes from agricultural villages had heard read in a private setting, aside from the Qurʾān. For a villager in Khuzistan, the Sawād of Kufa, or Tāzrūt, his first handling of a booklet made from paper must have been intensely exciting.

Receiving "the oath of the intimates [of God]" (*ʿahd al-awliyāʾ*) is the seminal transformative moment in the life of a believer. It is the point when a prospective convert formally joins the daʿwa. The oath represented the first of a series of ritualized epiphanies that mark the adept's ascent in the mission hierarchy. These are marked by the payment of dues, each named to represent the believer's rank. His "birth"—that is, his initiation into the daʿwa, was marked by his payment of a silver dirham. This was called "the creation" (*al-fiṭra*). After a major impurity such as sexual intercourse or menstruation, he or she would pay "the exile" (*al-hijra*). Upon reaching the rank of missionary, the believer would pay "the maturation" (*al-bulgha*). Ibn Rizām reports that this was seven gold dinars, a large sum; the believer would receive a special meal sent by the Mahdī consisting of sweets that came from paradise. At a further stage, the missionary ʿAbdān instituted "friendship" (*al-ulfa*) in his "island" in Iraq. Upon reaching this rank, the missionary's property became shared among senior members of the mission. Ibn Rizām wrote that those who achieved this rank "collected everything they had in one single place, and in this way they all became equal, and no one surpassed his comrade and brother through possessions of any kind. . . . It signified to them that they had no need of possessions at all."[54]

According to Ismāʿīlī sources, it was the acquisition of knowledge (*ʿilm*) that facilitated a believer's ascent to increasingly higher ranks (*ḥudūd*). Of what did this knowledge consist? One central question was the identity of the Imām. This was of grave concern, as the Imām was the intercessor between the believer and God, the lifeboat who would carry him or her to the afterlife. For Shīʿites, the succession to Imām Jaʿfar al-Ṣādiq (d. 765), the great-great-grandson of the Prophet Muḥammad's cousin ʿAlī and daughter Fāṭima, had been problematic.

Jaʿfar al-Ṣādiq had publicly proclaimed that his second son, Ismāʿīl, would succeed him as the Imām (the legitimate leader of the Islamic community); Ismāʿīl then died before his father. After Jaʿfar's death, some followers held that either his eldest surviving son, ʿAbd Allāh ibn Jaʿfar (d. 148/765), or younger son, Mūsā ibn Jaʿfar (d. 183/799), was their father's rightful successor. Others claimed that because his father Ismāʿīl had never served as Imām (because of his premature death), Muḥammad, Ismāʿīl's son (and Jaʿfar's grandson), was the rightful Imām. In maintaining the Imāmate of Muḥammad ibn Ismāʿīl, this third group upheld two Shīʿite principles. First, as an Imām, Jaʿfar al-Ṣādiq was incapable of error and thus could not have erred when he proclaimed that his son Ismāʿīl would succeed him. Second, after al-Ḥasan (d. 49/669) and al-Ḥusayn (d. 61/680), the Imāmate could not pass from brother to brother.

When Muḥammad ibn Ismāʿīl died without leaving an heir, many of his followers transferred their allegiance to one of his brothers. According to Imāmī heresiographers, one such group asserted that Muḥammad ibn Ismāʿīl had not died, but was in hiding, and would return at the End of Days.[55] Initiated by ʿAbd Allāh the Elder, this group constituted the beginning of the Ismāʿīlī movement.[56]

Besides the imminent arrival of the Qāʾim and the End of Days, Ismāʿīlī believers were introduced to other secrets. Among these is the story of divinity's emanation. A series of hypostases emanate from God in a supernal realm beyond the celestial spheres. This pleroma consists of two parts: a supernal dyad referred to as Kūnī and Qadar ("Be!" [fem.] and "fate"); and a supernal triad called Jadd (gravity), Fatḥ (opening), and Khayāl (imagination).

God
Kūnī Qadar[57]
God[58]

In one source that is clearly Gnostic in character, the origins of this pleroma take the form of a drama: after emanating from God, the original principle "Kūnī" arrogantly believed that she, rather than God, was the creator.[59] God commanded Qadar to emanate from Kūnī to show her that He alone is the Creator; Kūnī then recanted and recited the testimony of faith in the one God. The seven letters that spell Kūnī and Qadar (k w n y q d r) were apportioned to be bequeathed to the seven nāṭiqs (speaker-prophets) when the earthly daʿwa below unfolded.[60]

The triad Jadd, Fatḥ, and Khayāl, the secret names for the angels Gabriel, Michael, and Serafel, mediate between the pleroma and sublunar worlds. While there are few descriptions of this supernal pentad, its elements were frequently invoked in correlations between it and the cosmos and earthly daʿwa below.

The Ismāʿīlī theory of "hiero-historical" cycles was also a teaching of the early daʿwa. Thus far history has unfolded in a series of six cycles. Each cycle (*dawr*) was initiated by a speaker-prophet (nāṭiq) who was accompanied by a legatee (waṣī). After overcoming his enemy, the speaker-prophet compiles a law, and the legatee discloses its inner sense (*bāṭin*). The speaker-prophet is then followed by a heptad of Imāms, the seventh Imām of which enjoys a special status as the "completer" (*mutimm*) of the cycle.[61] He is either replaced by (or in some sources, himself becomes) the nāṭiq of the next cycle. The missionaries taught that they were currently coming to the end of the sixth historical cycle. The seventh cycle differed: instead of initiating another heptad of Imāms, the Imām would be the redeemer who would terminate history and religious law, reveal the hidden sense of all scriptures and laws, and initiate the End of Days during which believers who were part of the daʿwa would be rewarded, and wrongdoers, outside it, punished for their unbelief.

There were different versions of the identity of the seven speaker-prophets and legatees (waṣīs). The following list is among the most common.

NĀṬIQ	*WAṢĪ*
Adam	Abel
Noah	Shem
Abraham	Ismail
Moses	Aaron
Jesus	Simon-Peter
Muḥammad	ʿAlī
Al-Qāʾim	

Variations in the identity of the waṣīs in early sources suggest that this list was not yet fixed. However, the basic paradigm of six speaker-prophets and waṣīs followed by a heptad of Imāms emerged prior to the advent of the Fāṭimid caliphs.[62]

Finally, taʾwīl—the claim that there is a true, hidden sense underlying key phrases of the Qurʾān, religious praxis, and realia—was, from the beginning of the daʿwa, the main vehicle through which the above doctrines were expressed.

This summary of Ismāʿīlism's doctrines are not found in a clear creedal statement in any Ismāʿīlī source, but once delineated, these doctrines would not be difficult to master; clearly, salvific knowledge did not come from the content of these concepts alone. Rather, it was not merely learning doctrines, but rather, internalizing these schemes and forms so that one could produce them, that constituted "rearing" in knowledge. In the language of the sources, this was referred to as the missionary's capacity "to speak."

Up to this point, I have depicted the beginnings of the daʿwa as a group that North American scholars of contemporary religion would term a "new religious movement," that is, a group that experiences tension with both their "parent group(s)" and the external dominant societies.[63] The daʿwa was also, from the beginning, a militant political movement, a mission to replace the ʿAbbāsid caliph with the rightly guided Imām. When twenty-first-century persons learn of a movement that combines religious ideals with a militant political agenda that includes the use or threat of violence to subvert the sociopolitical status quo, we are predisposed to understand the former as mere rhetoric to serve the latter. Medieval Muslims, too, assigned ulterior motives to the Ismāʿīlī missionaries. They wrote that these "bāṭinīs" (esotericists) only claimed to be Muslims, but were, in fact, pagan philosophers, Jews, or Manicheans posing as Muslims to subvert the community of Muslims from within. Both of these sets of claims tell more about those making them than they do about Ismāʿīlism.

Ismāʿīlī sources themselves present the earthly political state as a vehicle for salvation in the next life. Fāṭimid-Ismāʿīlī doctrinal sources teach that human history alternates between periods of "screening" (*satr*) and periods of "appearance" (*ẓuhūr*); there are periods in which the adherents of truth must remain hidden and periods in which they can appear openly. This theory is, in fact, an idealization of realities that first appear on the ground in the late ninth century with the shift in the daʿwa's strategy from secret cells to the establishment of mountain fortresses and open war against the ʿAbbāsids and their client statelets.

Around the last decade of the ninth century missionaries in Yemen, Iraq, North Africa, and the Arabian gulf shifted tactics and began to proclaim their opposition to the ʿAbbāsid state openly in circumscribed safe havens of differing scope. Al-Qāḍī al-Nuʿmān reports that in a village in the Sawād (the agricultural region) of Kufa in 890, "the missionaries gathered and decided to create a place for themselves that would serve as a place of refuge to which they could emigrate and where they could assemble. They chose a village named Mahtamabad . . . among the Aramaen population. . . . There they piled up a great many stones, and built a well-fortified wall all around the village . . . along with a large moat. On the inside they built a large structure where men women and children were brought. The complex was called a *dār hijra* (place of refuge)."[64]

In that same year in Northern Yemen, the missionaries there built a fortress in Bayt Rayb in the villages in the Laʿa mountains in Yemen. The missionaries collected funds and purchased iron, tools, stone masonry, and weapons to defend it.[65] In eastern Arabia the dāʿī al-Jannābī converted clans of Bedouin warriors around 899/267, occupied the coastal city al-Qātif, and built a dār hijra there. Akhū Muḥsin reports that there, the missionaries ruled like traditional *amīrs* (princes). They resided in an oasis palace and offered the farmers military protection in exchange for taxes.[66]

The missionaries framed these safe havens in religious terms. The hijra, or emigration, was the seminal event in the Prophet Muḥammad's career. Since the early ninth century in Yemen, the Zaydīs used the term "dār hijra" for an encampment within which descendants of the Prophet and their partisans were protected from an unjust *suzerain.* The Ismāʿīlī missionaries drew from and expanded this vocabulary. Following the language of the first generation of Muslims who converted during the life of the Prophet, those who had come from outside the dār hijra were called the emigrants (*muhārijūn*); local adepts were called the Anṣār (helpers). Under the rule of the missionaries, Islamic law was strictly enforced; those who did not obey were subject to banishment. In the daʿwa in North Africa, the top missionaries lived an ascetic life, renouncing wealth. Like in Iraq the high-ranking missionaries in the North African dār hijra around Abu ʿAbd Allāh pooled their property. There was a sense of *communitas* and dedication. "They were brothers, and called each other as such," al-Nuʿmān reported.[67]

The "island" in North Africa was not a mere military encampment or fortress, but a vast territory known as Tāzrūt (a region encompassing what is today sections of modern Algeria and Tunisia). Educated scholars from Shīʿite backgrounds, particularly in the city of al-Qayrawān, were counted among the converts. But most were peasant Kutāma tribesmen. Prior to joining the daʿwa, these tribes had been only lightly "Islamicized" and were governed by tribal mores. Some of these customs, such as the sharing of wives with honored guests, were not in keeping with Islamic statutes. The leading missionary Abū ʿAbd Allāh al-Shīʿī proscribed these non-Islamic practices. To each village he sent a young missionary he called an "elder" as a teacher and spiritual guide. These missionaries held Majālis al-ḥikma (sessions of wisdom), the same term for "lessons" that was used in Iraq, and, later, in Fāṭimid times. In these sessions, men and women believers learned both Islamic teachings and their interior daʿwa sense.

By the end of the second/ninth century, missionaries had initiated several generations of believers who had learned that the rightly guided Imām, Muḥammad ibn Ismāʿīl, would soon appear to usher in the End of Days and reward his followers. Based on their allegiance to and identification with this mission, they had realigned their political and social commitments and, in some cases, put their lives at risk. They had tied their lives, and their hopes for salvation in the afterlife, to the figure of Muḥammad ibn Ismāʿīl.

In 899 the leadership in Salamiyya told the chiefs of the "islands" stunning news: the Mahdī (rightly guided redeemer) was not, as they had long been told, Muḥammad ibn Ismāʿīl. Rather the Mahdī was a certain ʿAbd Allāh, a descendent of Jaʿfar al-Ṣādiq's first son, ʿAbd Allāh ibn Jaʿfar (and thus Muḥammad ibn Ismāʿīl's uncle). Muḥammad ibn Ismāʿīl was but a cover name to protect the true Mahdī from his enemies.

The Announcement of the Mahdī

The believers had been expecting the Mahdī to usher in the End of Days and provide them with a bountiful award. In the Qurʾān the apocalypse is evoked frequently, and for the previous century Shīʿites had expanded on these allusions. The earth and heavens are to be rent asunder, stars will plummet, and mountains will be leveled.[68] After two blows of a trumpet, the bodies of the dead will be resurrected and all humans judged for their deeds. Unbelievers will be sent on the path sloping downward toward hell, while the believers will ascend a bridge that crosses over the fire into paradise.[69] The End of Days would be preceded by terrible war and bloodshed, the sun would rise from the west, and, mirroring it, the Mahdī, a young man, would arise from the west to govern the world with justice just as it was now ruled with tyranny.[70]

In light of these prophecies, the announcement of the Mahdī must have been disappointing. When he appeared not only did the climactic events described not occur, but also the Kutāma Berbers who first viewed him could not help but notice that he was not young. The Mahdī was thirty-five years old, and accompanied by a sixteen-year-old son.

It was up to the missionaries to use taʾwīl to placate the believers and explain this dramatic shift in doctrine. One might expect that this would be a lost cause. The sociology of messianic movements shows that the opposite is often the case: it is common for participants in chilliastic movements to accept rationalization when expectations are not met. When the world's end did not come to pass as predicted for a chiliastic UFO cult in North America in the 1970s, rather than declare their former beliefs erroneous, members increased the level of their committment.[71] Subsequent research has shown that the greater the social commitment and sacrifice of the believers, the further they are willing to adapt their ideas to maintain their commitment to the movement's vision.[72]

Rather than deny the pre-Fāṭimid doctrines, the Fāṭimid Ismāʿīlī missionaries reinterpreted them to suit the regime's aims. They used taʾwīl to show that ʿAbd Allāh did indeed initiate the End of Days; the eschaton, however, would comprise several periods. The reign of the Mahdī and his offspring was only the initial phase of the End of Days, during which the role of the Imām was to expand the rule of God eastward. In other words, for the immediate future, it was empire building, not the eschaton, that would occupy the believers.

His first obstacle, however, was convincing the missionaries of the various islands that he was, in fact, God's rightly guided deputy. At this he and his followers would have mixed success.

Islands of Apostasy

While early Ismāʿīlī doctrine has many features, it is the identity of the Imām himself that is, for any Shīʿite group, its sine qua non. The daʿwa was, after all, a "call" on behalf of this Imām in whose hands its members put their faith in this world and the hereafter. For some fifty years, Ismāʿīlīs had linked their salvation to the figure of Jaʿfar al-Ṣādiq's grandson Muḥammad ibn Ismāʿīl. When in 899 the leading missionaries ʿAbdān and Ḥamdān-Qarmāṭ were told that "Muḥammad ibn Ismāʿīl" had been just a cover name and that the real Mahdī was a "youth" named ʿAbd Allāh, they refused to accept it. ʿAbdān was immediately put to death by one of the leaders in Salamiyya; Ḥamdān-Qarmāṭ escaped and went into hiding. For much of the next century, the daʿwa was divided between those who accepted the Mahdi and his progeny as the rightly guided Imāms, and those who rejected them and continued to wait for Muḥammad ibn Ismāʿīl to return. Let us first consider the response of the various Qarmāṭian islands to the advent of the Fāṭimids in North Africa.

In Yemen two chief missionaries, Ibn Ḥawshab Manṣūr al-Yaman and ʿAlī b. al-Faḍl, founded dār hijras in the mountainous northern highlands several decades before the split. After his forces took control of Ṣanaʿa in 299/912, ʿAlī b. al-Faḍl repudiated his allegiance to the Fāṭimids and claimed himself to be the Mahdī. Ibn Ḥawshab and later his son Jaʿfar ibn Manṣūr al-Yaman—the name to which most Ismāʿil taʿwīl has been ascribed—would stay loyal to ʿAbd Allāh and the Imāms who followed. Yemen was thus at first split, but after several years of battles ʿAli b. al-Faḍl's forces were defeated, and Yemen was firmly in the hand of the Fāṭimid Imāms.

In Iraq and Syria it was a Fāṭimid partisan who had assassinated ʿAbdān, a missionary named Zikrawayh, who initially posed the greatest threat to the Mahdī. After going into hiding, Zikrawayh sent his two sons al-Ḥusayn and Yaḥyā—known in the sources by the colourful sobriquets the "Man with the Birthmark" (Ṣāhib al-shāma) and the "Man with the She-camel" (Ṣāḥib al-nāqa)—to lead a daʿwa, perhaps on behalf of Muḥammad ibn Ismāʿīl, from whom they claimed to be descended. In 290/903 the sons of Zikrawayh occupied Ḥimṣ, Hamāh, Maʿrrat al-Nuʿmān, Baʿalbakk, and Salamiyya itself, where the Man with the Birthmark ordered the slaughter of ʿAbd Allāh's kin (the Imam had vacated the palace in Salamiyya precisely fearing the Qarmaṭian attack).[73] The Man with the Birthmark was eventually captured and killed by the ʿAbbāsids in 391/905. Zikrawayh continued leading Qarmāṭian revolts in Syria until he too was killed in 907. The movement in the Sawād was, in 295/907–8, continued by a missionary named Abū Ḥātim al-Zuttī who forbade his followers to slaughter animals, and thus became known as "al-Baḥrayn" (the Cattle-ites).

The mission in Baḥrayn (in medieval nomenclature, "al-Bahrayn" connoted not just the territory of the modern state, but the entire Gulf coast of Arabia) had, a decade before the Fāṭimid-Qarmāṭī split, been established by a missionary named Abū Saʿīd al-Jannābī who had been sent there by Ḥamdān. After the schism al-Jannābī assassinated a Fāṭimid missionary who had been sent from Yemen and established a daʿwa in the name of a descendent of Muḥammad ibn al-Ḥanafiyya, announcing that Ibn al-Ḥanafiyya was expected to appear in the year 300/912 to usher in the eschaton. Abū Saʿīd himself would be murdered in that year, but under the leadership of his son, Abū Ṭāhir al-Jannābī, the Baḥraynī daʿwa again became active after 923. Once again they forecast the imminent End of Days, this time at the moment of the conjunction of the planets Jupiter and Saturn in 316/928. Abū Ṭāhir's daʿwa was joined by the Qarmāṭīs outside Kufa, and by neighbouring tribes led by a relative of ʿAbdān named ʿIsā b. Mūsā. Together, they threatened Baghdad in 316/927. In its most notorious act, Abū Ṭāhir's group attacked the pilgrims in Mecca in 317/930 and seized the Black Stone of the Kaʿba, presumably to demonstrate the end of the era of Islam and the beginning of the End Times.

The following years did not go well for the Baḥraynī island. After declaring a young Persian from Isfahan as the Mahdī—again in correlation to yet another date for the onset of the End of Days in the year 319/931—the youngster cast as redeemer ordered the cursing of all prophets and the worship of fire and, according to a witness, commanded that Qurʾān leaves be used as toilet paper. Abū Ṭāhir recanted his choice and had the young Persian imposter killed.

Despite this debacle the Baḥraynī island survived. Abū Ṭāhir came to terms with the ʿAbbāsid caliph and, in 339/951, returned the Black Stone to Mecca (now under the control of the ʿAbbāsids) for a ransom. From the years 357/968, under the leadership of al-Ḥasan al-Aʿṣam, the Qarmāṭīs of Baḥrayn came into active military conflict with the Fāṭimids, attacking points within Syria, which had been under Fāṭimid control. These Qarmāṭī-Fāṭimid skirmishes persisted until a truce was reached with the Fāṭimid caliph al-Muʿizz li-dīn Allāh in 974.

The islands in Northwest Iran and Transoxania had been active since the 860s. The region of al-Ṭaleqān (in present day Northwest Afghanistan) became a center from which missionaries were sent to other regions. After the schism of 899, there is evidence that both the Fāṭimids and Qarmaṭīs had supporters in the region, with the former based in Nishapur, and the latter in al-Rayy and, within al-Rayy, Marwarrūdh.[74] The latter enjoyed greater success. The head of a Qarmaṭī island named Ghiyāth converted the ruler of Marwarrūdh, Amīr al-Husayn ibn ʿAlī al-Marwazī, in 290/903. The head of the "island" in al-Rayy, Abū Ḥātim al-Rāzī, sent missionaries to Ṭabaristān, Isfahan, Azerbaijan, and Jurjān and forged ties with the Qarmāṭīs of Baḥrayn. In the first decades of the tenth century amīrs, courtesans, generals, and "the headmen of the towns, potentates, squires and leading scribes of the bureau" ascribed to the cause in the Samanid court and administration. Thus the Samanid Amīr Naṣr b. Aḥmad (r. 301/914–331/943) was converted along with, according to a report by al-Thaʿalabī, his boon companion Abū Bakr al-Nakhshābī, his private secretary Ashʿath, his chamberlain Aytash, the governor of Ilaq Ḥasan Mālik, and an army inspector, Abū Manṣūr al-Ṣāghānī, among others.[75] The most enduring contribution of the Qarmāṭī dioceses were not, however, success in missionizing. Rather it was their innovative reformulation of doctrine.

Ismāʿīlism did not begin as a system of speculative philosophy, but its character, an abstract, universalistic set of doctrines in which metaphysics played a key role, was conducive to a philosophical interpretation. Even the early daʿwa's teachings touched on such topics as the nature of God's unknowability, His first emanations, the primordial pleroma, the movements of the celestial spheres, and the nature of matter, form, and natures. In one of the earliest surviving tracts a demiurge is depicted as the world's creator—clearly, a gnostic theme.[76] Other elements have been termed Pythagorean.[77] The early sources lack the systematic, speculative rigor that would have been familiar to the denizens of court life who were trained in logic and *falsafa*—philosophy in the Neoplatonic Greek tradition of al-Kindī and the Baghdad school. The missionaries of Transoxania and Northwest Iran developed these speculative systems to compete with philosophers at court.

The most prominent members of this school whose works are extant (or excerpted in the works of others) are Muḥammad b. Aḥmad al-Nasafī (d. 332/943) in Samanid Transoxania and Khurāsān,[78] Abū Ḥātim al-Rāzī (d. 322/934) in Al-Rayy in Northern Iran, and Abū Yaʿqūb al-Sijistānī (d. ca. 365/975) in Khurāsān and later Sijistān.[79] The aim of these daʿīs was not to become philosophers in the Greek tradition. Rather they intended to demonstrate to those at court—most importantly, the amīr ruling the statelet—that the teachings of their mission were superior to falsafa. Greek philosophers were a useful target, for this allowed the missionaries to position themselves as an Islamic alternative to the pagan Greek sciences. Unlike ḥadīth scholars the Ismāʿīlī missionaries employed universalistic concepts and logic that could compete with philosophers on their own terms. Since the taʾwīl composed during the period of the caliph al-Muiʿzz included thinly veiled attacks on these dioceses, they are particularly important for this study.

After their break with the Fāṭimids, the leaders of these daʿwas created theories of leadership to account for the extended absence of the Mahdī Muḥammad ibn Ismāʿīl. Al-Nasafī held that until Muḥammad ibn Ismāʿīl returned, twelve "lieutenants" (*lawāḥiq*) or heads of individual dioceses should rule. It is unclear if one of these twelve was the leader, or if they were all to lead cooperatively. Abū Ḥātim al-Rāzī wrote that the present period was an "interim" (*fatra*)—a period between cyclical periods. In such interim periods during which a completer-Imām has not appeared to usher in a new cycle, one of the twelve lieutenants serves as chief and deputy (*khalīfa; mustakhlaf*) of the absent Imām until his return. Al-Rāzī did not, however, recognize the Fāṭimid Imān in North Africa as this deputy; he likely viewed himself in this role.[80]

It was thus not the Fāṭimids but a non-Fāṭimid Ismāʿīlī who introduced the concepts of khalīfa (caliph) and fatra (interim) into the conceptual vocabulary of Ismāʿīlism. Unlike for Sunnī Muslims, for whom khalīfa connoted "deputy of the Prophet of God," for al-Razī the caliph was the deputy of the rightly guided Qāʾim Muḥammad ibn Ismāʿīl.

Early in his career, al-Nasafī's student al-Sijistānī adopted his teacher's view. He wrote that until the return of Muḥammad ibn Ismāʿīl there would be no Imāms, only the twelve lawāḥiq. Toward the end of his career, however, al-Sijistānī altered his views, suggesting that after the arrival of the Qāʾim, Imāmate was in the hands of Muḥammad ibn Ismāʿīl's descendants.[81] This shift suggests that al-Sijistānī recognized the Fāṭimids as deputy-Imāms, perhaps as a result of the reforms instituted by al-Muʿizz li-dīn Allāh.[82]

A second related topic of dispute was the status of the law in the period of the first speaker-prophet Adam. It was expected that the Qāʾim would return the world to the religion of Adam. The first and final periods were thus closely associated; consequently the career of Adam was controversial. When al-Nasafī claimed that Adam's form of worship did not require laws or works, for Adam was able to worship God directly in His unicity, this implied that during the period of the Qāʾim, law and works would also be unnecessary. Abū Ḥātim al-Rāzī strongly rejected al-Nasafī's conception that during the period of Adam, religion did not entail "works." Abū Ḥātim held that Adam must have received prophecy and a law, for these were the primary vehicle to worship God.[83] As Madelung notes al-Rāzī's position was likely due to the extreme antinomianism of the Qarmāṭians in al-Baḥrayn discussed above. These political concepts and Neoplatonic interpretations were adopted by the Fātimids during the reign of al-Ḥākim.

For our purposes the most important point is that Fāṭimid taʾwīl was composed in the context of Ismāʿīlī groups who challenged Fāṭimid legitimacy and power. Fāṭimid responses to these challenges leave their mark on taʾwīl, castigating those who challenged the divinely chosen leader. But even among the Fāṭimids, the relationship between the state and daʿwa was less clear-cut than has frequently been presented.

The Imperial Island: The Fāṭimid Caliphs and the Ismāʿīlī Daʿwa, 909–1010

Unlike the dioceses described above, the North African region led by Abū ʿAbd Allāh al-Shīʿī was, in the beginning, enthusiastically behind the Mahdī ʿAbd

Allāh. Abū ʿAbd Allāh al-Shīʿī, who had been trained as a missionary in tribal Yemen. He had studied the tribal governance of Berber North Africa, and, as he put it in a communication, mastered the customs of "these simple people" and earned their trust. First by proselytizing the Shīʿites, and then by leveraging this success with political and military stratagems, he motivated almost all the Kutāma tribes (Ijjāna, Laṭāya, Jīmala, Malūsa, Danhāja, and Ūrīsa) to join the daʿwa. Based in Tāzrūt, Abū ʿAbd Allāh al-Shīʿī had effectively become the ruler of a small theocratic statelet. "The Friends of God" (as the *dāʿīs* were known) dedicated themselves to educating the Kutāma Berbers in Islamic law and Ismāʿīlī doctrine. Between 906 and 909, the state moved from the agricultural regions to the cities of Ṭubna and eventually al-Qayrawān and al-Raqqāda, displacing the Aghlabids (a tributary of the ʿAbbāsid caliphs). Before the Mahdī had even appeared, an administrative system of governors had imposed Shīʿite ritual forms in the mosques: the Shīʿite call to prayer (which adds the phrase "come to the best of works") was mandated. In addition supererogatory prayers (*tarāwiḥ*) that are encouraged by Sunnīs were disallowed. In sermons preachers mentioned the virtues of ʿAlī, Fāṭima, al-Ḥasan, al-Ḥusayn, and their descendants. The (Sunnī) notables and scholars, terrified at this turn to a Shīʿite theocracy, fled the city.

After his arrival the Mahdī assumed the position of Imām and the title Commander of the Faithful.[84] The Mahdī toured different tribal territories. In one a poem praised him as "the new Moses" and "son of Fāṭima, a Fāṭimid Imām." The Mahdī preached in a Friday sermon that his Kutāma tribal peasant army, "like the Israelite tribes," were the elite of an emerging empire. They were destined to displace the tyrants to the east and rule the world. ʿAbd Allāh had his judges enforce Shīʿite principles in law. (His genealogical lineage, and specifically his descent from Jaʿfar al-Ṣādiq, was adjusted several times and was an internal matter privy only to the elite.) Outwardly the state was referred to variously as "al-Dawla al-Nabawiyya" (the prophetic state), "al-Dawla al-ʿAlawiyya" (the ʿAlid state), "Dawlat al-Rasūl" (the state of the Messenger [of God], or simply, "Dawlat al-Ḥaqq" (the state of the True God).[85] The shift from the appellation "al-Mahdī" (the divinely guided one), an epithet with clear messianic overtones, to the regnal title "Mahdī billāh" (the one guided by God) reflects this transition from chiliasm to caliphate.

In principle, the Fāṭimid Imām was to assume two roles: he was a divine guide charged with the spiritual welfare of humankind; and, he was the ruler of an empire. As spiritual leader, the Fāṭimid Imām was charged with leading his followers to salvation by teaching the secret sense of the law. As ruler, his responsibilities were not unlike caliphs in other Islamic empires: he founded palace cities and grand congregational mosques, led the Friday prayer, collected taxes, protected and expanded the borders, supervised the designs for coinage, appointed judges and market inspectors, and patronized scholars, scientists, and littérateurs.

For Fāṭimid missionaries, these two roles were viewed as perfectly complementary. In *al-Mūjaza al-kāfiya fī adāb al-daʿwa wal-ḥudūd*, an epistle on the correct comportment and manners for missionaries, the Fāṭimid dāʿī Aḥmad al-Naysābūrī's (thrived mid fourth/tenth century) described state and daʿwa (mission) as perfect complements: "Kingship is the guardian of religion; and the spread of religion and the success of the daʿwa strengthens the state. The followers of the Imām reside either within the empire's domains (*fī ḥadratihi*) or in different islands of the daʿwa. They are his army (*jund*)."[86] According to al-Naysābūrī, the Imām's dual role as head of mission and state was a straightforward proposition: the ruler supports the mission, and the mission strengthens the state.

There were, however, clearly moments when the Fāṭimid Imām's position of ruler chafed against his role as spiritual leader. At times there were problems in reconciling the comportment of the Mahdī with the Shīʿite theocratic state forged by Abū ʿAbd Allāh al-Shīʿī. Before the Mahdī's appearance in al-Raqqāda, the Kutāma "Friends of God" had adopted Abū ʿAbd Allāh al-Shīʿī's ascetic values. Their mentor wore rough wool clothes, lived humbly, forbade alcohol under punishment of death, imposed a nightly curfew, and divided the revenue that he received equitably among the believers. Once ensconced in his castle in al-Raqqāda, the Mahdī wore fancy silks, drank from gold vessels, and distributed large amounts of money, expensive clothes, and other prizes to the Kutāma chieftains. There were charges that he drank wine and enjoyed the company of Greek eunuchs. According to reports, one of the senior Kutāma elders among the Friends of God, a certain Hārūn ibn Yūnus, confronted the Mahdī, accusing him of whore-mongering, drinking wine, sodomy, and lying, and challenging him to perform a miracle to prove his divinely-guided status. The Mahdī had all those involved executed, including Abū ʿAbd Allāh al-Shīʿī, the founder of the Fāṭimid state in Tāzrūt.[87] Such incidents suggest that at times serving as a ruler in the manner of caliphs could conflict with the role of spiritual guide.

Modern historians have tended to downplay such incidents and, like al-Naysābūrī, presented the Fāṭimid Imām's two roles, divinely-guided leader and head of state, as complementary. When they do so, they allude to a number of factors. First, Fāṭimid-Ismāʿīlī doctrine legitimized the position of the Fāṭimid claimant to rule the world; doctrine thus served as the vehicle of empire.[88] Second, the Fāṭimid Imāms sponsored the Majālis al-ḥikma (sessions of wisdom); instruction in doctrine was a state-administered project. Third, the later Fāṭimid caliphs appointed judges steeped in Shīʿite law, one caliph, al-Mansūr, wrote a legal treatise,[89] and, under al-Ḥākim, the Fāṭimids established a chief-judge from the Ismāʿīlī *madhhab* (school of jurisprudence). Fourth, although it is unlikely that the Bāb al-abwāb ("gate of gates" or chief missionary) was an institutional rank in the early period, after the year 1001, it was clearly a state sponsored institution, and thus from this point a missionary held a clearly defined role in the state apparatus. Fifth, we know that in North Africa and Egypt, the Imām would authorize the works of his missionaries in matters of doctrine; he thus occupied a clear role in formulating doctrine.[90] Sixth, we know that during the Fāṭimid period, the Fāṭimid missionaries and the Imām himself corresponded with believers in the different Ismāʿīlī islands to correct points of doctrine. Finally, several historians have suggested that public ceremonial—mosque and coin inscriptions, court symbols and decorum, and festivals—held an Ismāʿīlī doctrinal valence.[91] Historians have thus presented the source of legitimacy of the Fāṭimid caliphs as steeped in Ismāʿīlism.

However, there is good reason to believe that these two positions of caliph and Imām were not always easy to reconcile. There is little evidence that the Fāṭimids encouraged local populations under their rule to convert to Ismāʿīlism; the missionaries proselytized for the daʿwa outside the Fāṭimid territories. When the Fāṭimid missionaries taught at the Majālis al-ḥikma in the caliphal palace, only those already in the Ismāʿīlī fold were permitted to attend.[92] One would expect a regime concerned with strengthening the daʿwa to have done more to institute it as part of the state apparatus, and to have called for communities near the palace city to join it.

The notion that the Fāṭimids founded an "Ismāʿīlī legal school" should also be qualified. First, it has yet to be established that Ismāʿīlī jurists comprise a madhhab in the sense that traditionally applies in Islam: a network of teachers and students over successive generations and commentaries on the seminal texts of a founding jurist such as we find in the Ḥanafī Sunni, Zaydī-Hadawī, and Akhbārī Twelver *madhhabs*, for example. Poonawala's *Guide* lists little evidence that al-Qāḍī al-Nuʿmān's *Daʿāʾim al-islām* became the basis (*aṣl*) for a scholastic madhhab of commentaries, ancillary works, and super-commentaries by networks of scholars—the typical basis for an Islamic madhhab—during the Fāṭimid period. Rather, al-Nuʿmān's work served as a type of legal code for Ismāʿīlī communities. Wilferd Madelung's recent discovery of a legal treatise purportedly penned by the Caliph al-Manṣūr billāh is interesting in part because the work never became well known; like Ibn al-Muqaffaʿ's legal treatise for the ʿAbbāsid Caliph al-Manṣūr, the fact that it was not widely disseminated suggests that his treatise represented an aborted project by a Fāṭimid Imām to formulate law.[93]

In substance, al-Qāḍī al-Nuʿmān's jurisprudence was really an interpretation of Jaʿfarī law, the teachers of Jaʿfar al-Ṣādiq and the preceding Imāms. Al-Nuʿmān's *fiqh* has been described as a mixture of Twelver law and Zaydī law; in other words, it seems again to be a compromise jurisprudence that would have appealed to a wide range of Shīʿites.[94] In this light, it is noteworthy that al-Nuʿmān composed several works devoted to traditional Shīʿite (rather than partisan Ismāʿīlī) works such as the *Kitāb al-manāqib li-ahl al-bayt* (The Book of Virtues of the Family of the Prophet) and the *Sharḥ al-akhbār faḍāʾil al-āʾimma* (The Book of Reports regarding the Virtues of Imāms). It is difficult to view the jurisprudence and related genres produced by Fāṭimid-Ismāʿīlīs as evidence of Ismāʿīlism's role as the Fāṭimid state religion. On the contrary, it could just as easily be read as an attempt to present the Fāṭimid Imām's commitment to reaching out to all ʿAlids.

Historians have presented Fāṭimid public ceremonial and architecture as an opportunity for the Fāṭimid Imām to surreptitiously bring the teachings of the daʿwa into the public sphere. Paula Sanders suggests that the Fāṭimids' court ceremonial held a secret Ismāʿīlī sense,[95] while the art historian Rene Bierman has gone further, arguing that the Fāṭimids' inscriptions on mosques and other distinctive Fāṭimid forms such as the concentric designs on the Fāṭimid coinage was reflected in taʾwīl. "To those who saw the concentric circle format, it was a sign of Fāṭimid rule and law. To Ismāʿīlīs among them, it was that and more. It was a sign of Ismāʿīlī ideology."[96]

In fact, subsequent scholarship by art historians has not born out claims that there was an Ismāʿīlī secret sense to Fāṭimid public texts. Sheila Blair's work has refuted the notion that the floral Kufic style of the Fāṭimid inscriptions on mosques was political or ideological in nuance; it likely had more to do with local artisans than caliphal policy.[97] Bloom, too, finds that Fāṭimid architectural design reflects an interest in project splendor, rather than polemic.[98] And *pace* Bierman, to the degree that they could be considered sectarian, Fāṭimid ceremonial and public texts (mosque inscriptions, coinage, and congregational mosque sermons) tended to be more pan-ʿAlid than Ismāʿīlī. The epistles issued by the Fāṭimid Imāms emphasized the primacy of the Prophet's rightly-guided descendants, their sermons described the Imām as Noah's ship, and the festivals they sponsored such as ʿAshūra and Ghadīr Khum were broadly Shīʿite, not specifically Ismāʿīlī. Inscriptions on mosques, too, adduced seminal verses of the Qurʾān—hardly a sectarian source. The Fāṭimid nomenclature for the hierarchy discussed by Paula Sanders is extremely rich, but differs from the names for the Ismāʿīlī daʿwa hierarchy in taʾwīl. And the Fāṭimid ceremonial emblems—the Imām's parasol, ʿAlī's staff, and the distinctive Fāṭimid turban, are not prominent themes in Ismāʿīlī taʾwīl.[99] Even the unofficial name of the regime, "Fāṭimid," based on Fāṭima the mother of al-Ḥasan and al-Ḥusayn, could be viewed as an attempt at inclusivity, reaching out to those who identify with both these ʿAlid sub-branches of the Hāshimite family (but still tweaking the ʿAbbāsids who were Hāshimites unrelated to Fāṭima).

Fāṭimid coinage reform brings up a particularly interesting case from which to explore the connections between state and sectarian rhetoric. The date and provenance of coins is certain--the issue date and place are provided on the flan of the coin. The legends are sufficiently discrete to observe shifts over time. It is clear from a review of early Fāṭimid coinage that there were significant shifts in Fāṭimid official rhetoric during the reign of the fourth caliph, al-Muʿizz li-dīn Allāh (ruled 341-365/953-975).

The first extant coins come in the period when Abū ʿAbd Allāh al-Shīʿī, the revolutionary who proclaimed the arrival of the Messiah ʿAbd Allāh, struck dinars soon after entering the Aghlabid capital Raqqāda issued at al-Qayrawān in 296/908.[100] The first issue, which is also attested in documentary sources, has on its obverse, the testimony of faith (shahāda) by itself; on the reverse is the *ḥamdala* (praise of God). The following year, 297/909, also in al-Qayrawān, coins were struck with new legends. On the obverse was inscribed "*balaghat ḥujjat Allāh*" (May the proof of God be complete) on the reverse, *tafarraqa aʿdāʿ Allāh* (May the enemies of God be dispersed). The same year we have dinars issued with just the shahāda on the obverse, with *lillāh*/al-Mahdī (To God / al-Mahdi) on the reverse. Another issue of dinar the same year has on the obverse, *'Abd Allāh / amīr al-muʾminīn* (ʿAbd Allāh / Commander of the faithful); on the reverse, al-Imām / al-Mahdī billāh (The Imām / The One Guided by God). This last type is not extant for the year 298/910, but is the type used for every issue of al-Mahdī's reign until 322/933. In his notes on the coins that the Islamic numismatist Michael Bates made available to me, he orders the issues of these years as follows: Abū ʿAbd Allāh's arrival to al-Qayrawān; al-Mahdī's liberation or arrival to Raqqāda; and finally the assumption of authority of ʿAbd Allāh with full titles.[101]

These changes on the coins reflect the transition from a sectarian, chiliastic movement to an emerging caliphate. The legends on the reverse of the early 297/909 issue, *tafarraqa aʿdāʾ Allāh* (may God's enemies disperse), includes a petitionary prayer against God's enemies. On the obverse, "*ḥujja*," a term used by Shīʿite sectarians both for the Imām and his head missionary, would have resonated broadly among Shīʿite sectarians. The phrase "*balaghat ḥujjat Allāh*" ("may the *ḥujja* be complete") would certainly have inspired interest among an Imāmī Shīʿite population awaiting the re-appearance of the Imām whom they held had been in occultation since 260/873.

The coinage design shifts significantly after the year 909. The 909 title, al-Mahdī, carries a millenarian resonance. In 298/910, the name "al-Mahdī billāh" (the One Rightly Guided by God) was clearly intended as an honorific, regnal title. This latter type also provides the ruler's proper name (ʿAbd Allāh), status as al-Imām, and formal title "Amīr al-Muʿminīn" (Commander of the Believers). This process is similar to the shifts in the early titulature of the early ʿAbbāsid caliphs.[102]

There are several significant shifts in coins issued by ʿAbd Allāh's son al-Qāʾim (ruled 322-34/933-945). The issues from al-Qāʾim are all from al-Mahdīya, what was a new Fāṭimid city (in what is today Tunisia). Like its predecessor, on the obverse is the caliph's name (Muḥammad Abū l-Qāsim), the shahāda (in two lines), and title (al-Mahdī billāh); on the reverse was "al-Imām / al-Qāʾim bi-amr illāh / Muḥammad rasūl Allāh / amīr al-muʾminīn." On all dinars in all provinces, a second marginal legend was added outside the date-mint formula, *tammat kalimatu rabbika ṣidqan wa-ʿadlan lā mubaddila li-kalimātihi wa-huwa al-samīʿu l-ʿalīm*; "The words of your Lord are the completion of truth and justice; no one can alter his words, for He is the Hearing, the Knowing" (Qurʾān 6:115). The coinage of al-Manṣūr (ruled 334–341/945–952) at first follows al-Qāʾim's coinage. The sovereign's names are located above and below the central formula in both the obverse and reverse, a double linear circle divides the fields from the margins, and there are stylized floral inscriptions. But in 336/947, coins with a new design were issued. On these coins, field and marginal inscriptions are bounded by inner and outer linear circles. These dinars and dirhāms were minted at al-Mahdiyya in 336–338/947–949. Then, a slightly modified version of the initial type was struck for the next three years.[103]

Al-Muʿizz li-dīn Allāh (ruled 341-365/953-975) introduced significant changes to Fāṭimid coinage. In both the dinars and dirhāms issued in 342/953 the legends in the middle of the flan were presented in concentric form and bordered by circles. This is the first issue with entirely concentric legends in Islamic coinage.

> Obverse
> Glory is God's / [shahāda]/and Ali is the legatee of the messenger, the representative of the favored, and the husband of the radiant, pure FATIMA
>
> Reverse
> The power is God's / ʿAbd Allāh Maʿadd Abū Tamīm al-Imām al-Muʿizz li-dīn Allāh is the Commander of the Believers / The reviver of the sunna of the Prophet, lord of the messengers, heir of the rightly-guided Imāms / In the name of God, Who possesses the clear truth [Mint date]

In the following year, the al-Muʿizz administration again changed the legends. The central field legends ("Might / Power is God's") were replaced by a single dot; hence the modern designation of these dinars as "bulls-eye coins."

> Obverse
> ʿAlī is the best of the legatees, the helper of the best one of those who had been sent
>
> Reverse
> Al-Muʿizz li-dīn Allāh (The Glorifier of the religion of God) is the Commander of the Believers / The Imām summons to the unity of the eternal God.

This initial type is grander and more "Shīʿite" than the latter. In the latter, the praise of ʿAlī is briefer, there is no mention of Fāṭima, and the claims that al-Muʿizz is "reviver of the sunna" and "heir to the Imāms" has been removed. Al-Muʿzz is described as the one who "calls [the believers] to the unicity of God," a belief, of course held by all Muslims. The coins provide evidence of a shift in state rhetoric from a more partisan Shīʿite to a broader ʿAlid stance.

As Wilferd Madelung first established, al-Muʿizz was responsible for important shifts to Fāṭimid-Ismāʿīlī doctrine. Al-Muʿizz revoked his great-grandfather al-Mahdī's claims that Muḥammad ibn Ismāʿīl had been a mere cover name. His missionaries held that Muḥammad ibn Ismāʿīl was indeed the awaited final redeemer. Until his reappearance, his descendants, the Fāṭimid Imāms, would rule in his place. When he returned, Muḥammad ibn Ismāʿīl's reappearance would not be corporeal, but spiritual; just as the End of Days has different stages, so too does the nature of the Qāʾim Muḥammad ibn Ismāʿīl. He had briefly appeared in corporeal ḥadd (limit), disappeared during "the period of the hidden Imāms," and returned as ʿAbd Allāh the Mahdī at the beginning of "the period of disclosure." In the present period, he is in his "spiritual limit" (*ḥadd rūḥānī*) and is represented on the earth by the Fāṭimid caliphs. These shifts were intended to reach out to the Qarmāṭian dioceses in Iran. More broadly, they were part of al-Muʿizz's strategy to expand the empire to the east.[104]

Contrary to how Fāṭimid public rhetoric has been portrayed, rather than Ismāʿīlī, I would suggest that the Fāṭimid state vacillated between partisan Shīʿite (the public cursing of the companions, the celebration of ʿAshūra and Ghadīr khum, the announcement of "come to the best of works" in the call to prayer) and broadly ʿAlid (extolling ʿAlī, Fāṭima, and their progeny as the bequest of the Prophets). Both entailed the Fāṭimids' attempt to appeal to an audience sympathetic to the claim that legitimate rule should rest in a descendant of ʿAlī and Fāṭima. Thus when al-Muʿizz first arrived in Egypt after his troops had taken the city, a contemporary wrote that al-Muʿizz addressed the scholars there. A near contemporary is reported to have recalled al-Muʿizz's entry to Egypt in the following terms.

> He was not coming to Egypt so as to enlarge his empire, nor for the sake of money. Rather he wished to help the truth attain its due, to perform the pilgrimage, and to conduct the jihād. He wished to devote his life to pious deeds and to do what his ancestor the Prophet had commanded. His address moved many listeners to tears. In response, the Egyptian jurist and historian Ibn Zulāq made a speech in praise of the Prophet Fāṭima, ʿAlī and their descendants, the true Imāms. Al-Muʿizz honored him with a camel litter.[105]

A pan-ʿAlid rhetorical strategy made sense in a period in which the star of Shīʿite regimes as well as a general sympathy for the family of the Prophet (*tashayyuʾ hassan*) was rising. The century of 950–1050 would see, in addition to the Qarmāṭians and Fāṭimids, the rise of Shīʿite Buyyids in Iraq and Iran, the Imāmī Ḥamdānids in Syria, the ʿUqaylids in the Ḥijāz, and a Zaydī Imāmate in the Caspian and Yemen. Even Sunnī statelets needed Sayyids (descendants of the Prophet) for their legitimacy. It was also in this period that the position of the naqīb, the representative of the Prophet's family, was established. During a period in which the ʿAbbāsids' legitimacy waned, the Fāṭimids used their Ṭālibid pedigree to woo support.

The Fāṭimid daʿwa continued as well, and the Fāṭimid Imām was head of that, too.[106] Primarily, his role in the daʿwa was not to expound on doctrine himself, but rather, to provide his charismatic imprimatur to the missionaries' works and, when necessary, reign them in.[107] As Madelung wrote, the first Fāṭimid Imām al-Mahdīh

> had little sympathy for the Ismāʿīlī daʿwa. He had come to distrust it every since the breakaway of ʿAbdān and many of the eastern Ismāʿīlī communities. This distrust was only enhanced by the disloyality of Abū ʿAbd Allāh al-Shīʿī and his brother Abū l-ʿAbbās which affected many of his Kutāma followers. Al-Mahdī was worried about both antinomian tendencies and excessive veneration and expectations concerning the Imāms in the teaching of the daʿwa which could foster aversion and opposition among the Sunnī population. After an outbreak of riots and street fighting in al-Qayrawān between the inhabitants and the Ismāʿīlī Kutāma soldiers, he forbade the daʿwa to teach and to proselytize for a long time. . . . There are frequent reports about his severe punishment of missionaries who had provoked public offense. In 309/921, he ordered . . . to round up 200 dāʿīs in al-Qayrawān, Bāja, and Tūnis who had openly drunk wine and eaten pork during Ramaḍān. Most of them were left to die in prison.[108]

The rounding up of antinomian Ismāʿīlī missionaries represents a far different reality than the integrated daʿwa-dawla roles depicted by al-Naysabūrī. While state and religious mission were both important to the Fāṭimid Imāms and the leading missionaries, their trajectories were distinct and should not be conflated. From the vantage point of the Ismāʿīlī missionaries who composed taʾwīl, their allegiance to the Imām focused on his role as savior to the believers. The daʿwa sources were for internal consumption, meant to buttress the commitment of the community and elevate their spiritual status through mastering ʿilm knowledge. The state may have provided a safe-haven, but it is the Imām's role as a source of saving knowledge that was crucial for the daʿwa.

The remainder of Ismāʿīlī history, that is, after the caliphate of al-Ḥākim bi-Amr Allāh to the present, is only indirectly related to this book, but there are good reasons for briefly recounting Ismāʿīlism's story. These early sources of taʾwīl were copied and read by Ismāʿīlīs in the later communities; it is, as I recount in the following chapter, due to the efforts of later communities that such sources are extant. It is worth recalling that as in the case of any literature meant to endure over time, its impact is not limited to its moment of composition: early Ismāʿīlī taʾwīl may have been composed in a time and place, but its impact transcends these circumstances.

Ismāʿīlism, from al-Ḥākim to the Present

Under the caliph al-Ḥākim bi-Amr Allāh's (r. 386/996–411/1021) industrious and influential dāʿī, Abū Ḥamīd al-Kirmānī, Fāṭimid-Ismāʿīlī doctrine again changed course.[109] From philosophers in the Neoplatonic tradition, al-Kirmānī incorporated a system of ten intellects into Fāṭimid Ismāʿīlism. Al-Kirmānī also responded to Druze sectarians who had broken from the Fāṭimid Ismāʿīlī camp, worshipped al-Ḥākim as God in human form, and declared the corporeal End of Days here and now. Al-Kirmānī emphasized the importance of the external form religious praxis and rejecting any allegorical interpretation that resulted in the relaxing of a law.[110] In al-Kirmānī's thought aspects of Islam that had once been allegorized now must be accepted prima facie: Muslims must believe that "paradise and hell are true," that "the dead will be resurrected," and that Adam was merely the father of mankind who brought the first law (and not the secret principle behind all the speaker-prophets and Imāms). The Fāṭimid caliphs were human, and neither divine nor, as earlier texts in the Ismāʿīlī corpus at times hinted, a series of Qāʾim saviors. The law of Islam would never be abrogated, not now, nor in the future End of Days. When the Qāʾim arrives at the End of Days, he will merely dismantle the daʿwa's earthly hierarchy; God's law will continue to apply. In correcting Druze excess, al-Kirmānī dampened aspects of Ismāʿīlī doctrine that were inconsistent with non-Ismāʿīlī Islam, rejecting many tenets that had been at the heart of Fāṭimid-Ismāʿīlism forty years prior.[111]

Some years after the caliphate of al-Ḥākim, strife along ethnic lines (Berbers, Turks, and sub-Saharan Africans) within the Fāṭimid military, as well as plague and famine, weakened the regime. The decade after 1060 is referred to as the period of "strife" (*fitna*) and "crisis" (*shidda*) in the sources.[112] The Fāṭimid ministers rose in power, and, by the end of the eleventh century, the caliphs were figureheads for their Turkish ministers. The Ayyūbid dynasty (1171–1250) formally ended the Fāṭimid caliphate in 1171. Statelets affiliated with Ismāʿīlism continued to rule in Yemen (the Ṣulayhids) and, for a brief period, in Iraq (the ʿUqaylids); the longest-ruling Ismāʿīlī statelet controlled a territory in western Iran from 1090–1256 from a mountain fortress in Alamut.

As was the case during the early Fāṭimid period, so too after the late eleventh century, Ismāʿīlism was marked by fissures. When the Fāṭimid caliph al-Mustanṣir named his first son, al-Nizār, to succeed him, his powerful Turkish minister Badr al-Jamālī, whose daughter had married al-Mustanṣir's son al-Mustaʿilī, politicked for al-Mustaʿilī to be chosen as the successor. The Persian Ismāʿīlīs were loyal to al-Nizār. When al-Mustanṣir died in 1094 and al-Nizār was purportedly assassinated that same year, the Persians defected from Cairo, claiming that al-Nizār had not died, but continued to rule in occultation. Their leader, Ḥasan-i Sabbāḥ, and his cadre captured a castle fortress in Alamut in al-Nizār's name; from there the Nizārīs launched an open rebellion against the ʿAbbāsids in Baghdad and their Seljuk overlords. Persian missionaries from Alamut migrated to mountain villages in Syria and pursued a policy of assassination, terrorizing both ʿAbbāsid and Fāṭimid leaders, including the Fāṭimid caliph al-ʿĀmir. Islamic law was periodically suspended during several revolutionary phases of the movement.

The Nizārī rulers of Alamut sometimes ruled as ḥujjas of the Imām, and sometimes as the Imām himself, and vacillated from chiliasm and antinomianism to conservative, traditional Islamic positions. Thus the Imām Ḥasan ʾala Dhikrhi l-Salām proclaimed the advent of the End of Days and the resurrection of the dead (*qiyāma*) and interpreted Islamic law symbolically, whereas his successor, the Imām Jalāl al-Dīn Ḥasan, repudiated these views and invited Sunnī jurists of the Shāfiʿī madhhab to teach the Ismāʿīlī about community law.[113] Crucial to these sweeping shifts in doctrine was the principle that as an impeccable source of God's knowledge, the Imām possessed authority to make and remake doctrines to suit the age, a doctrine first adopted by the ḥujja Ḥasan-i Ṣabbāḥ (r. 1090–1124).

One genealogical line of Imāms that claimed descent from Alamut through a certain Shams al-Dīn Muḥammad, who claimed descent from ʿAbd Allāh the Elder, surfaced in Iran in the village of Anjudan under the name Qāsim Shāh.[114] In the fifteenth and sixteenth centuries in Central Iran, Nizārī Ismāʿīlism became intertwined with the Niʿmatallāhī Sūfī order, and attracted large numbers of Gujrati converts.[115] The Qāsim-Shāh line played an important role in Iranian politics in the sixteenth and seventeenth centuries. This line was given the title the Aga Khans (princes) in 1828. After a failed revolt on Kirmān, the Aga Khan moved to British India in 1845. Following steps initiated by his grandfather Sulṭān Muḥammad Shāh Aga Khan III (d. 1376/1957), the current Aga Khan, His Highness the Prince Shāh Karīm al-Ḥusayni Aga Khan IV, has led the Nizāri-Ismāʿīlī community since 1957. He has developed an international organization, the Aga Khan Development Network (AKDN), an international, nongovernmental, intrastate institution devoted to serving the welfare of Ismāʿīlī communities and the societies in which they live worldwide. They have been devoted to such issues as health care, education, and economic development.

Aga Khan IV (r.1957–present), in particular, has devoted himself to institutional success of the AKDN and, in his speeches, seems to suggest a theory of Imāmate as an abstract principle, rather than residing in his person. Aga Khan

III and Aga Khan IV have developed a liberal, modernist theory of leadership that finds its expression primarily in institutional structures, the identity of the communities, and the office of the Aga Khan itself.[116]

The Persian Ismāʿīlīs who accepted Mustaʿlī as al-Mustanṣir's successor became known as Mustaʿlī Ismāʿīlīs. They too later endured a succession dispute; those who claimed descent after the twenty-first Mustaʿlī Ismāʿīlī Imam al-Ṭayyib ibn al-ʿĀmir went into "screening" (satr) in 524/1130 and became known as the Mustaʿlī-Ṭayyibīs. Since this point the group has been led by a series of chief dāʿīs, or dāʿī muṭlaqs, based first in Yemen and then, after 946/1539, in Surat in western India. During the twentieth century the movement has been led from Mumbai by Sayyidna Tahir Sayf al-Din and Sayyidna Muhammad Burhan al-Din, who claim far reaching authority. Other subsects, such as the Sulaymānī and Dawudī Bohras, claim different lines of descent for leadership of the movement in lieu of the screening of the Imām.[117]

In January 2014 the death of Burhan al-Din led to a succession dispute between his sons. Abbas Hamdani and Ismail Poonawala, prominent Mustaʿlī-Ṭayyibi scholars and reformers in the United States, have published a manifesto calling for the end of the dāʿī muṭlaq position and the far-reaching power to tax and excommunicate that the position implies. They call for it to be replaced by a daʿī-nāẓim, who would serve in an administrative position without religious authority that accepts input from board members democratically elected by local community councils (*jamaʿāt*).[118]

Conclusion

This brief summary of the history of the Ismāʿīlī daʿwa demonstrates the cyclical recurrence of a particular constellation of doctrinal-historical elements and dynamics. In his social history, William Sewell writes that a particular society's historical narratives are filtered frameworks and "logics" that play a role in their genesis. While each of the historical turns recounted above is of course infinitely more complex and should not be reduced to disputes of succession or theology, the persistence of these concepts to legitimize power well over a millennium demonstrates Ismāʿīlī doctrine's durability and capacity to respond effectively to historical change. Thus the doctrine of "screening" (satr) of the Imām and daʿwa, obedience to Islamic law, and repudiation of antinomian elements vacillates with other periods of disclosure (ẓuhūr) of the Imām and imminent eschatology and antinomianism. What is clear is that during times of upheaval or uncertain succession of the Imām, Ismāʿīlism's schematized theory of history provides ready made options. A leader or dissident can declare the End of Days, or, conversely, declare the present a time of "screening" when the authentic Imām is hidden. In a certain sense, it could be said that once formulated, such concepts do more than allow responses to historical events. By setting the terms by which events are conceived and experienced and through which potential rulers can claim authority, such doxa generate history.

In early taʾwīl similar fissures find echoes in the daʿwa sources. The importance of a missionary not transgressing one's proper rank, for example, is a recurrent theme that could be invoked against subsects attempting to interpret aspects of daʿwa knowledge for purposes contrary to the leadership of the movement.

Ismāʿīlī Taʾwīl and Daʿwa Literature

CHAPTER 2

In medieval Arabic sources, the word *taʾwīl* most often connotes Qurʾānic exegesis. It is thus unsurprising that the few previous articles on Ismāʿīlī taʾwīl have taken comparison with tafsīr, traditional Qurʾānic exegesis, as their point of departure. Tafsīr is, as Bruce Fudge has succinctly put it, "a genre of commentary based on the glosses on difficult or problematic passages in the Qurʾān" that brought to bear such subfields as lexicography, tradition, historical reports, the study of grammar, jurisprudence, and theology to serve the intellectual and ideological concerns of its authors.[1] As a scholastic genre, most tafsīr was composed by ʿulamāʾ (scholars) for ʿulamāʾ; they assembled all available knowledge in comprehensive, line-by-line commentaries of the entire Qurʾān. In his important analysis of al-Thaʿlabī al-Naysabūrī's (d. 1035) *Kashf wal-bayān ʿan tafsīr al-Qurʾān,* Walid Salih describes tafsīr as a "genealogical" tradition. Rather than replacing older methods of interpretation, an exegete added his approach while preserving those that preceded his.[2] Thus al-Thaʿālabī's work was composed in dialectic with the scholastic network of which he was part and should be read in light of this broader exegetical tradition. Saleh thus proposes a synoptic analysis in which each commentary under scrutiny is compared to works that preceded and followed.

This synaptic approach is well suited for the textual, scholarly world of the ʿulamāʾ. However, this sort of philological, source-critical approach is, I would argue, less useful to analyze the sources produced within the activist world of the Ismāʿīlī missionary. Ismāʿīlī sources describe taʾwīl as an interpretive vehicle to unveil the *noumena,* the hidden truths behind the ephemera of the external world for believers who make up the daʿwa. Although it is true that decoding the Qurʾān's "true sense" is among the authors of taʾwīl's stated aims, the ultimate object was not the elucidation of the Qurʾān. This is true in several senses. First, the missionaries interpreted many sources, not just the Qurʾān. And second, and most importantly, the real aim of taʾwīl was not to elucidate a source, but to spiritually transform its audience.

Within Ismāʿīlism, taʾwīl is used to connote a body of doctrinal literature, a hermeneutical technique, and a rhetorical claim to know the "true sense" of a passage or theme. It is useful to disentangle these different senses of the term. I shall refer to the corpus of written taʾwīl sources as "daʿwa literature," and the hermeneutical practice as "taʾwīl." The aim of taʾwīl, to view the world as it truly is, I refer to as "daʿwa knowledge."[3]

Taʾwīl According to the ʿUlamāʾ

Although taʾwīl has become associated with Ismāʿīlism in Western scholarship, it is, in fact, a common word in Arabic Islamic sources. According to the medieval Muslim lexicographers, taʾwil is a verbal noun etymologically linked to the word "first" (*awwal*); this form of the word can have a causative sense as in "to return something to its first or original [state]."[4] In several verses of the Qurʾān, taʾwīl means the coming to pass of an event that had been predicted (Qurʾān 10:39) or the outcome of an event (Qurʾān 4:59, 17:39). In other verses it refers to an interpretation or explanation of a dream (Qurʾān 12:6, 21). But the primary sense adopted by medieval Muslim scholars is that of Qurʾān 3:7, where taʾwīl connotes scriptural commentary, a synonym of the more frequently used word "tafsīr." Abū Jaʿfar ibn Jarīr al-Ṭabarī (d. 310/923), Muḥammad ibn Manṣūr al-Māturīdi (d. 333/944), and Maḥmūd ibn Ḥamza al-Kirmānī (active twelfth century) all used the word *taʾwīl* to mean "commentary" in the titles of their works of Qurʾānic exegesis. This suggests that for them taʾwīl's primary meaning was Qurʾānic exegesis.[5]

Although most commentators took tafsīr and taʾwīl as synonyms, it is clear from al-Suyūṭī's (d. 911/1505) *Kitāb al-Itqān fī ʿulūm al-Qurʾān* that some commentators used taʾwīl as a more specific technical term. They held that tafsīr explicates a word, and taʾwīl, a sentence; or that tafsīr explicates an expression (*lafẓ*), and taʾwīl, its underlying signification (*maʿnā*); or, that tafsīr is concerned with *riwāya* (the transmission of reports) and taʾwīl with *ḍirāya* (deriving the meaning of the verse with the intellect).[6] The second/ninth-century Kufan exegete al-Farrāʾ held that taʾwīl connoted "the reconstruction of [a word's] original meaning" that was "often concealed" and "not obvious from the form itself"—in other words, etymology.[7]

The notion that taʾwīl entails exegesis through recourse to the interpreter's intellect was particularly important for those steeped in the *ʿaqlī* (rationalist) science of dialectic theology. Muʿtazilī and Māturīdī scholars used taʾ wīl to explain anthropomorphic images of God in the Qurʿān inconsistent with their understanding of God's unicity.[8] For example, since the Qurʾān's reference to God's hand (Qurʿān 3:73, 38:75, 48:10, 5:64) could not refer to material hands like those that humans' possess, scholars such as the Zaydī Imām Qāsim ibn Ibrāhīm (d. 246/860) took "hand" to connote God's promise, might, and wisdom.[9] They referred to such rationalist interpretation as taʾwīl.

From an early period, certain traditionalist scholars condemned recourse to intellect to interpret scripture. Taking support from Qurʾān 3:7, which they read as associating taʾwīl with "those who attempt to sow dissension," the proto-Sunnī exegete Muqātil ibn Sulaymān (d. 150/767) distinguished between Qurʾānic interpretation that can be known by humans, tafsīr, and that which is known to God alone, taʾwīl. This view is repeated by later Sunnī scholars, some of whom forbid taʾwīl, which they began to associate with "bāṭinism" (esotericism), again using Qurʾān 3:7 for support.[10] Pickthall's translation of the verse reads:

> He it is Who hath revealed unto thee the Scripture wherein are clear revelations [*muḥkamāt*]. They are the substance of the Book. And others [which are] allegorical [*mutashābbihāt*]. But those in whose hearts is doubt pursue, forsooth, that which is allegorical [taʾwīl] seeking [to cause] dissension by seeking to explain it. None knoweth its explanation [taʾwīl] save God. And those who are of sound instruction say: We believe therein; the whole is from our Lord; but only men of understanding really heed.

According to Pickthall's translation of the passage, scripture comes in two types, "clear" (*muḥkam*) and allegorical (*mutashshābih*). The clear verses can be known by humans; the allegorical sense is known only to God. Those who seek to apply taʾwīl (the word Pickthall translates as "interpretation") to the latter do so only to cause mischief and dissension. In this translation Pickthall was clearly influenced by the Sunnī *riwāya* (ḥadīth oriented) exegetical tradition transmitted by scholars opposed to taʾwīl.

Those who held that taʾwīl is licit such as the Muʿtazilite al-Zamakhsharī interpreted the verse differently. Those verses that Pickthall refers to as "ambiguous" and "known only to God" they translated as "multivalent." In the words of al-Zamakhsharī, "Their expression is singular, but their senses are various" (*lafẓuhu wāḥid wa-maʿānīhi mukhtalifa*). The taʾwīl of such verses is known to God and the "rāsikhūn fī al-ʿilm" (those of sound instruction). Such an interpretation is possible because Arabic allows for both it and the prior translation, depending on whether one parses "those of sound instruction" as apposite to God, or as beginning a new sentence. Al-Zamakhsharī held that "those of sound instruction" were scholars with sound mastery of religious knowledge (*thabatū fīhi watamakkanū*), which, for al-Zamakhsharī, meant those well trained in Arabic grammar and lexicography, dialectic theology, tradition, and other Islamic sciences that he valued.[11] Conversely the fourth/tenth-century Imāmī exegete al-Qummī claimed that "those of sound instruction" refers to "the Prophet and his family to whom was sent down the entirety of the revelation and its interpretation."[12] The Prophet and Imāms alone have access to these sources unavailable to others.

It could be said that proto-Sunnī and Imāmī scholars agreed that the Qurʾān had a hidden sense, but disagreed on who had access to it: God alone, properly trained scholars, or particular divinely guided descendants of the Prophet. During the late Umayyad period, a number of Shīʿite groups applied the third option to fuel various millenarian movements.

Taʾwīl and Esotericism in Early and Pre-Buyyid Shiism

A number of militant Shīʿīte sects from the Umayyad and early ʿAbbāsid period in Khurāsān in Western Iran amplified the view that there were special figures who knew secret, true knowledge of the Qurʾān's hidden sense. Although we do not have many of the sources they produced, later descriptions in histories and heresiographies recorded their views. Among these views is that their leader had supernaltural powers, could speak to angels or bygone prophets, or held the secret knowledge behind scripture. The Bayānīya, the followers of Bayān ibn Samʿān (thrived the first half of the third/eighth century), purportedly interpreted the Qurʾān allegorically.[13] The leader of the Manṣūrīya, Abū Manṣūr al-Ijlī (d. c. 740), claimed to have ascended to heaven and received prophecy, and that he had been given the secret, authentic interpretation of the Qurʾān. The heresiarch al-Mughīra, too, held that the Qurʾān had a *bāṭin* (interior) sense that takes priority over its exterior meaning. Al-Mughīra held that this hidden sense was known only to the redeemer, which he decoded through letter interpretation.[14]

Two claims commonly made by Shīʿite sectarians, the notion that prophecy continues through the savior's link with God, or that this savior has the secret, hidden knowledge of scripture that is extant, had the capacity to serve a similar function. Each claim could provide the group with the sense that what was once hidden was now being disclosed to them alone, a phenomenon they associated as a sign of apocalypse. Thus both the reopening of prophecy and esoteric interpretation are linked to the sense that the End of Days is nigh.

Our knowledge of these militant groups is limited because they produced few sources, and those that were produced are difficult to authenticate to a particular author, time, and place.[15] We know more on the exegesis of the Imāmī Shīʿites of the late third/ninth and fourth/tenth century, as, rather than activists, quietist ʿulamāʾ, scholars devoted to the preservation of knowledge. Meir Bar-Asher has described the early fourth/tenth-century Imāmī Qurʾān commentary that reflected Imāmī scholarly circles in Qumm, Kufa, and Baghdad in the works of Imāmī scholars Furāt al-Kūfī (thrived early fourth/tenth century), ʿAlī ibn Ibrāhīm al-Qummī (d. ca. 307/920), Muḥammad al-ʿAyyāshī (thrived first half fourth/tenth century), and Muḥammad al-Nuʿmānī (d. 971). Imāmī ʿulamāʾ held that there is an interior (*bāṭin*) sense encoded in phrases and lines in the Qurʾān, and that this hidden sense, which was transmitted from ʿAlī to the

Imāms, refers to ʿAlī, Fāṭima, and their progeny.[16] They held that the Imāms alone possess all true knowledge, including the Qurʾān's hidden sense.[17] Other aspects of early Imāmī tafsīr are the use of exegesis by ḥadīth on the authority of the Prophet and his family; a focus on verses of the Qurʾān that bear on the Imāmate; and hostility to Sunnīsm and its heroes, the companions of the Prophet.[18]

Bar-Asher describes pre-Buyyid Imāmī tafsīr as selective and typological. It is selective in that exegetes interpret isolated expressions as clues to be deciphered, and typological in that it connects these passages to the Imāmīs' heroes and teachings. Such an exegetical strategy is similar to that of the church fathers when they find references to church dogma in the Old Testament. In Imāmī scholastic circles, this approach, and the various exegetical strategies employed (variant readings, the addition of words, the use of secret language), authorized its communities' central narratives, made seminal texts and stories directly relevant to its community, and polemicized against competing views.[19]

The Secondary Literature on Ismāʿīlī Taʾwīl

Ismāʿīlī taʾwīl has been analyzed to describe Ismāʿīlī doctrine. That is, scholars such as Stern, Madelung, and Halm have derived a coherent set of doctrines from these unruly sources.[20] This is clearly useful but should be distinguished from the consideration of taʾwīl as a hermeneutic genre.

There have been several substantial articles on Ismāʿīlī taʾwīl as a genre of Qurʾānic exegesis, and two other works that offer contributions to its study. In the most important of these, "Ismāʿīlī taʾwīl of the Qurʾān," Ismail Poonawala describes taʾwīl and its status in Ismāʿīlism through sources composed by the missionaries al-Qāḍī al-Nuʿmān (d. 363/947), Jaʿfar ibn Manṣūr al-Yaman (d. c. 349/960), and Abū Yaʿqūb al-Sijistānī (d. ca 365/975). The bulk of Poonawala's article describes the metaphysics and rhetorical claims upon which Ismāʿīlī taʾwīl is based.

As opposed to the exterior knowledge produced by tafsīr, taʾwīl reveals the inner truth, the *bāṭin*. Taʾwīl is unchanging and complete in its conveyance of truth and reality (*ḥaqīqa*).[21] The Imām recognizes the *ḥaqāʾiq* through God's *taʾyīd* (support). Al-Sijistānī describes the relationship between *tanzīl* (revelation) and taʾwīl to that of the raw materials of wood to the highly refined chest. "The wood's worth and benefit become manifest only after it receives the craftsman's craftsmanship. The craftsmanship puts everything in its proper place. . . . Similarly, the *tanzīl* consists of putting things in words. Beneath those words lie the treasured meanings. It is the practitioner of the taʾwil who extracts the intended meaning from each word and puts everything in its proper place."[22]

Al-Sijistānī suggests that the Qurʾān, Islamic law and ritual, and stories of ancient prophets are merely raw materials; they are pure potential. Only a divinely aided (*muʾayyad*) Imām has the capacity to draw from them the "treasured meanings." This is accomplished, in the words of al-Sijistānī, by "putting everything in its proper place." This approach, the recovery of the structure of all objects of interpretation into their true, divinely ordered hierarchy, is a key principle for taʾwīl.

In *al-Taʾwīl: Ususuhu wa-maʿnīhi fī al-madhhab al-Ismāʿīlī* (*Taʾwīl: Its Foundations and Meanings in the Ismāʿīlī School*), al-Habeb al-Fekki describes taʾwīl ascribed to the early Fāṭimid judge and missionary al-Qāḍī al-Nuʿmān. The latter half of al-Fekki's book consists of critical editions of portions of several of al-Qāḍi al-Nuʿmān's sources that have since been edited in full.[23] The book's contribution lies in the thoroughness of what we might call a phenomenological approach in part three of the book: al-Fekki lists the taʾwīl for seventy-five most common themes in the literature.

In his monograph Michael Ebstein situates Ismāʿīlī taʾwīl with other esotericist literatures that were composed in the same period in North Africa and Andalusia—the works ascribed to Ibn Masarra and Ibn al-ʿArabī. Ebstein argues that despite the fact that these traditions are part of the same intellectual heritage, their affinities have gone unnoticed because Ibn al-ʿArabī and Ibn Masarra are labeled "mystical" whereas Ismāʿīlī taʾwīl is not. Ebstein finds that all three lines of esoteric thought drew from common Gnostic, Hermetic, and Neoplatonic traditions.[24] On this point Ebstein is undoubtedly right. However, despite his thorough treatment, he does not uncover direct influence or the sharing of identical sources, only affinities between these traditions. The widely different social contexts in which these sources were produced raises the question as to what the presence of such affinities tells us.

Bar-Asher's recent article on Fāṭimid taʾwīl is the most important work on the topic since Poonawala. Besides summarizing the sources composed by the Fāṭimid missionary-authors, Bar-Asher sets an intellectual context for this material in its broader Shīʿite milieu. He writes that Ismāʿīlī taʾwīl is similar in its basic approach to that of pre-Buyyid Imāmism—it is selective, allegorical, and typological, with Ismāʿīlī missionaries valorizing their own Imāms as heroes, and, like the Imāmīs, attacking the illegitimate sources of knowledge such as the companions of the Prophet Abū Bakr and ʿUmar.[25]

While there are clearly similarities between Imāmī tafsīr and Fāṭimid-Ismāʿīlī taʾwīl, these literatures were produced in different sociopolitical contexts. Imāmī exegetes were ʿulamāʾ (scholars) whose aim was to preserve knowledge and authorize the doctrines of their school. In contrast the early Ismāʿīlī authors were missionaries who composed taʾwīl as part of a covert daʿwa on behalf of a hidden Imām who would soon reappear to usher in the End of Days. They were activists, and their taʾwīl was a tool meant to sow revolution.[26] The ethos of these early missionaries was closer to the militant, chiliastic Shīʿite sects described above than it was to Imāmī scholastics. Even after the announcement of the End of Days and the arrival of the Fāṭimid Imām, the Ismāʿīlī missionaries produced material meant to maintain a revolutionary, sectarian consciousness among the true believers.

Ismāʿīlīsm's and Imāmī Shīʿism's different social contexts left their mark on the sources each produced. While the tafsīr produced by Imāmī scholars focused on the Qurʾān, Ismāʿīlīs prioritized the results of interpretation, and the Imām who discloses it. The Imām is at times referred to as the "speaking scripture" (as opposed to the "silent scripture," the Qurʾān). In the words of al-Qāḍī al-Nuʿmān, "What is in the Torah and the Gospels is similar to what is in the Qurʾān: there are amthāl, signs, and symbols, and the exterior requires taʾwīl, which is the stored-away knowledge (*ʿilm makhzūn*)."[27] As the ḥaqāʾiq (noumena) behind all scriptures, rituals, and realia, taʾwīl is not merely commentary, but divinely aided revelation (*kashf*).

In consequence, while the Qurʾān is an important object of interpretation, it is by no means the only one. In Ismāʿīlism the taʾwīl of the divinely guided interpreter-Imām has parity with, or perhaps even priority to, its objects of interpretation, just as, in al-Sijistānī's metaphor, the role of the craftsman in fashioning a finely made chest is of equal importance to the wood from which it is crafted.

Fāṭimid Ismāʿīlī taʾwīl is also distinguished from Imāmism in that while the latter valorizes the Imāms and family of the Prophet, in Ismāʿīlism the "daʿwa" itself is a topos. Not just the Imāms, but also all the stations of the *daʿwat al-ḥaqq*, the mission of God on earth, are extolled. The daʿwa's stations of hierarchy on earth, the believers learn, is the purest form of the patterns of the universe: the angels, celestial spheres, plants and animals, and mineral world reflect this divinely ordered scheme. Thus when believers join the mission and ascend through its ranks, they not only learn to recognize these truths; they themselves become part of its purest expression. Taʾwīl allows them to see that they too, in al-Sijistānī's words, "have been put in their proper place."

Previous studies of Ismāʿīli exegesis have focused on taʾwīl of the Qurʾān; however, the missionaries interpreted a wide range of objects. Ibn al-Haytham marveled at the Berber missionary Aflaḥ b. Hārūn's capacity to improvise by drawing on objects of taʾwīl to suit his audience. "I listened to the way he proselytized the women, using references in his discourse that their understanding could comprehend, and which made an impression on them. When he spoke to women, he would generally draw his example from a jewel or a ring, from earrings and diadems, from necklaces, foot bracelets, or arm bracelets, from clothing and kerchiefs, from spinning and weaving, from coiffure, wardrobe, and other things with which women adorn themselves. He would speak to the craftsman of his art, to the tailor of such things as needle and thread, eyelet and shears, to the shepherd of his staff and cloak, of his flock and his pouch."[28]

Aflaḥ's virtuosity notwithstanding, there were a great number of favorite objects of interpretation. Themes such as the numbers two (the twin supernal "roots") and seven (for the speaker-prophets), water (for taʾwīl), birth (for conversion to the daʿwa), and birds (for missionaries) recur frequently. Such symbolic forms became intrinsic to their signification within the world of daʿwa knowledge, signifiers that point to the ḥaqāʾiq.

I think it useful, then, to refer to taʾwīl less as a literature, than as a rhetorical status for "the truths" taught by missionaries in the field. According to the missionaries, through taʾwīl, the believers join a higher, spiritual world to which those in the mission alone had access. Henry Corbin has described early Shiism's cosmology and history as based in part on hierohistory, the sense that through the Imām, God works through the events of history.[29] In a similar vein, Ismāʿīlī taʾwīl could be termed "hiero-interpretation," a hermeneutic that provides the sense that God can be felt in the workings of the present. In other words, taʾwīl is a tool to instill a particular way of interpreting the world, a cognitive retraining that binds the community of believers to God's mission. This training is referred to in the sources as *tarbiya* (rearing).

If we refer to taʾwīl for the practice of interpretation of missionaries in the field, we need a separate term for the written sources. I refer to doctrinal sources that record a substantial amount of taʾwīl and that were produced in the context of the Ismāʿīlī mission as "daʿwa literature." Daʿwa literature thus consists of sources composed by Ismāʿīlī missionaries for other missionaries to instruct the believers in the teachings of God's and His Imām's daʿwa.

The Sources

We have limited knowledge of the biographies of Ismāʿīlī authors and the context of the composition of daʿwa literature they composed. This is for several reasons. First, according to Ismāʿīlī sources, daʿwa works were disclosed only to inspired (*muʾāyyad*) members of the family of the Prophet—ʿAlī and his offspring, including, in the Fāṭimid period, the Fāṭimid Imāms. Thus when a taʾwīl source is ascribed by the tradition to a missionary such as Jaʿfar ibn Manṣūr al Yaman, it is implied that while Jaʿfar may have compiled this work, it ultimately derived from the current Imām of the period under whom he served. Second, missionaries were trained to work in environs where it was necessary to hide their identities. It is then unsurprising that they did not discuss the circumstances surrounding a source's composition. It also explains the reason that ancillary genres such as the biographical dictionary were not developed in Ismāʿīlism. It is then not surprising that until relatively recently, few manuscripts of taʾwīl were available to outsiders. From the absence of collation and readership statements in daʿwa literature manuscripts copied by Ismāʿīlī scribes in Gujarat, it is likely that even for those within the Ismāʿīlī community, access to these sources was limited.

In light of these factors, the composition and authorial attribution of works of daʿwa literature often cannot be determined with certainty. I have discussed this issue at some length elsewhere.[30] Here I will briefly provide examples of several tools that have been used to establish a *terminus post* and *ante quem* for Ismāʿīlī sources.

Wilferd Madelung provides one such device. He argues convincingly that if the Imām Muḥammad ibn Ismāʿīl is mentioned in a source that was composed during the Fāṭimid period, we can be certain that it was composed during or after the reign of al-Muʿizz li-dīn Allāh (d. 975).[31] This is because it was al-Muʿizz who updated Fāṭimid doctrine by reestablishing Muḥammad ibn Ismāʿīl in the role of final redeemer in Fāṭimid doctrine. Similarly, if a source possesses reference to a metaphysical scheme with ten intellects, it is certain that it dates after the period of the celebrated missionary Ḥamīd al-Dīn al-Kirmānī, who introduced this scheme into Fāṭimid-Ismāʿīlism at the end of the fourth/tenth century. It is worth emphasizing that the obverse point cannot be maintained—a source with metaphysics that does *not* contain the ten intellects may have been composed after al-Kirmānī.

Another useful tool to establish the date of sources or fragments within sources are what we might call otiose elements—formulations of themes that are antithetical to Ismāʿīlism's "mature" doctrine of the Fāṭimid period, and thus unlikely to be fabricated. For example Abbas Hamdani verifies the authenticity of an epistle ascribed to the first Fāṭimid Imām ʿAbd Allāh by noting that his genealogical pedigree presented in the source was soon dropped in subsequent generations; Hamdani concludes that the source likely dates to the period of ʿAbd Allāh's rule when this genealogical claim was operative.[32] Another example of an otiose theme is the formulation of a primordial creation myth in which a feminine demiurge is guilty of hubris, an act that brings about the creation of the universe. The myth was attributed to the Fāṭimid missionary Abū ʿĪsā al-Murshid but, as Stern noted, was clearly based on an earlier pre-Fāṭimid doctrine that was updated in Fāṭimid times.[33]

The above examples pertain to establishing the date and authenticity of a source. A related question is how closely the text in the nineteenth-century manuscripts in which a particular work was preserved corresponds to the original source composed a millennium earlier. Halm has shown that the *Kitāb al-fatarāt wal-qirānāt* was updated over successive generations of missionaries. And, in his analysis of *al-Risāla al-mudhhiba,* Daniel De Smet shows the significant variation between manuscripts and between the manuscripts and the published edition. Paul Walker has noted that the published editions of Ismāʿīlī sources, often based on only one or two manuscripts, must be treated as if they were manuscripts themselves, rather than critical editions.[34]

These examples show that scholars who interpret daʿwa literature must proceed source by source, and, in some cases, subsection by subsection within a source, to establish the date and provenance of a text. Inevitably such analyses will likely find that many of our sources of "early taʾwīl" were significantly reworked by later hands.

These difficulties need not prevent analysis of taʾwīl, but they do limit the nature of the conclusions we can draw. Obviously the uncertainly of the date of the sources in the form that comes down to us precludes an interpretive approach that depends on a particular historical moment for its interpretation. As a framework for analysis, we are on safer ground considering a source's themes and form that transcend any particular historical moment. Many themes reflected in taʾwīl—a missionary overstepping his role in the hierarchy; succession from one Imām to the next; failure to recognize the proper Imām—transcend any particular moment in the history of the Ismāʿīlī mission. It is worthwhile to recall that while each taʾwīl and subsequent "update" was composed to address the concerns of particular moment, this was a literature read by future generations of missionaries. Since its impact transcended its original composition, so too can our analysis consider themes and strategies that transcend any single historical moment.

With the above proviso of the uncertain state of the sources in place, we turn to the pre-Fāṭimid and Fāṭimid daʿwa sources consulted in the chapters that follow. To be clear: This is by no means a list of all Ismāʿīlī sources from this period; my criteria for selection was largely based on the sources' availability to me during my years of research, and the similarity of their style. All these sources are free of the extensive philosophical speculation that al-Kirmānī introduced into Fāṭimid taʾwīl.

The periodization below is based largely on prior scholarship.[35] After providing a brief description of the work, I list the extant manuscripts and their date and provenance listed in the manuscript catalogues of the Institute of Ismaili Studies. Ismail Poonawala's biobibliography surveys and describes all known Ismāʿīlī literature, published or in manuscript, and includes surveys of private Indian libraries inaccessible to those outside the Bohra community.[36]

Pre-Fāṭimid Works (c. 870–909)

Kitāb al-kashf (The Book of Revelation), Anonymous

This is a collection of six brief treatises. The third and fifth treatises form a unit and are likely from the pre-Fāṭimid period—the expectation of the Mahdī is central, that he will complete all laws and will seal all prior eras. The source includes cryptographic writing and obscure references to "the greater ʿayn," "Greater Maryam," and "Greater Fāṭima" that are not found in other sources. The rest of the treatises are likely from the early Fāṭimid period. The compilation was probably completed during the reign of al-Qāʾim.[37]

The work was edited by R. Strothman from two manuscripts, the first in Berlin and the second in the Fyzee collection.[38] A second edition was made by

Muṣṭafa Ghālib.[39] Poonawala lists five additional manuscripts in private collections in India.[40]

Kitāb risālat taʾwīl al-ḥurūf al-muʿjama (The Taʾwīl of the Alphabet)
This is a taʾwīl of the letters of the alphabet. This work combines elements of early Ismāʿīlism such as the heptads of cycles of letters and a focus on the Mahdī, with topoi typical of the Nuṣayrīs such as reference to the *ism* and *maʿnā* and reference to Jaʿfar al-Ṣādiq's near contemporary Muḥammad ibn Sinān, a figure known for ghuluww and adduced in Nuṣayrī sources. Two manuscripts of this work are extant, a manuscript copied by the Syrian Nizārī community that was edited by Guyard,[41] and a second manuscript, IIS Ms. 1283, an undated work that was transmitted by the Bohra community that is in the Institute of Ismaili Studies.[42] This title should not be confused with a different work under the same title, but ascribed, most likely correctly, to Jaʿfar b. Manṣūr al-Yaman.

Kitāb al-ʿālim wal-ghulām (The Book of the Scholar and the Pupil), Abū al-Qāsim al-Ḥasan b. Faraj b. Ḥawshab b. Zādān al-Kūfī (hereafter Manṣūr al-Yaman) (?)
The work is notable for its unusual literary form, a dramatic dialogue in which an Ismāʿīlī missionary, the learned one, successfully convinces "the youth" to join the daʿwa. There are parallels between speaker-prophets and waṣīs during humanity's seven historical periods and between the luminary spheres and the earthly mission, taʾwīls of Qur'anic passages, and creedal statements. What makes this work unusual is that the taʾwīl found in other sources is here situated in the context of an emotive narrative. Pace Morris, it is unlikely Jaʿfar b. Manṣūr al-Yaman composed the work; it is more likely that Jaʿfar's father composed the work.[43]

The book has recently been edited and translated by James Morris, who describes the manuscripts of the work that are extant.[44]

Kitāb al-rushd wal-hidāya (The Book of Guidance and Direction), Ibn Ḥawshab Manṣūr al-Yaman (?)
This is a taʾwīl of Qurʾānic verses. The focus is on the coming of the Mahdī, who will be the culmination of the seventh era of speaker-prophets; he alone is said to combine the role of prophet and waṣī. The work was edited by Muḥammad Kāmil Ḥusayn.[45]

Fāṭimid Works (909–c. 990)

Kitāb al-farāʾid wa-ḥudūd al-dīn (The Book of Prescriptions and Proscriptions of Religion/Book of Obligations and the Hierarchy of Religion),[46] Abū al-Qāsim Jaʿfar b. al-Ḥasan b. Faraj b. Ḥawshab (hereafter Jaʿfar b. Manṣūr al-Yaman)

This is a taʾwīl of Sūrat Yūsuf, Sūrat al-kahf, Sūrat al-nūr, and other sections of the Qurʾān. Also embedded in the work is an epistle by ʿAbd Allāh al-Mahdī that contains a genealogy of the Fāṭimid Imāms which claims that Muḥammad b. Ismāʿīl was a cover name for the Imāms during a period of screening when their identities could not yet be disclosed. As this doctrine was initiated by ʿAbd Allāh al-Mahdī but would soon be replaced, it is likely that it was composed under the first Fāṭimid caliph.

The source has not been edited but is preserved in a number of manuscripts. IIS Ms. 1106 was copied in Hyderabad in 1331/1913;[47] IIS Ms. 1236 was copied in Hyderabad in 1358/1939;[48] IIS Ms. 1194 was copied during the mid-nineteenth century;[49] IIS Ms. 928 was copied in the nineteenth century; and IIS Ms. 520 (no date) is likely mid-nineteenth to twentieth century.[50] Poonawala lists eleven manuscripts in India.[51]

al-Shawāhid wal-bayān fī ithbāt maqām amīr al-muʾminīn wal-aʾimma (Textual Evidence and Clarification Regarding the Proof of the Status of the Prince of the Believers and Imāms), Jaʿfar b. Manṣūr al-Yaman

The focus of the taʾwīl is the speaker-prophets and Imāms. The Bohra ascription of the source to Jaʿfar b. Manṣūr al-Yaman is plausible based on its content and terminology. The dating of the source to the period of the Mahdī ʿAbd Allāh comes from the identity of the redeemer as al-Qāʾim al-Mahdī who has yet to arrive, but is expected as the culmination of a series of heptads of Imāms following ʿAlī.[52]

The source has not been edited but is extant in a number of manuscripts at the Institute of Ismaili Studies. IIS Ms. 1135 was copied in the middle of the nineteenth century, and IIS Ms. 734 was copied in 1384/1965.[53] Poonawala lists six manuscripts in private collections in India.[54]

Kitāb taʾwīl al-zakāt (The Book of the Allegorical Sense of Alms), Jaʿfar b. Manṣūr al-Yaman.

This work, a taʾwīl of verses and Islamic rituals such as prayer and alms, was likely composed during the period of al-Muʿizz. In this source the End of Days occurs in cycles, and in its final stage, the dead will be resurrected, the law abolished, and "works" no longer necessary. The Mahdī, who is clearly yet to come, exceeds the status of the speaker-prophets.

It has been edited by Ḥusām Khaddūr. He does not describe the manuscript(s) on which he depended.[55] There are three manuscripts at the Institute of Ismaili Studies, Ms. 1141 ARI ZA, which was copied in 1875, Ms. 1028, which was copied in 1291/1874,[56] and Ms. 216 which was copied in 1384/1965.[57]

Taʾwīl sūrat al-nisāʾ (The Allegorical Sense of the Chapter "Women" [in the Qurʾān]), Jaʿfar b. Manṣūr al-Yaman

This is a taʾwīl of the fourth chapter of the Qurʾān. Although the source has not yet been authenticated, its style and themes are consistent with other works by Jaʿfar ibn Manṣūr al-Yaman, and thus the Bohra copyists' ascription to Jaʿfar ibn Manṣūr al-Yaman is likely correct. The work is extant in a unicum, IIS Ms. 1103, a late thirteenth/nineteenth-century manuscript.[58]

Kitāb al-riḍāʿ fī al-bāṭin (The Book of Suckling in the Interior [Sense]), Jaʿfar ibn Manṣūr al-Yaman
This is a taʾwīl of prayer, fasting, pilgrimage, other rites, and *Laylat al-qadar* (Qurʾān 22:47). Its style and themes are consistent with other works by Jaʿfar ibn Manṣūr al-Yaman.

Manuscripts include IIS Ms. 1172, which was copied in 1889, IIS Ms. 1143 (no date), which was likely copied in the eighteenth century,[59] and IIS Ms. 167 (no date), which was likely copied in thirteenth/nineteenth century.[60] Poonawala lists nine copies in manuscripts in India and one in Berlin.[61]

Sarāʾir al-nuṭaqāʾ; Asrār al-nuṭaqāʾ (The Secrets of the Speaker-Prophets), Jaʿfar b. Manṣūr al-Yaman; Pseudo-Jaʿfar.
These two related works are a taʾwīl of stories of ancient prophets. The first section of the two titles are nearly identical. The *Asrār* adds a heresiography of the erring sects after Jaʿfar al-Ṣādiq and, in one manuscript, claims that 120 years have elapsed since the death of Ḥasan al-ʿAskarī (d. 260/873). Based on this manuscript, Ivanow suggests that this piece must have been written around 380/990.[62] The claim that the *Asrār* represents a reworking of the early *Sarāʾir* during the fifth Fāṭimid caliph al-ʿAzīz is the most plausible current hypothesis.[63]

The *Asrār al-nuṭaqāʾ* was published under the title *Sarāʾir wa-Asrār al-nuṭaqāʾ* by Mustafā Ghālib.[64] It should be treated as a manuscript rather than a true critical edition based on multiple manuscripts.

Manuscripts of the *Sarāʾir al-nuṭaqāʾ* include IIS Ms. 1150, which was copied in 1853;[65] IIS Ms. 178, copied in 1316/1898; IIS Ms. 17, no date; and IIS Ms. 737, copied in 1384/1965.[66] Manuscripts of the *Asrār al-nuṭaqāʾ* include IIS Ms. 1126, which is dated 1883;[67] IIS Ms. 239, copied in 1336/1918;[68] IIS Ms. 738, copied in 1384/1964 and signed in Gujarati;[69] and IIS Ms. 16 (no date) mid-fourteenth/twentieth century.[70] Poonawala mentions that he has seen manuscripts of the *Sarāʾir* and *Asrār* transcribed in 742/1241–42 in Yemen that were in the possession of A. A. Fyzee and lists six additional manuscripts of the *Sarāʾir,* along five copies of the *Asrār.*[71]

Risālat taʾwīl ḥurūf al-muʿjam (Taʾwīl of the Alphabet) Jaʿfar b. Manṣūr al-Yaman (?)
This is a taʾwīl of the Arabic alphabet. The author focuses on the shape of letters and the number of letters in the spelling of each letter to generate dyads

and triads that become the basis of more elaborate taʾwīl. The terminology employed is consistent with other works of Jaʿfar.

There are two manuscripts of the work, both from Bohra collections, IIS Ms. 1209 (no date),[72] and IIS Ms. 716, which is dated 1861.[73] The work should not be confused with a different composition ascribed an identical title and preserved in IIS Ms. 1283 (see above).

Kitāb al-fatarāt wa-l-qirānāt (The Book of Interims and Conjunctions), Jaʿfar b. Manṣūr al-Yaman (?)
This work is a genethlialogy to show the reign of the Fāṭimid Imāms occurred in accord with the conjunction of the heavenly spheres. Heinz Halm has shown that the work contains several strata from different periods, perhaps from the period of al-Manṣūr (d. 341/953) to al-Ḥākim bi Amr Allāh (d. 411/1021).[74] The author of the last strata is unknown, and the ascription to Jaʿfar ibn Manṣūr al-Yaman of the sections composed earlier is uncertain.

Three manuscripts at the Institute of Ismaili Studies and one in Tübingen were the basis for my critical edition of the prologue to the text.[75] Ms. IIS 726 was copied in 1355/1936; Ms. 1254 is undated; Ms. 1134 was copied in 1358/1939; HS Tübingen Ms. VI 297 is undated.

Kitāb asās al-taʾwīl, Abū Ḥanīfa al-Nuʿmān b. Manṣūr b. Aḥmad b. Ḥayyūn al-Tamīmī (hereafter al-Qāḍī al-Nuʿmān)
The source presents the hiero-history and taʾwīl of the nāṭiqs (speaker-prophets). As Madelung points out, it is clear that the End of Days has not yet arrived, and the work seems at times devoted to dampening chiliasm. It was likely composed during the reign of al-Muʿizz.[76]

The *Asās al-taʾwīl* was published by ʿĀrif Tāmir based on two manuscripts; the first was copied in Syria in 1183/1769 and the second copied in Uganda in 1033/1623.[77] The Institute of Ismaili Studies has three copies, Ms. 1148 was copied in 1262/1846; Ms. 110 was copied in the second half of the ninteenth century,[78] and Ms. 1441, a Persian translation of the work, is dated 1307/1890.[79] Poonawala lists eighteen copies of the work in various private collections.[80]

al-Risāla al-mudhhiba, pseudo–al-Qāḍī al-Nuʿmān (?); pseudo–Ibn Killis (?)
This work, whose author and date is uncertain, is a pastiche of metaphysical discussions that provides a daʿwa interpretation of astral governance of this world. The celestial spheres are merely likenesses of the angelic supernal heptad and duo-decade that actually govern this world. The work has been ascribed to Ibn Killis and al-Qāḍī al-Nuʿmān. For a review of the problems with the source, see Daniel De Smet's recent article.[81] The work is preserved in the Muḥammad-Shah, Nizārī community in Syria. The four manuscripts that are attested yield very different texts. The edition by ʿĀrif Tāmir, attributed, most likely falsely, to al-Qāḍī al-Nuʿmān, must be used with caution.[82]

Ismāʿīlī Manuscripts and Their Transmission

With the exception of several manuscripts copied in Iran, Syria, and Yemen, most works of daʿwa literature in manuscript that are extant were produced by the Ṭayyibi-Mustaʿlī Ismāʿīlīs in the nineteenth and twentieth centuries in western India. In other words the earliest manuscripts to which we have access were copied some eleven centuries from their time and place of composition.

A number of factors explain the disappearance of Ismāʿīlī sources from Egypt and North Africa, as well as the relative lack of manuscripts generally. Outside of Ismāʿīlism, when a well-known medieval Muslim scholar composed a new work, he did so as part of a scholarly network of cohorts and students. His work would be audited and disseminated in a wide network of scholars. Conversely, in Ismāʿīlism, daʿwa literature was closed to outsiders and restricted to those inhabiting the upper ranks among the daʿwa hierarchy. Sometimes this was in order to protect the community from the sources falling into the hands of their enemies. In other contexts the concealing of sources served other communal purposes. At other times sequestering key sources may have served as a means of social control by the community leaders over its members. The absence of Ismāʿīlī works from Egypt and North Africa is also due to the fact that the Ismāʿīlī daʿwa never attempted to aggressively proselytize near the caliphal center, and thus Ismāʿīlism never represented a substantial segment of the population.[83]

After conquering Egypt from the Fāṭimids, the Ayyūbids destroyed a great many Ismāʿīlī manuscripts. The historian al-Maqrīzī describes the destruction of Ismāʿīlī works held in the library attached to the Dār al-ʿulūm (House of Knowledge) attached to the caliphal palace in Cairo.[84] Since the daʿwa held the manuscripts in the palace library, many sources, Ismāʿīlī and non-Ismāʿīlī, were likely erased by this violent intervention.

Approximately seventy works from the pre-Fāṭimid and Fāṭimid periods did survive, and in his recent article, Ismail Poonawala outlines the trajectory of their transmission. He focuses on the importance of the mission in Yemen, one of the earliest strongholds of the Ismāʿīlī daʿwa, in preserving these sources. As a result of instability in Cairo, under the Sulayḥids, a tributary of the Fāṭimids who ruled the Yemeni highlands from 439/1037 until 532/1138, Yemen became a crucial site for the preservation of Ismāʿīlī sources. In 454/1062, during the reign of the Fāṭimid caliph-Imām al-Mustanṣir (r. 427/1036–487/1094), the missionary Ḥātim b. Ibrāhīm al-Ḥamidī sent a deputation headed by the chief judge Lamak ibn Mālik al-Ḥamdānī to Cairo. Recognizing the instability in Cairo, the chief missionary, al-Muʾayyad fī al-dīn al-Shirāzī (d. 470/1078), sent many Ismāʿīlī sources to Yemen with Lamak when he returned. They thus survived their later destruction when the Fāṭimids in Egypt were overrun by the Ayyūbids.[85]

The transmission of many of these sources from Yemen to India was facilitated by connections between Yemen and western India after the sixth/twelfth century. When the Imām ʿĀmir was assassinated by a Nizārī missionary in 524/1130, the regent for his infant son, al-Ṭayyib, claimed to be the leader of the movement under the name al-Ḥāfiẓ li-Dīn Allāh. The Sulayḥid Queen Sayyida ʿArwa bt. Aḥmad upheld the Imāmate of al-Ṭayyib and proclaimed the missionary Dhuʿayb b. Mūsā al-Waḍiʿī as a "dāʿī muṭlaq," a missionary with unlimited authority to manage the state in the absence of the Imām, who was in occultation. The chain of dāʿī muṭlaqs continued in Yemen until 946/1539, when it passed to Yūsuf b. Sulaymān of India. During the sixteenth and seventeenth centuries, the center of the "Ṭayyibī" sect shifted from Yemen to India.[86]

Poonawala's article complements Abbas Hamdani's and François de Blois's account of the transmission of the Hamdani family library from Yemen to India. A large number of Ismāʿīlī sources that had been transferred from Cairo to Yemen by Lamak ibn Mālik in the eleventh century were preserved by the Mustaʿlī-Ṭayyibī Ismāʿīlīs, among them, the Hamdani family. A group of the Hamdanis crossed over to the mountainous Ḥarrāz region of Yemen with their sources (they became known as "Yaʿbūrīs"—those who crossed over). After the Ṭayyibīs shifted the seat of the dāʿī muṭlaq, the leader of the community, from Yemen to India, many manuscript were relocated to western India. Thus the aforementioned thirty-ninth dāʿī muṭlaq Ibrahim Wajih al-Din (d. 1754) invited ʿAlī ibn Saʿīd ibn al-Ḥusayn ibn ʿAlī al-Yaʿbūrī al-Ḥamdānī to come to India and to bring with him his collection. According to Abbas Hamdani, "Copying of old Yemeni manuscripts proliferated in the study circles (*ḥalqas*) of his grandson Fayḍ Allāh (d. 1876) and his great-grandson (Muḥammad ʿAlī (d. 1898) who built a large library."[87] Abbas Hamdani, a reformist Ismāʿīlī scholar who was a professor at the University of Wisconsin in the United States, donated most of his family's collection to the Institute of Ismaili Studies in 2002.

The Institute of Ismaili Studies (IIS), which makes such manuscripts available to non-Ismāʿīlī scholars, has played a crucial institutional role in making sources such as the Hamdani collection, available. The IIS reflects Ismāʿīlism's turn toward liberalization and modernity nearly a century in the making. The turn began with the forty-eighth Imām of the Nizārīs, Sir Sultan Mohammed Shah Aga Khan III (1877–1957), who allowed the Russian bibliographer and scholar Wladmir Ivanow (d. 1970) to study his manuscripts. Ivanow was a book collector and librarian, and he purchased Ismāʿīlī manuscripts in Iran and India during the 1950s. This policy of intellectual liberalization was extended further by Karim Aga Khan IV, who has led the movement since his ascension in 1957 until the present. The Ismaili Society of Bombay and the Ismaili Association for Pakistan, Karachi, were opened, and Ivanow donated his collection to these centers. The manuscript collections of these centers were greatly enhanced by the work of Chhotu Lakhani, a member of the Khoja Ismāʿīlī community who forged close ties with different Ismāʿīlī communities in India, and was able to acquire a great many important Bohra manuscripts for the Ismaili Society of Bombay. Mention should also be made of the scholar Asaf Ali Fyzee, a prominent member of the Sulaymānī-Ṭayyibī community and a Cambridge-trained scholar and attorney, who, in addition to being a prominent advocate in the High Court in Bombay, served as the secretary of the Ismaili Society of Bombay. He donated his family's extensive manuscript collection to the University of Bombay.[88]

In 1977 the Aga Khan founded the Institute of Ismaili Studies, an academic institute dedicated to the academic study of Ismāʿīlism, Shīʿism, and Islam. In 1979 the manuscript collections were transferred from India to the Institute in London, and from the 1980s until the present, manuscripts from the Bohra, ʿAlawī-Ismāʿīlī, and Sulaymānī Ismāʿīlī communities have been acquired, either through donation or purchase. These collections grew substantially when several extremely learned members of prominent Bohra-Ismāʿīlī families in India who possessed manuscript collections donated them. These donors include ʿĀbid ʿAlī, the descendant of the important scholar Zahid ʿAlī (d. 1958), and Husayn Hamdani (d. 1962) and his son ʿAbbas Hamdani.[89] These figures were themselves scholars (Zahid ʿAli had a doctorate from Oxford, and Husayn Hamdani from the School of Oriental and African Studies in London; and Ismail Poonawala and Abbas Hamdani were, until they recently retired, professors at the University of California, Los Angeles, and the University of Wisconsin, respectively.) In effect the Institute of Ismaili Studies now serves as a center for Ismāʿīlīs from different communities who believe that the sources of their tradition should be open to investigation. A number of catalogues have been produced, and digital images of the manuscripts are provided to researchers upon request.

Conclusion

Written compositions of Ismāʿīlī taʾwīl, daʿwa literature, were likely composed by missionaries, for missionaries. The extant copies of these sources survive mainly in manuscripts that were copied in the nineteenth and early twentieth centuries in India. Recent lower-text critical studies of these manuscripts demonstrate that some sources have been updated over the generations. Taʾwīl itself, the disclosure of the hidden sense behind the object of interpretation, was primarily taught orally.

CHAPTER 3

Rearing

Ismāʿīlī missionaries used taʾwīl to call potential acolytes from the darkness of the exterior sense of scripture and religion to the light of the mission of God and His rightly guided Imām, and to further teach those who joined the mission God's secret knowledge (ʿilm).[1] Taʾwīl led the acolyte to read scripture and tradition in a radically different way, one that pointed to the importance of allying oneself to the mission of God's rightly guided Imām.

My aim is to analyze daʿwa literature to map the habits of mind that make particular interpretations possible, an approach that borrows from theories of cognition and ethnographies of contemporary communities of believers. In other words, rather than analyzing literary sources as such, I view them as exemplars of symbols, patterns, and logics—the consciousness—that made their composition possible. I call the new mode of cognition that the Ismāʿīlī missionaries perpetuate and impart, "daʿwa knowledge."

My assertion that the Ismāʿīlī missionaries created a new cognitive world, is, I concede, a rather grand claim. I think, however, that the grand claims within daʿwa literature invite such a model. The literature describes an acolyte's conversion to the daʿwa as "birth," and his gradual acquisition of daʿwa knowledge as "rearing." It was the dissemination of this special, saving knowledge that was meant to facilitate this radical transformation. In other words the literature itself signals that it intended to have a dramatic impact on its audience. In addition the unconventional style and form of taʾwīl, particularly the repetition of patterns and symbols, invite a cognitive reading. Several Ismāʿīlī conversion narratives exemplify the response taʾwīl was meant to inspire.

Recognition

Several conversion narratives in Ismāʿīlī sources clarify the impact of secret knowledge to prospective acolytes.[2] In particular the accounts in the *Kitāb al-ʿālim wal-ghulām* (The Book of the Master and the Disciple), a literary depiction of the conversion and training of a young adept, and the *Sīrat ibn Ḥawshab* (The Biography of Ibn Ḥawshab), a first-person conversion account by the famous missionary Ibn Ḥawshab (Jaʿfar ibn Manṣūr al-Yaman's father), are particularly rich.[3] These are idealized accounts, stories that exemplify how conversion to the mission *ought* to unfold, rather than the naïve reports of converts. But as such accounts were composed not long after the conversions in question, they likely reflect the experience of many early converts.

Sīrat Ibn Ḥawshab (The Life of Ibn Ḥawshab), a biography of Jaʿfar ibn Manṣūr al-Yaman's father, Ibn Ḥawshab, is preserved in several Fāṭimid histories.[4] The account is narrated in the first person, an autobiography of the author recounting his conversion at some later period. Ibn Ḥawshab describes himself walking alone on the river during prayer time in a state of distress, mulling over the spiritual crisis that had befallen his community. He stops to pray, reciting a Qurʾānic chapter that recounts the "Companions of the Cave" (known in ancient literature as "the tale of the seven sleepers"), a story of a group of true believers who seek refuge in a cave for protection until God awakens them three hundred years later. While Ibn Ḥawshab is reciting, an old scholar and his attendant appear.

> I sat reflecting upon my situation. Then I began reciting the Qurʾān, starting with the chapter *The Cave.* While I was reciting it, suddenly an old man, accompanied by another man, approached me. By God, never before had my eyes gazed upon anyone who filled my heart with greater reverence than that old man! He sat down and another man sat in front of him, both some distance from me. Out of respect for him, I interrupted the recitation, but continued to gaze at him. Suddenly, the young man approached, walking boldly. He came near me. . . . I asked, "Who are you?"
>
> He replied, "A descendant of al-Ḥusayn."
>
> I wept and said, "By my father, al-Ḥusayn, may God's blessings be upon him, the one stained with blood, to whom this water was denied."
>
> I saw then that the old man looked at me. . . . I noticed the tears flowing on his beard. . . . He asked me, "Who are you who speaks of al-Ḥusayn thus?"
>
> I replied, "A Shīʿite."
>
> He asked, "What is your name?"
>
> I replied, "al-Ḥasan ibn Faraḥ ibn Ḥawshab."
>
> He said, "I know your father adhered to the Twelver school."
>
> I said, "Indeed."
>
> He asked, "Do you follow the same path?"
>
> I hesitated.[5]

The story begins with Ibn Ḥawshab in distress, alienated from his community. In 860, approximately a decade before this scene, Ibn Ḥawshab's Imāmī madhhab (school) was dealt a traumatic blow when the Imām al-Ḥasan al-ʿAskarī died without having sired a son to succeed him. This contradicted a central pillar of Imāmism. Since the Imām is the "proof of God" (ḥujjat Allāh) on earth without whom the world ceases to exist, it should be impossible for an Imām to die without leaving a son to succeed him. Imāmī doctrine would come to hold that al-Ḥasan *did* have a son, a certain Muḥammad. This Muḥammad entered into "occultation" (ghayba) and would return at the End of Days in the distant future (thus the Twelver Shīʿites' doctrine until today). But this doctrine took time to be accepted. Ibn Ḥawshab's autobiography reflects a period during which anxieties among this community concerning this situation persisted.

When the elder mentions al-Ḥusayn, Ibn Ḥawshab's anxiety is transformed to grief—both he and the elder weep at mention of the martyr al-Ḥusayn, the Prophet's grandson who was killed attempting rebellion against the tyrannical Umayyad caliph Yazīd. Al-Ḥusayn is the symbol of the family of the Prophet's unjust deprivation of their rightful position as rulers of the Islamic community. Their shared pathos over the tragedy of al-Ḥusayn's martyrdom leads the two figures to disclose their Shīʿite identity to one another. Their mutual sharing of their allegiance with the family of the Prophet forged a complicity, a powerful bond between the missionary and potential convert. This is undoubtedly why missionaries were sent to regions inhabited by Shīʿites.[6]

> When asked about his affiliation, Ibn Ḥawshab is reticent to speak.
>
> "Speak, for I am one of your brothers!"
>
> I said, "I used to be a follower of that [Twelver] path until it was proved invalid. I am out here in this place because of my distress regarding this issue . . ."
>
> He said, "I see that you are alert, for I listened to you while you were reciting. Why did you cease the recitation?"
>
> I replied, "I swear, may God support you, only reverence for you silenced me."
>
> He said, "Recite, just as you had been reciting."
>
> So I continued from where I had stopped until I reached: "then they proceeded until, when they met a young man, he slew him" [Qurʾān 18:74]. He then signaled to me with his hand to be quiet. He asked, "Are you a believer in God's Justice and Unity?"
>
> I replied, "Yes, that is my creed."
>
> He asked, "What justice is there in slaying an innocent one who had slain none, except what [God] said: 'and We feared that he would grieve them by obstinate rebellion and unbelief [Qurʾān 18:80]'?"
>
> I remained silent. He said,
>
> "Speak!"
>
> I asked, "What shall I say?! By God, it as if I had never read the verse. I lack the knowledge thereof, so if you consider explaining the matter to me, then do so."

He said, "Before accomplishing that, one must deal with a thin veil."

I said, "Would that you remove the veil for me! May I be your ransom!"

He said, "That will happen when it is possible, if God, the Exalted, wills."[7]

The Qurʾānic verse claims that it was justified for Moses's anonymous companion to slay an innocent youth on the grounds that once grown, the youth would have oppressed his parents with unbelief. The premise behind the verses is that the youth's future was predetermined and that humans do not possess free will (*qadar*) over their actions. Such a belief runs contrary to the Muʿtazilite theological principles held by many Imāmīs in the period that emphasized God's justice and humans' free will. Thus ʿĀṣim ibn Abī Ṣabāḥ al-Jaḥdarī (d. 745), a transmitter later adduced by the Muʿtazilite al-Zamakhsharī (d. 538/1144) in his Qurʾānic exegesis, explains that God knew that the youth had already begun to pervert his parents and was thus guilty before being slain.[8]

When interrogated by the elder, Ibn Ḥawshab is unable to explain the passage. "It is as though I have never read this verse before!" Through the missionary's questioning, the youth becomes aware of his own ignorance. He recognizes the inadequacy of his school's doctrines and the need for help.

The *Kitāb al-ʿālim wal-ghulām* is a dialogue between a missionary and a youth whom he converts. The missionary is instructed to target Shīʿites, for it is they who will sympathize with the Ismāʿīlī movement. The missionary goes to a village where a group of men are discussing theological matters in a public setting. He listens to them and, in an opportune moment, makes a speech laden with Qurʾānic allusions on the gulf that separates the political ideal of God's rule through rightly guided leaders and the Muslims' current state of affairs living under tyrants. The speech leaves its audience in tears. One young man becomes the missionary's student. He eventually is administered the oath of allegiance and converts his father, and they proceed to convert the entire village.[9]

The two narratives follow a similar pattern. In each an anonymous missionary goes to a locale with Shīʿite leanings. The missionary reaches out to a young man in spiritual crisis. The missionary forges an emotional and intellectual connection with the acolyte, hinting that he knows the identity of the true Imām and the special knowledge he possesses but does not disclose it. Non-Ismāʿīlī historians also portray individual missionaries propagating the mission alone.[10] It is likely that these accounts represent literary expressions of actual Ismāʿīlī conversion narratives.

After attracting the potential convert, the missionary tests his devotion. Ibn Ḥawshab is made to wait for the old man's attendant for several days before he is permitted access to training and, eventually, to take the secret oath of allegiance and formally join the mission. Similarly the youth in the *Kitāb al-ʿālim wal-ghulām* must first undergo preliminary instruction before he is finally administered the oath. Throughout the anecdotes, and in taʾwīl itself, the believer is told that he is on the cusp of having his current state of darkness illuminated by access to the secrets.

Wielded properly, a secret can be an extremely potent device. It forges and maintains an intimate and intense psychological bond; it separates those who carry the secret from those excluded; and it protects the knowledge concealed from skeptics who would diminish its status.[11] In his discussion of the esoteric, secret literature produced by the communities at Qumran, Samuel Thomas points out that the act of concealment and its corollary, disclosure, function as mechanisms through which we navigate our intersubjectivity, the nexus between our intimate personal and public social existence.[12] Those participating in the secret create a new sense of self in which the member consciously chooses to participate. The rhetoric of "concealing" and "revealing" becomes a strategy to reclaim power from those outside the sect who would criticize or, as in our context, destroy the movement.[13] By opening himself to this secret knowledge and movement, his understanding of this world, as well as his understanding of the path to reward in the afterlife, are altered. In early Ismāʿīlism conversion to the movement placed the adept in danger; this undoubtedly strengthened the bond and intimacy forged by the secret.

When the missionary is satisfied that the adept is ready, he is considered a mustajīb (one who seeks the answer). The missionary accepts the acolyte's request to be administered the ʿahd al-awliyāʾ, "the oath of the friends of God" and formally joins the mission of God.

Birth: The Oath of Allegiance

The ʿahd al-awliyāʾ is a formal testimony of allegiance to the mission. Upon being administered the oath, the acolyte becomes a muʾmin or mustajīb (believer or acolyte), a member of the mission.[14] The oath meant entering a new religio-social world and forsaking all that had been familiar. It must have been a terrifying experience for the convert.

Several steps preceded the oath. First the missionary formally accepted the acolyte's request to be administered the oath by the missionary who had recruited him. He was told that the oath was the same as the one that had been administered to the prophets and Imāms. The oath was preceded by a three-day fast followed by ritual ablutions.[15] The missionary al-Ḥusayn al-Ahwāzī instructed Ḥamdān Qarmāt to perform ablutions in a canal before administering to him the ʿahd.[16]

We do not have a full text of the secret oath in medieval Ismāʿīlī sources. Excerpts are preserved in several medieval histories (again on the authority of Ibn Rizām). Heinz Halm has shown that these passages are similar to the oath sworn by the modern Bohra-Ismāʿīlī communities.[17]

The oath began with the missionary asking the acolyte to swear absolute secrecy.

> "You will keep secret what you are going to hear and everything you have already heard, everything you know, and everything you will know, everything you have experienced and everything you will experience—concerning me and concerning the ones who reside in this city for the Lord of truth. Do you agree?"
>
> "Yes."[18]

The missionary commands the acolyte to uphold the law of the Prophet Muḥammad "in its external and internal sense." The initiate must be "a friend to the friends of the Imāms and an enemy to their enemies from whom he must now disassociate." After each stipulation the believer is asked to respond "yes."

The missionary then refers to the current Imām, from whom all real knowledge derives. The acolyte is told he will be nourished (*rabba*) with knowledge and principles via the Imām. The missionary stipulates to the new initiate that he must not reveal any of the things pledged by this oath, nor betray those bound by it. To do so is to: "renounce God, the Creator of heaven and earth . . . His earlier and later messengers, the mighty Qurʾān, the Torah, the Gospel, the Psalter and the Wise admonition, every religion sanctioned by God. . . . You leave the party of God and His intimates (*awliyāʾ*), to God's unconcealed disappointment. But He will soon bring retribution and punishment upon you, and you will walk in the fire of Hell, in which there is no mercy."[19]

To break the terms of the oath is to renounce God and all the prophets and scriptures. It is noteworthy that all the scriptures, not only the Qurʾān, are listed. While of course ancient prophets and their scriptures are prominent in the Qurʾān, in Islamic discourse the former are referred to as precursors to Muḥammad and God's book. The believer's oath would have been the first time that the Qurʾān, Torah, and Gospel were presented as a group of scriptures.

According to another report, the oath terminated with a gesture. After the missionary Abū ʿAbd Allāh al-Shīʿī received the oath from acolytes, he would "place his finger on their mouths," a speech act prescribing silence.[20]

The pledge imposed a dramatic reorientation on the believer. He moved to a new social order and set of relationships: other believers were now his only confidantes, and their enemies were now his enemies.

The first task of the convert was to convert his family and trusted comrades. We can assume that most would have enjoyed mixed success, and thus that many families and friendships were disrupted. The Fāṭimid-Ismāʿīlī jurist al-Qāḍī al-Nuʿmān reported in his account of the early mission that after a conversion, the family and friends of the acolyte were aware of this shift. "When his best acquaintance, his closest relative, or his dearest friend asked what sort of enterprise it was that he had joined, and what they had taught him there, he would only answer, 'Go there, and you will find certainty.'"[21]

The daʿwa also reformulated the criteria for divisions of social status. In classical Islamic society, the literary elites classified themselves as the *khāṣṣa,* "the elite," and the nonliterate as the *ʿamma,* "the hoi polloi." Upon joining the movement, initiates from all segments of society learned that they, the divinely favored believers, were the *khāṣṣā* and that those outside the mission were the *ʿamma.* Status was allocated on sectarian lines.

After conversion the initiate learned that the oath, "his birth," was only the first of a series of steps from ignorance to knowledge. After being administered the oath, the convert in *Kitāb al-ʿĀlim wal-ghulām* was interrogated by a higher-ranking missionary who demonstrates to the new acolyte that he is only at the beginning.

> Scholar: What is your name?
>
> Youth: ʿAbd Allāh ibn ʿAbd Allāh [literally: "the slave of God, son of the slave of God"].
>
> Scholar: Are you a free person or a slave?
>
> Youth: I am a free man, son of ʿAbd Allāh [literally: "son of a slave of God"]
>
> Scholar: And who freed you from servitude, so that you are a free man?
>
> The youth points to the missionary who called him to the mission.
>
> Youth: This wise man set me free!
>
> Scholar: If he himself were now unfree, could he then set you free?
>
> Youth: No, he could not.
>
> Scholar: Then what is your name?
>
> The youth stands with downcast eyes, unable to find an answer.
>
> Scholar: Young man, how can something be known and right [*maʿrūf*] which does not even have a name yet, even if it is a newborn baby?
>
> Youth: So I have been born to you. Give me a name!
>
> Scholar: This will happen, after seven days have elapsed.[22]

When asked his name, the adept responds that his name is "ʿAbd Allāh ibn ʿAbd Allāh," literally, "a slave of God, the son of a slave of God." This is a pun; each missionary in the daʿwa is called "a servant of God," and "his father" refers to the missionary who administered the oath to him. The new convert claims to be free, but the scholar points out that it is impossible for one to be freed by a slave. Clearly it is not the missionary who can set the youth free, but the one whom this servant serves—the Imām himself. Thus since the acolyte still does not yet know the identity of the Imām, he has yet to learn his own name. The "seven days" the adept must wait corresponds to the seven days before an infant is circumcised. The anecdote reminds the new convert that, from the vantage point of the mission, he is still a newborn who has yet to receive a name.

Such passages suggest that the oath is but the first of a series of ranks in the mission hierarchy. For the believers the ascent through the stages of the mission was no mere metaphor. These ranks were part of the divinely sanctioned hierarchy, the ḥudūd (limits); they held ontological priority over the corporeal world of ephemera. In the *Asrār al-nuṭaqā'* (Secrets of the Speaker-Prophets), a ta'wīl of Qur'ān 3:49, in which Jesus breathes life into a clay bird statue, proves the existence of this spiritual birth. "Since we have only witnessed [birth] among the beastly or human animals . . . through coitus—sexual intercourse through the semen coming from the loins of the male to the womb of the female, [a clay statue coming to life] is quite impossible to consider, if it did not have a ta'wīl to explain it."[23] After being "impregnated" with secret knowledge, the acolyte is spiritually reborn. This spiritual birth (*tawallud ruḥānī*) is more significant than his corporeal birth.[24]

This spiritual birth is followed by a series of ceremonially marked ranks of ascent through the different ranks of the daʿwa. These were at times marked by the payment of dues. The believer's "birth" (*tawallud*) is marked by *al-fiṭra* (the creation) and a payment of a silver dirham. Upon reaching the rank of missionary, he would pay "al-bulgha" (maturation?) and become a dāʿī balāgh (a reporting missionary?). The Ismāʿīlī apostate Ibn Rizām reports that upon reaching this rank, the believer deposited seven gold dinars, for which he received a special meal sent by the Imām said to be sweets that came from paradise. In the Iraqi mission, the missionary ʿAbdān instituted another rank called *al-ulfa,* "friendship," at which time the believers' property became shared among the senior members of the "island."[25] The theme of "rearing" (tarbiya) is frequently evoked,[26] as are a number of symbols apposite to the life cycle (sperm, womb, coitus, birth, infants and children, marriage, parenthood, divorce, death).[27]

The sources suggest that "rearing" entailed mastering the saving knowledge channeled from God to His Imām.

Daʿwa Knowledge

The believer's experience of "unveiling" was facilitated by the training of his teacher. My aim in this section is to identify the forms and logics that occasioned this shift. In other words, I read ta'wīl as providing exemplars of daʿwa knowledge, a particular mode of cognition.

In the social sciences, "cognition" refers to primary processes through which sensory and cultural data is first organized.[28] It begins with the observation that sensory stimula are never experienced without cognitive mediation; we organize our experience of "raw" stimulus through mechanisms that function on a preconscious level.[29] Among these mechanisms is language. Through language, we process stimuli through "conceptual packets," mental spaces that organize and provide meaning to discourse at a preconscious level of processing. This preconscious processing is learned.[30] Studies in cognitive psychology show that repeated exposure to forms and images can shift the way we process sensory data. "Priming" subjects by repeating words or images impacts their memory and cognition at a presemantic level.[31]

Scholars of sectarianism in Second Temple Judaism and early Christianity such as Ilkka Pyysiäinen, Vernon Robbins, and Jutta Jokiranta have shown the utility of cognitive models for textual analysis.[32] When literary forms mix different cultural frames, the ensuing "conceptual blend" produces new meanings beyond the content of the linguistic forms themselves.[33] Taking stock of not just the literary forms at work, but the organizing principles of the mind from which they emerge, provides an opportunity for a deeper reading of the sources.

In the study of religion, the shift of the object of inquiry from text to mind informs Tanya Luhrmann's recent ethnography of the Vineyard, a renewalist Protestant church in Chicago. Luhrmann writes that the congregants' internalization of the language of faith and practices of prayer shapes the congregants' understanding of their own experience, as well as the experience itself. It is through the adoption of a new cognitive framework reflected in symbol, story, and practice that congregants learn to "hear God's voice." Drawing on cognitive psychology to interpret her fieldwork, Luhrmann shows that even on the level of primary "unconscious" processing, the experience of religious forms and how we interpret them is learned. Congregants who receive instruction describe their experience of prayer and "listening to God's voice" differently.[34]

This is a simple but powerful insight. If primary processes constitute the bases of our preconscious interpretation of sensory input and reason, and these processes are shaped through habituation to new patterns of thought, then we have a clear explanation for one of taʾwīl's primary stylistic features: repetition. Through repeating the same daʿwa forms and the causal links that connect them, the believers internalized these forms.

In his "philosophy of culture," Ernst Cassirer anticipated some conclusions of cognitive science regarding the study of religion. Cassirer wrote that what he called the "mythical consciousness" reflects an irreducible cognitive order, a consciousness that differs from the "rational" or "scientific" cognitive mode. Mythical consciousness consists of structures, principles, and unarticulated theories of causality that underlie mythic thought and their expression in particular myths. He shows that in these frameworks, contiguity in space, congruence in time, comparable sounds or letters of two words, similarity in shape of objects, and correspondence in number can be viewed as causally related. Cassirer liked to use the example of denizens of cultures who believed the coming of the swallows *caused* the coming of the spring. Cassirer calls these logics or tacit theories of causality "modes of configuration." The themes expressed through these modes of configuration he termed "symbolic forms."[35]

Cassirer's theoretical move and terminology is consonant with social science models of "primary processes" through which individuals first organize cultural data. Rather than analyze literary sources as such, this approach reads particular interpretations for the modes of causality that made them possible.[36] A Cassirerian analysis reads texts as exemplars of the cognitive structures and principles that produced them.

I shall refer to Cassirer's "symbolic forms" as "symbols" and his "modes of configuration" as "logics." In the language of the daʿwa, symbols are the *mathals* (signs) and *mamthūls* (that which is signified) that are so commonly applied that their presence suggests that they exist as part of a pattern. "Logics" refer to the *tarākīb* (patterns), the bases by which these symbols are set in parallel. I call the combination of symbols and logics "daʿwa knowledge."

Repetition

It is difficult to exaggerate the amount of repetition in taʾwīl. The same symbols, terms, and logics for their apposition recur on practically every page, linking all phenomena to the daʿwa hierarchy. For example, in several pages of *Kitāb al-Shawāhid wal-bayān,* the vehicles seven and twelve are the basis for a series of interpretations. "God made His creation built upon what His religion was based," the author declares and then proceeds to show that both the universe and Islam are rooted in the numbers seven and twelve. Thus, the author claims, God created seven heavens, seven land masses, seven seas, seven minerals, seven "lower lights" in the sky (Sun, Moon, Mars, Mercury, Jupiter, Venus, and Saturn), the seven days and seven nights of the week. The author then shifts to the number twelve: there are twelve constellations, twelve islands, twelve hours of the day, twelve hours of the night, and twelve months in the year.[37]

He then turns to the human form. A human being's length is seven spans, he has seven limbs (hands, forearms, arms, trunk, legs, thighs, feet), seven composite aspects of his body (brain, bones, flesh, blood, veins, nerves, skin), seven "levels" to his formation in the womb. There are seven days of celebration for the bride-groom, an ill person recovers on the seventh day, a newborn is circumcised on the seventh day, the corpse is prepared for burial in seven sections, and seven leaves of lotus are placed on its body.[38]

The author then shifts to the topic of religion. God revealed the Qurʾān in seven dialects. There are seven *ḥawāmīm* in the Qurʾān (chapters that begin with the letters *ḥāʾ* and *mīm*). There are seven verses to the Fātiḥa (the opening chapter of the Qurʾān). The words "in the name of God" have seven letters. To vocalize the Qurʾān, there are seven parts of the body that are utilized (the lungs, chest, larynx, uvula, tongue, and two lips). During the ḥajj pilgrims circumambulate the house of the Kaʿba seven times. They make seven trips between Ṣafwa and Marwa; they throw seven stones at the devil, seven times.[39]

The author then returns to the number twelve. There were twelve gates to the Prophet's mosque. The Prophet married twelve women. The people of Moses had twelve tribes; when Moses struck a stone with his staff, twelve springs came forth. The Prophet send twelve naqībs. Jesus had twelve disciples. "Thus," the author comments, "[God] made his stations and levels in seven and twelve and made these creations as mathals, as evidence for them and as signs of them."[40] He goes on,

> As we previously mentioned, when God created His religion, He set His prophets, Imāms and their links [*asbābahum*], their stations and ranks, into sevens and twelves. He made His creations evidence of them, mathals for them, signs alluding to them. He named them *ayāt* [signs; verses] in the interior [sense]. Where "ayāt" are mentioned in the Qur'ān, He means "the Imāms," peace be upon them. Thus He said, "We will show you our signs, in their horizons, and in their souls, until we clarify of them that He is the Truth," meaning: they show you the Imāms and messenger-prophets "in the horizons, and in their souls" through seven and twelve, and all the evidence of them. For they [the works of creation] suggest them through their mathals, until it is clarified for them that the religion and command of God is the truth, and it is "He who made the things, all of them." It is He who imposed the *sunna* for them, established it, and bequeathed the messenger-prophets and guides, and put them in levels in His religion.

This type of comment is as close as we come to a theory of taʾwīl in sources ascribed to Jaʿfar ibn Manṣūr al-Yaman. According to the narrator God created the world through sequences of heptads and duo-decades (sequences of twelve) to provide evidence of the truth of His religion. In other words the empirical world parallels the order of the Qur'an and Islamic ritual and demonstrates its divinity. The author then links both of these to the earthly daʿwa hierarchy.

> So God [Exalted is He] established seven messenger-prophets as speakers of the religious laws. Each messenger prophet has twelve naqībs. And He made seven mutimm-Imāms between two speaker-prophets. Each Imām possesses twelve ḥujjas. The skies are mathals for the speaker prophets; the seven illuminated stars are mathals of the mutimm-Imāms. The seven land masses are mathals of the waṣīs, just as God the Exalted and All-Powerful, said "seven heavens and from the earth like them are the commands descends among them," meaning: the command of God descending among the messenger-prophets and legatees, and from each messenger to his legatee. Also, the days of the week are mathals of the speaker-prophets, and the twelve hours of the day are mathals of the naqībs. Just as each day has twelve hours, so too does each speaker-prophet have his naqībs. And the seven nights are mathals of the interior Imāms, and the hours of the night are mathals of the ḥujjas. Every night has twelve hours, and each Imām has twelve ḥujjas.[41]

In this concluding summary paragraph, the narrator connects the mathals of sevens and twelves in religion and realia to the upper stations of the daʿwa, the speaker-prophets, waṣīs, and naqībs, and Imāms and ḥujjas. Images of clarity and openness such as day and light refer to the laws received by the speaker-prophet and the naqībs whose role is public and open. Darkness and the hours of the night refer to those figures who possess secret, hidden knowledge such as the waṣīs and ḥujjas.

More than any other stylistic feature, it is the sheer amount of repetition of the same structures, patterns, and symbols that distinguishes taʾwīl from other interpretive literatures in Islam. By repeating symbols and patterns, the missionaries habituated their audience to this new knowledge and the principle of its organization, rearing a believer to experience the world through this interpretive prism. At that point the believer "learns to speak," that is, becomes a missionary who has gained sufficient mastery over daʿwa symbols and logic that he is able to teach others.

Daʿwa Symbols

Sources composed by different missionaries show that each drew from a shared palette of concepts and symbols. In the list below, I show that there was a common core of symbols that were widely attested across different "islands" (Ismāʿīlī dioceses) between 890 and 990. Missionaries across Ismāʿīli dioceses shared a common core of symbols.

The list, which is meant to be representative rather than exhaustive, is derived from sources composed during Ismāʿīlism's first four generations (c. 870–990) in pre-Fāṭimid, Fāṭimid, and non-Fāṭimid Ismāʿīlī sources.[42]

Numbers
two;[43] three;[44] five;[45] seven;[46] twelve[47]

Terms of Apposition
mathal (likenesses);[48] bāṭin/ẓāhir (interior/exterior);[49] ḥadd (limit);[50] taʾyīd (support)[51]

Hypostases of the Pleroma and Noumena
al-aṣlān (the two roots);[52] al-Sābiq/al-Tālī (the preceder and the follower);[53] al-Mubdiʿ/al-mubdaʿ (the emanating one and the emanated one);[54] ibdāʿ (emanation);[55] jadd/fatḥ/khayāl (gravity, opening, and imagination);[56] ḥaqāʾiq (noumena);[57] ʿilm (knowledge);[58] ʿaql /nafs (intellect and soul)[59]

Time and the Celestial Spheres
day/night;[60] sun/moon;[61] the twelve astrological constellations;[62] seven days of the week;[63] dawr (cycle);[64] fatra (period);[65] celestial spheres;[66] qiyāma (the rising);[67] (periods of) satr/kashf/ẓuhūr[68]

Daʿwa Ranks
nāṭiq (speaker);[69] wāṣī (legatee);[70] mutimm (completer);[71] asās (fundament);[72] khalīfa (deputy);[73] ḥujja (proof);[74] bāb (gate);[75] dāʿī muṭlaq (absolute missionary);[76] dāʿī balāgh (report-missionary);[77] dāʿī maʾdhūn (permitted missionary);[78] mustajīb (acolyte);[79] Qāʾim (arising one);[80] Mustawdiʿ-Imām (caretaker Imām);[81] lāḥiq (wing)[82]

Hiero-historical Figures
Adam/Seth;[83] Noah/Shem;[84] Abraham/Ismāʿīl;[85] Moses/Joshua[86] (or Aaron);[87] Jesus/Simon-Peter;[88] Muhammad/ʿAlī;[89] Pharaoh;[90] ḍidd (adversary);[91] qiyasīya (analogists)[92]

Human Life Cycle
sperm;[93] womb;[94] birth;[95] circumcision;[96] tarbiya (rearing);[97] infants and children;[98] marriage;[99] coitus;[100] impregnation;[101] parenthood;[102] divorce;[103] death[104]

Scripture/Revelation
taʾwīl;[105] letters/alphabet;[106] al-jārī (the flow);[107]mawādd (the resources);[108] al-ṣāmit (the silent one);[109]al-kitāb (the book; scripture)[110]

Religion/Ritual
ṣalāt/sujūd (prayer/prostration);[111] shahāda (testimony of God's oneness);[112] Torah;[113] Gospels;[114] ahl al-kitāb;[115] the Cross[116]

Nature
water;[117] light/shade;[118] earth/mud;[119] birds[120]

Daʿwa Institutions
ʿahd/mithāq (pact);[121] dār hijra (abode of refuge);[122] daʿwa (mission);[123] jazāʾir (islands);[124] sirr/kitmān (secrecy)[125]

These symbols constitute the units of analysis for taʾwīl. Once internalized, the presence of one such symbol can initiate a sequence of interpretations. For example, "the earth" is a symbol that commonly signifies "the mission." In Jaʿfar ibn Manṣūr al-Yaman's *Taʾwīl al-zakāt*, a reference to those who *yafsidūn fī al-arḍ* (sow corruption on earth; Qurʾān 2:27) refers to those who "leave the mission and swerve from allegiance to the Imāms and their ḥudūd"—those who apostatize. In *Taʾwīl sūrat al-nisāʾ*, Jaʿfar interprets Qurʾān 4:11, a verse pertaining to bequest, as a reference to the daʿwa hierarchy. "The father and mother are a mathal for the nāṭiq and asās; the brothers are the Imams, peace be upon them. The children are their ḥujaj. Their relations on the father's side are the missionaries. The believers are the orphans." The mention of just one of these ranks in the daʿwa was considered sufficient for the missionary to rehearse the entire daʿwa hierarchy.

Other symbols include Islamic ritual prescription such as prayer, pilgrimage, testimony of faith, and alms, as well as themes from non-Islamic symbols and rituals such as the Christian cross, the Torah, and Church hierarchy. It includes themes from nature (water, shade, light, and birds) and themes in the human life cycle (birth, rearing, and death). Other strata of symbols pertain to hiero-historical cycles of speaker-prophets, and metaphysics and the supernal world (the "originator" and "originated," the intellect, and the soul).

In the list above, I do not differentiate between the symbol and that which is signified, the mathal and mamthūl. Based on his analysis of al-Qāḍī al-Nuʿmān's writings, al-Fekki provides a list of common mathal-mamthūl collocations. These include the ranks of the earthly daʿwa hierarchy, the concepts "interior and exterior" (ẓāhir and bāṭin), and special, saving knowledge.[126]

OBJECT OF INTERPRETATION	TAʾWĪL
Two parents	Imām and ḥujja
Newborn	New convert
Children	Missionary ranks
Fingernails	Exterior (ẓāhir)
Skin	Exterior (ẓāhir)
Under the fingernails	Interior (bāṭin)
Bones	Interior
Hands	Imām and ḥujja
Breaking of fast	Converstion to daʿwa
Ritual slaughter	Taking oath of allegiance
Defecation	Idolatry
Preejaculate (*madhī*)	Doubt
Removing clothes	Showing interior (meaning)
Scripture	Imām
Torah	Exterior
Qurʾān	Exterior
Gospels	Interior
Islam	Exterior
Faith	Interior
Seven-fold circumambulation	Seven speaker-prophets
Prostration	Speaker-prophet
Divine presence (*sakīna*)	Imāmate
Wisdom	Taʾwīl
Water	Knowledge
Washing with water	Purification with knowledge
Circumcision	Discovering interior sense
Sun	Speaker-prophet
Moon	Wāṣī

Sea	Exterior
Night	Secrecy
Seven days of week	Seven speaker-prophets
Ship	Mission
Agriculatural land	Mission
Plants	Adjunct missionaries
Birds	Missionaries
Camels	Imāms
Ants	Maʾdhūn missionaries
Milk	Knowledge of interior
Lavatory	Mission

These lists demonstrate that while the mathals, the objects of interpretation (or in classical rhetoric, "vehicle") are many, the mamthūls or hidden meanings, are few. Most refer to the ranks of the daʿwa hierarchy, special knowledge, the supernal hypostases, and taʾwīl itself. The world becomes a prism that reflects back the mission and the special, secret knowledge upon which it subsists.

A believer's mastery over the special "daʿwa sense" of these symbols was crucial to forge a shared understanding with others in the mission. Thus knowing that the sun and moon often indicated Muḥammad and ʿAlī, that water signified knowledge, and that birds referred to missionaries provided the believers a shared symbolic vocabulary of specialized words and terms. Argots and cryptolects were not uncommon in medieval Islam.[127] It is possible that this technical terminology was at times used as a code for missionaries to communicate in secret.

Logics: Harmony and Hierarchy

By "logics," I refer to the basis of the causal connection that underlie two or more different objects of interpretation in taʾwīl. Since taʾwīl commonly likens one object to another, these logics are largely based on apposition. In Ismāʿīlī taʾwīl the two most important underlying principles of apposition are harmony and hierarchy.[128]

For our purposes harmony refers to two or more entities that are deemed identical in structure according to a shared system of order. A key concept in taʾwīl that serves the principle of harmony is the mathal. "Mathal" occurs eighty-eight times in the Qurʾān, often in the sense of metaphor but also as parable or aphorism. The mathal "represents other than what it literally depicts. . . . It is like it but it is not the thing itself."[129] The most frequent formulation is expressed as "X is a mathal for Y" where X, the mathal or *ishāra* (indication or sign) is the exterior (ẓāhir) sign, and Y, the mamthūl (that which is signified), is the "true reality" (ḥaqīqa). In a taʾwīl of Qur'an 3:49, "I fashion for you out of clay the likeness of a bird," God's creation of a bird from clay is a mathal for the

Imām's appointment of a missionary. I suggest, however, that when missionaries made this parallel, they did not mean merely that in the Qurʾān, God spoke in an allegorical language. Their claim is more fundamental. For them the bird in the passage is, in its ontology, parallel to the missionary. In other words taʾwīl's claims are not merely rhetoric, that is, based on the analysis of language. Rather they are metaphysical and based on the ontological presupposition that things in the world exist in parallel.

The most common basis for harmony is number. In a treatise on the alphabet most likely composed by Jaʿfar ibn Manṣūr al-Yaman, the number of letters with which a letter of the alphabet is spelled is the basis to draw parallels between that letter and other forms. Since the letters *bāʾ* and *tāʾ* are each spelled with two consonants, they indicate the ranks of legateeship and Imāmate. Explanations based on the harmony of dyads, triads, pentads, and heptads fill Ismāʿīlī taʾwīl.

Like harmony, hierarchy, the principle that objects are ranked, pervades the sources. For our purposes hierarchy may be defined as the principle that things occur in highly ordered ranks, and that these ranks are part of their ontology, the nature of their existence. The key term is ḥadd (plural ḥudūd). In Arabic ḥadd usually connotes "limit," or "definition" of a word or term. In Islamic law it is a technical term for prohibitions proscribed directly by God in the Qur'an. In Ismāʿīlism ḥadd carries a different range of meanings. It often refers to a high-ranking dāʿī. Thus early in his career the first human Adam ascends "from ḥadd to ḥadd" in the daʿwa hierarchy until he reaches the ḥadd of speaker-prophet. In another source it is clear that one rises within a ḥādd after mastering everything to be learned within it, and then one ascends to the next one. But it also carries a more abstract sense, as in moving from the ḥadd of materiality to the ḥadd of immateriality, or from the ḥadd of the celestial spheres to the ḥadd of the pleroma.

The Ismāʿīlī sense of ḥadd is similar to the Pythagorean term *pera* (limit; boundary), the units that divide the undifferentiated *apeiron*.[130] These limits are not arbitrary; they are built into nature. Pythagoreans liked to use the example of a single-stringed instrument to explain this reality. In principle there are an infinite number of places that one could divide the string by placing one's finger down; it is, nevertheless, discernable to even an untrained ear that there are divisions that correspond to the notes on a scale. These are not culturally determined; they occur naturally—they are built in to the universe. The Aristotelian tradition extended this claim of naturally occurring divisions to the genera and species of the material world. Each species in the world of minerals, plants, and animals represents a particular, naturally occurring limit from among the infinite possibilities, a pera of the infinitely undivided apeiron.[131]

Similarly Ismāʿīlī missionaries believed that the supernal pleroma, the celestial spheres, and the material world are, too, divided into "limits." But it was

God, not nature, who fixed them. The purest form of these ḥudūd are found in the daʿwa hierarchy, but evidence for them is found everywhere—hence the constant citation of parallels between the earthly and heavenly ranks. Nāṣir al-Dīn al-Ṭūsī (thrived mid-thirteenth century), a Shīʿite scholar extremely well-read in Ismāʿīlī sources, aptly described the early Ismāʿīlī tracts of ʿAbdān as "Pythagorean."[132]

In taʾwīl these principles of harmony and hierarchy were expressed in a variety of vehicles. Among the most common of these were numerology (correspondences between numbers and pairs of numbers); wordplay (homophony, metagraphy, synecdoche, *istinbāṭ* (changing the order of letters in a word); and cyclical history (correspondences in historical scenerios; telescoping from one historical moment to another).

Another stylistic element of taʾwīl is the use of dissonance, the pairing of anomalous sources. This can take the form of the taʾwīl of a symbol, which, in and of itself, is anathema in Islam, such as the Christian cross or the taking of the Eucharist. Or it might entail juxtaposing and combing themes culled from wildly different intellectual idioms—for example connecting Islamic ritual law with Greek science. The bricolage created by these combinations would have been heard as jarring to its audience. Such dissonance provided a sense that the believers were learning the secret harmony accessible only to the believers, for they alone can perceive the unity behind these aberrant or discordant forms. Cognitive linguists have shown that units of language come in "packets" that are tagged in a preconscious state. Creativity comes through combining these packets of meaning in new ways.[133]

Harmony: Noah and the Daʿwa

The story of Noah, an important motif in Shīʿite lore, demonstrates the distinctiveness of Ismāʿīlī daʿwa knowledge. The Imāmī ʿulamāʾ transmitted historical traditions of Noah's ark that resonated with or even explicitly affirmed Shīʿite doctrine. On the authority of the Imāms, they adduced traditions that Noah's ark paused above Karbala, the site of al-Ḥusayn's future martyrdom; that the ark landed on dry land on the tenth day of the month of Muḥarram, the date on which al-Ḥusayn was later martyred; and that like ʿAlī, Noah was buried in Najaf. Bar-Asher has noted that interpretations such as these are typological: They authorize the role of Imāmism's early heroes by showing that they were prefigured in the stories of ancient prophets. Ismāʿīlī missionaries' handling of the Noah story was different. It employs the logics and symbols discussed above to reinforce daʿwa knowledge.

In his taʾwīl the Fāṭimid Ismāʿīlī jurist al-Qaḍī al-Nuʿmān first rehearses the commonly accepted *akhbārī* (traditional) account, and then provides the true, hidden story. After humankind had fallen into a state of corruption and ignorance, having altered and neglected the divine law previously revealed to

Adam, God sent Noah a new revealed law to teach humankind how to properly worship God in His unicity. Al-Nuʿmān wrote that in Noah's day, the ʿulamāʾ of the period refused to respond to his call. They doubted his claim that he was a prophet and strayed from God's path. In response God told Noah that he would send down rain to destroy the ungrateful ʿulamāʾ and their followers. The narrator comments that this rainwater coming from the sky alludes to God's secret knowledge coming from the nāṭiq. Knowledge is a salvation for those within the daʿwa but will doom the ʿulamāʾ to drown in its depths. This mocks the ʿulamāʾ using one of their own expressions, playing on the idiomatic sense of *baḥr* (sea) as a scholar who is extremely knowledgeable—"a sea" of knowledge.[134]

God provides Noah with the design of the ark and commands him to build it. The narrator reveals that the ship's design is a mathal for the daʿwa. The ark's two materials, wood and iron, allude to the al-aṣlān, "the two supernal roots," the twin hypostases of the divine pleroma. The ark's seven elements (two human leaders, a mast, crossbeam, sail, anchor, and rope) refer to the seven nāṭiqs (speaker-prophets) and to the seven Imāms who follow each of the first six speakers. The ark's twelve tablets refer to the mission's twelve lawāḥiq or "wings," the high ranking missionaries who direct the twelve islands into which the mission is divided.[135] The blueprint and materials for the ship thus encode the daʿwa.[136]

This taʾwīl depends on numeric equivalents two, seven, and twelve found in the ship and the daʿwa. Such an interpretation relies on, and reinforces, the principle that harmony expressed through number is salient for uncovering the archetypal reality beyond the apparent sense. It also illustrates a major difference between Ismāʿīlī and Imāmī interpretation.

While Imāmī interpretation draws parallels between the ship and the institution of the Imāmate, this Ismāʿīlī taʾwīl of Noah's ark encodes the entire daʿwa, from nāṭiq, to the believer, in its architecture. As in all taʾwīl, this is established through analyzing the story through the prism of daʿwa knowledge, finding numeric and phonetic harmonies between God's references to the Noah story and elements of the mission.

Elsewhere in his interpretation in the story of Noah, al-Nuʿmān compares the numbers of letters and sounds of words. Nuʿmān interprets the basmallāh ("in the name of God") in Qurʾān 11:41 as follows: "We say, 'bismi illāh' [through the name of God] is two words. They are like the two supernal roots. They are seven letters, like the letters of Muḥammad and ʿAlī, pen and tablet, and Imām and ḥujja. The mission flows through (*bi*) them, and settles onto those who rest with Him."[137]

Rather than the conventional understanding of the particle "bi" as "in" (the name of God), al-Nuʿmān translates "bi" as a particle of agency, or "through." It is thus "through" the words "name" and "God" that the mission flows. "Name"

(ʾ-*s-m*) and "God" (ʾ-*l-l-h*) consist of seven letters. These words parallel the two roots (al-aṣlān), also known as the pen and tablet (*q-l-m-w-l-w-ḥ*), the Prophet Muḥammad (*m-ḥ-m-d*) and legatee ʿAlī (ʿ-*l-y*), and the Imām (ʾ-*m-ā-m*), and ḥujjā (proof) (*ḥ-j-j*). Thus knowledge flows through the al-aṣlān (the "two roots" or supernal hypostases) to the Prophet Muḥammad and his legatee, ʿAlī, and then to the Imām and his lead missionary, the ḥujja. This passage thus appeals to harmony of number and also hierarchy in its broad sense as reflecting different strata to show that knowledge descends from the level of the twin supernal roots to the prophet and legatee, to the Imām and chief missionary.

Al-Nuʿmān explains that the word "merciful" in the verse indicates *taʾyīd* (support), a technical term for the connection between God and Prophets and Imāms. "Mercy [*raḥma*] is derived from womb [*raḥim*]. Similar to this is the effect of wisdom in the interior of the one supported [*muʾayyad*] [by God]. It descends like the falling of the sperm in the interior of the womb [*fī bāṭin al-raḥim*], taking nourishment in [the womb] ever so lightly, until the creation is completed and perfected."[138]

The homophony between the words "raḥma" (mercy) and "raḥim" (womb) suggests their apposition. Just as sperm impregnates the raḥim (womb) and takes nourishment from it, so too does God's raḥma (mercy), which is His wisdom, enter him who has been given God's support (taʾyīd) until this person reaches perfection.

The Imāmī narratives emphasize the historical connections between the ark and later key historical sites such as Kufa and Karbala. Nuʿmān's interpretation emphasizes the daʿwa.

> "It came to rest on [Mount] al-Jūdī (Qurʾān 11:44)." This means that the daʿwa came to the acolytes. The sense of this is that the unveiling [*al-mufātiḥa*] through the daʿwa and hidden knowledge flowed from the nāṭiq to the asās. It did not rest with him; rather, it flowed to the ḥujjas. It did not rest with them, but flowed also to the naqībs who are their adjuncts. Then, it flowed to the wings, being the missionaries. Then it flowed to the acolytes [mustajibīn]. It did not leave them, and came to rest, and persisted upon them.[139]

Thematically this aspect of taʾwīl—an emphasis on not only the rightly guided Imāms or family of the Prophet, but the entire daʿwa hierarchy—distinguishes Ismāʿīlism from other Shīʿite sectarians. The repeated inclusion of the missionaries and believers in the special scheme was useful for sectarians in forging a closely knit community of believers.

"Those Forbidden to You": Hierarchy and Daʿwa Knowledge

Like harmony the principle of hierarchy is omnipresent in taʾwīl. I have already discussed the pervasiveness of the ḥudūd, the "limits" or ranks of the supernal realms and earthly daʿwa. The repetition of the ḥudūd contributed to the believer's sense that he belonged to the daʿwa's intricate, divinely apportioned architecture.

Mathals for the different processes and ranks of the earthly hierarchy frequently draw on sex, gender, and phases of the life cycle. An acolyte's oath is his "birth" and "circumcision," his first stage of rearing. "A convert is like a baby—he first must be fed soft foods, and only later, solid foods."[140] "Men are Imāms, and women are the ḥujjas," and "every [act of] teaching is masculine and act of learning is feminine," the narrator of *Taʾwīl surat al-nisāʾ* claims.[141] The "flow" or "stream" (al-jārī) from the supernal hypostases to the missionaries is like the penis penetrating the vagina, according to the author of the *Kitāb al-ridāʿ fī al-bāṭin.* Just as this act is hidden from the light of the sun, so too is the spread of the mission by his ḥujjas out of the view of the Imām.[142] A taʾwīl of the Imāmī tradition that no one is permitted to have sexual intercourse in the mosque of the Prophet except for ʿAlī and Muḥammd,[143] is that missionizing should only be done through the scripture revealed by Muḥammad, and its hidden taʾwīl sense imparted by ʿAlī.[144] In a passage of the Qur'ān on bequest, the father and mother are taken as the nāṭiq and asās, "the brothers" as the Imāms, their children as the ḥujjaj, the agnatic relatives as the missionaries, and the uterine relatives from the women as the believers.[145] "Learning to speak" connotes becoming a mature dāʿī at a rank sufficient to proselytize.[146] Giving birth is like disseminating the daʿwa.[147]

Hierarchy is expressed in the repetition of these ranks, and in prohibitions against transgressing one's station. In Qur'ān 4:23 God prohibits men from marrying various classes of relatives. This passage provides an occasion for the missionary to discuss those who go outside the parameters of the daʿwa hierarchy.

> It is prohibited for us to enter into and remain in [a marriage] without the approval of the mission of the guardian [*walī*] of God, as was the case with the law of Moses when Jesus (peace be upon him) appeared. For he who grants permission to have intercourse with mothers is an accursed one, just as one who campaigns for the laws of the prophets without the approval of the Imāms and legatees is an accursed unbeliever.
>
> "Daughters" [refers to] a man who has been summoned, and who possesses wealth and ease; he gives the dowry with the support that is required of him. Proselytizing him is forbidden. He is named "a daughter" because he is forbidden [*muḥarram*] for he has not joined the rank of believers. . . .
>
> "Your sisters" indicates a man who has fulfilled his duty and his like has been determined, but then returned to doubting and calling the lie. He is prohibited from being received until he repents, undergoes purification, and takes the oath.

"Your [paternal] aunts" [refers to] the man without eloquence or clarity [. . .]. The guardian [on behalf of] God [set him] in the mission, but he contravened his command and did not fulfill his pact, so he is prohibited from proselytizing.

"Your [maternal] aunts" [refers to] the dāʿī who institutes the law of the guardian [on behalf of] God, but [then] he claims a ḥadd which he has not reached and for which [he] has not been commanded, so he is prohibited from proselytizing and [it is prohibited to] obey or listen to him, for he depends on the status of opinion and analogy.

"[Fraternal] nieces" refers to the hypocrites. They were our brothers in the religion of God, but the feminine noun was applied to them because of their lowness in the station of their faith and their hypocrisy, so it is forbidden to disclose any knowledge to them.

"Nieces" [through the sister refers to] those whom were called by one without permission to administer the oath; it is forbidden to accept them.

"Your milk-mothers who suckled you" are the ḥujaj [proofs] who received the knowledge of the caretaker of God, but then cut off the people of his diocese from the caretaker of God, claimed his place and disputed his priority in rank. All are forbidden to obey him [. . .].

"The good ones of the women who are married" are the people of previous laws. It is forbidden to accept and to proselytize them, for their interior [bāṭin] is forbidden.[148]

The most common reason for the censure of believers is that they have doubted, disobeyed, exceeded the bounds of their ḥadd, or otherwise contravened the wishes of the rightful leader, the *walī Allāh.* The prohibition against marrying one's sister is a mathal for disallowing the return of a former believer who had apostatized to return, one's paternal aunt is a mathal for the disobedient, the maternal aunt is a mathal for a missionary who has overstepped his bounds, and the uterine niece is a mathal for one who has been converted to the mission by one who did not have permission to proselytize. The milk mother is a mathal for former high-ranking missionaries who had received knowledge, but then dispensed it without recourse to the walī Allāh.

It is clear that the warning against acting without permission of the "walī Allāh," the leader of the community on behalf of God, is directed against Qarmāṭian proselytizing on behalf of Muḥammad b. Ismāʿīl, and do so without the sanction of the Fāṭimid Imām and the ḥudūd under him.

The Familiar and the Obscure

Certain combinations of themes suggest techniques for creating the sense of epiphany and recognition that was one of taʾwīl's aims. One such technique was to interpret a familiar theme in a radically new way. A number of taʾwīls of the first part of the shahāda, the declaration *lā ilāha illā Allāh* ("there is no god but God"), interpret the creedal statement in terms that would be repugnant to non-Ismāʿīlīs.

As S. M. Stern first noted, descriptions of a demiurge-creator through interpretations of the shahāda are among Ismāʿīlism's earliest elements. In a fragment nested within a treatise by the Egyptian missionary Abū ʿĪsā al-Murshid (d. ca. 369/980) Stern found evidence that the *tahlīl* (first part of the shahāda) is read as a speech by the first emanation from God. After "the First" emanation sprang forth:

> it saw no other beings besides itself. Thus, it conceived a proud thought that there is nobody but itself. Upon this, six dignitaries (ḥudūd) immediately emanated from it through God's power, in order to teach it that there is an omnipotent being above it from Whom it derives its power and upon Whose will all his actions depend [. . .] When the First saw that this happened neither through its own power nor according to its own will, it was convinced that there was something above it and acknowledged its Creator; it was then that it said: "There is no god but God"—that is, "I am not a god."[149]

In order to correct "the First's" hubris, God creates six ḥudūd to indicate that He, and not the First, is the actual Creator. Recognizing its mistake the First then testifies that "there is no God but God," that is, "I am not God" (*ay, lastu anā bi-lāh*). In so doing, from the First the second emanation, Qadar (power or fate), was generated. Elsewhere in the treatise, the First is called *Kūnī,* the feminine form of God's command "*Kun!*" ("Be!") (Qurʾān 3:47 et al.). Through Kūnī and Qadar God brought forth (*kawwana*) and determined (*qaddara*) all things. As Halm points out, Abū ʿIsā is the sole version of the myth that refer to the demiurge's "hubris," a motif found in many strains of late antique Gnosticism.[150] What interests me is not the symbol's origins, but its impact: the taʾwīl transforms the testimony of faith into a cosmogonic "prologue in heaven" that imagines a demiurge as the creator. Several anti-Ismāʿīlī tracts allude to this statement as clear evidence of Ismāʿīlism's polytheism. For the believers with whom such an account was shared, possessing forbidden knowledge bound the community members together.

Subsequent missionaries offered other interpretations of the shahāda. Qarmaṭian missionaries in Iran and Transoxania such as al-Nasafī, Abū Ḥātim al-Rāzī, and al-Sijistānī offered philosophical interpretations of the shahāda. Al-Sijistanī, for example, parsed it to describe the glorification of God by *al-Sābiq* (the "Preceder," al-Sijistānī's term for the First emanation).[151] Al-Qāḍī al-Nuʿmān divided it into two parts, *lā ilāh* (there is no god) and *illā allāh* (but God). He writes,

> In each part, there are two words. The first is connected to and lower than the second; the second is higher than [the first]. Likewise, the portion which is the confirmation is higher than the portion which is the negation, which precedes it. Thus the final ḥadd, which is the confirmation, is in the interior sense a likeness of the supernal ḥadd, just as the ḥadd which is the denial is in the interior sense a likeness of the lower ḥadd.

Thus al-Nuʿmān relates the drama in the pleroma to the different ḥudūd of God's supernal and earthly ḥudūd of the daʿwa.[152]

A line in Jaʿfar ibn Manṣūr al-Yaman's *Kitāb al-fatarāt wal-qirānāt* (The Book of Periods and Conjunctions) suggests the importance of this symbolic form. In discussing the celestial bodies, the author alludes to a testimony by a supernal being. "They [the planets] are similar to the divine device [*āla ilāhīya*] that had formerly, at the beginning of creation, sanctified the world of divinity when it took the oath on the descendants [*al-ʿahd ʿalā al-dhurrīya*] by confessing to His unicity."

The author refers to a "divine device," the first of the twin supernal roots, that testifies that there is no God but god. The testimony is referred to as "the oath of the descendants." The first emanation's testimony that "there is no god but God" is presented as an oath to join God's mission, connecting the oath of allegiance to the supernal "First" in the pleroma. This taʾwīl indicates that when believers are administered the secret oath, they imitate the words of the first emanation when it testified to the Creator's existence.[153] The Islamic understanding of the testimony that there is one God is thus transfigured, becoming a secret cosmological myth of creation in heaven.

Taʾwīl of familiar Qurʾānic verses, rules for daily prayer, and the rite of pilgrimage were similarly transfigured to apply to the elements of the missionary hierarchy. In a taʾwīl of Qurʾān 2:30, "Verily I will place on the earth a viceroy," Jaʿfar ibn Manṣūr al-Yaman claims that God in the Qurʾān actually refers to the speech of the Imām of the time.[154]

Although access to daʿwa literature and taʾwīl was restricted to Ismāʿīlīs, the few medieval Muslim ʿulamāʾ who gained access to this secret literature duly expressed their disapproval. Muḥammad al-Ghazālī (d. 500/1111), who devoted an entire treatise to the bankruptcy of Ismāʿīlī "bāṭinism" (esotericism), accused its exponents of emptying the Qurʾān of sense and converting it to mere symbols (*rumūz*) to suit their own agenda (*maṣlaḥa*).[155] The Zaydī Imām Yaḥya ibn Ḥamza (d. 749/1348) declared that in taʾwīl, Ismāʿīlīs mix the religious laws of the prophets with Greek philosophy; the result is a mishmash of symbols that have "no meaning in Arabic."[156] Taʾwīls of Qurʾānic passages which gloss "God" as "the Imām" surely would have been repugnant to contemporary

ʿulamāʾ, and the Ismāʿīlī missionaries would have been well aware of this when they used this imagery.

Just as joining the daʿwa meant taking an oath to maintain strict secrecy about the movement and its teachings, so too would gaining access to this type of transgressive material forge a bond at a later stage of participation in the mission. Thus taʾwīl transformed what was familiar into something hidden and dangerous.

Reconfiguring familiar themes was one taʾwīl strategy. The obverse, showing that unconventional objects of interpretation point to God's hidden signs, also provided special knowledge that bound the believers together. Thus missionaries composed taʾwīls on the church hierarchy, the clothes of the priests and monks, the Eucharist, and passages from the Bible in Hebrew or the Gospels in Syriac.[157]

In a taʾwīl in the *Kitāb al-fatarāt wal-qiranāt,* an anonymous sage explains that both the human body and the universe were created by al-aṣlān, "the two original roots" of the pleroma.

> Furthermore, the existence of the body [*al-juththa*] of the human was by the influence of the rising of the power from the two supernal sources [al-aṣlān] that were the cause of the existence of the macrocosm. Therefore, one of the ancient wise ones [*ḥukamāʾ mutaqaddimūn*] said that the beginning of existence is two lines, one on the other in the middle, in this shape:  . Because of this, the Messiah was mounted on the cross to exemplify it, indicating the two roots [al-aṣlān]. Then they became two circles, one on the other. One of the two was named "the [outermost] sphere" [*al-falak al-mustaqīm*] and the other "the sphere divided by the signs." The [outermost] sphere turns the divided sphere every day and night on its rotation, disposed [to go] from east to west. From its rotations, all of the heavenly and earthly worlds, the spiritual subtleties and natural crudities, are generated.[158]

This taʾwīl is based on a set of numeric and geometric equivalents based on the number "two." One of the "ancient wise ones" (*ḥukamāʾ mutaqaddimūn*) describes the beginning of existence as two lines (*khaṭṭān*), one on the other; these are parallel to the two original roots in the pleroma, and the two posts of the cross upon which Jesus was crucified.

References to "the outermost sphere" and "sphere divided by the signs" were familiar to fourth/tenth-century medieval Muslims from Greek astronomy. The conception of two lines forming the ecliptic and equator of the universe ultimately derives from Plato's *Timaeus,* a well-known source among the Baghdad school of falsafa (philosophy in the Greek tradition). The narrator describes these two lines as a cross, and, two paragraphs later, "the line" is explicitly referred to as the cross on which Jesus was crucified, suggesting that the author intended to highlight that this allusion came from a Christian source.[159]

In Qurʾān 4: 157, God declared explicitly that Jesus was *not* crucified on the cross, a point accepted by medieval Muslims. A popular tradition narrated that at the End of Days, Jesus would return and punish those who worshipped the cross, rather than God.[160] As a symbol for the doctrine of the trinity and the Christian empire, the parallel of the cross with foundations of the universe would surely have been repugnant to Muslim sensibilities.

The same point could be made regarding the philosophical dicta. In the fourth/tenth century, the ʿulamāʾ strongly objected to Greek sciences such as falsafa and astrology.[161] However, in taʾwīl sources such as the *Kitāb al-fatarāt,* the missionaries not only transmitted philosophical and scientific dicta but did so explicitly on the authority of "the ancient Greeks." The narrator repeatedly names Plato, Aristotle, and Euclid.

Comparison with other sectarian, esoteric sects provides insight into why Ismāʿīlī missionaries composed taʾwīl of unconventional objects such as the Christian cross and knowledge from pagan Greeks.[162] Samuel Thomas draws from sociological theories of sect formation and esotericism to analyze sources produced by the community at Qumran.[163] Drawing from Stark and Bainbridge, Thomas notes that sectarians seek to perpetuate a sense of tension with those outside the community by producing myths, doctrines, and practices objectionable to those outside the sect. These secrets create a new and different reality, a "second world" in which community members experience an alternative to the manifest world. Access to this alternative world is achieved through a radical transformation of the acolyte, a dramatic experience of receiving the hidden knowledge. For religious sectarians who employ this discourse, such learning creates a sense of difference from outsiders and binds the sectarians together. Thus esoteric literature can serve a sectarian ethos.

By demonstrating the unities underlying eclectic, disparate idioms, missionaries showed that this hidden sense was beyond the reach of those outside the daʿwa. It also demonstrated the universal scope of their Imām's knowledge. In the fourth/tenth century, when fields of knowledge had become highly specialized, the Imām showed that God gave him the capacity to decode the hidden signs behind all religions, falsafa, science, and astronomy.

Research in other contexts provides some context for uses of similar semierudition and the mixing of idioms among literate and nonliterate cultures. One of Maurice Bloch's conclusions to his classic study of the role of astrology as esoteric, privileged knowledge in Madagascar is that it is precisely the juxtaposition of forms of knowledge not usually found together that increases their value, and the value of the astrologer.[164] Taʾwīl's recourse to Greek science and Christology might represent a similar dynamic at play. To the missionaries the discovery of underlying, structural unities to material that was otherwise inaccessible created a sense of wonder to the semiliterate agricultural and villages and towns in tenth-century Yemen, North Africa, and Sind, where the daʿwa was propagated.

Conclusion: Daʿwa Reading and Daʿwa Knowledge

Taʾwīl relies on the repetition of symbols, patterns, and unconventional "logics," that is, bases for apposition between two components of the interpretation. Through taʾwīl believers were led to internalize these forms and logics and, once reaching maturity, propagated the mission and instructed those at a lower rank. This shared cognitive world bound community members together as it polemicized against external Shīʿite groups vying for the allegiance of the same community members.

A cognitive approach to the texts allows us to consider the sources as exemplars that reflected the habits of mind that the missionaries wished to instill. Ultimately, of course, such an approach still relies on the interpretation of literary sources. I would suggest, however, that by replacing textual analytic categories such as "themes" and "hermeneutics" with cognitive ones such as "symbols" and "logics," we better appreciate the interpretive stakes in question for these sources. Such an approach continues to rely on close analysis of texts but stresses their social role in a sectarian religio-political movement. The Fāṭimid Ismāʿīlī missionaries used taʾwīl not only to maintain a community of believers, but also to compete with other Shīʿite missionaries for their allegiance.

CHAPTER 4

Beyond the Qurʾān

Prophecy, Scriptures, Signs

Sectarian movements require profound trust among participants. When ʿAbd Allāh was declared the first Fāṭimid Imām by the mission's leadership, a number of leading missionaries rejected his claim. For the Fāṭimid missionaries, this constituted a breach of this trust, a threat to the integrity of the daʿwa, and an apostasy before God. This fissure within the community would occupy the Fāṭimid missionaries for the next century, and left its mark in daʿwa sources and taʾwīl.

A close reading of Jaʿfar ibn Manṣūr al-Yaman's theory of prophecy and of the narrative taʾwīl of speaker-prophets demonstrates a veiled Fāṭimid response to apostates within the Ismāʿīlī movement. Passages in the *Sarāʾir* suggest that Jaʿfar was aware of the doctrines of the (non-Fāṭimid) Iranian Ismāʿīlī missionaries, and incorporated some of their conceptual language into his taʾwīl. I argue that this was likely not, as has been suggested, an attempt to accommodate the Iranian Ismāʿīlīs who had left the fold. Rather Jaʿfar's taʾwīl was a riposte. In addition I show that Jaʿfar's model of revelation provides an epistemology that helps explain an unusual aspect of taʾwīl: the missionaries' propensity to interpret extra-Qurʾānic interpretation.

Prophecy and Scripture in Ismāʿīlism: The Iranians

In daʿwa sources we read that the speaker-prophet "composes a law" (*allafa sharīʿa*). This is not a common view in Islam. In the Qurʾān God declares that He "revealed" (*awḥā*; Qurʾān 42:51) or "sends down" (*anzala*; Qurʾān 29:50) verses of scripture; tradition clarifies that the angel Gabriel transmitted revelation aurally from God to *rusul*, messengers.[1] The word "messenger" implies that a prophet *transmits* prophecy, and this is what the scholars emphasized. Thus they interpreted Qurʾān 7:157 to mean that the Prophet Muḥammad was illiterate, and thus could not possibly have composed or compiled the Qurʾān.[2] In narratives of the early production of the first authorized Qurʾānic codices, traditions seldom use the word *allafa*, a word which can also connote "compile." According to early Islamic traditions, when the caliph Abū Bakr commissioned the companion Zayd ibn Thābit to produce an authoritative text of the Qurʾān from the versions circulating among the companions, Zayd is reported to have *jamaʿa* (gathered) the Qurʾānic fragments and versions. The word *jamaʿa* (gathers) implies that the codex of the Qurʾān's production was merely putting together what was available, and that there was little human intellectual engagement.[3] Islamic tradition thus emphasizes that there was little human intrusion in scripture's creation.

In stark contrast, in Ismāʿīlism, we repeatedly read that the first six nāṭiqs (Adam, Noah, Abraham, Moses, Jesus, Muḥammad) each composed (allafa) a law. The Qāʾim-Mahdī, the seventh and final speaker-prophet, will complete all the prior laws, reveal their secret meaning, and vanquish the tyrants to rule the world with justice just as it is now ruled with tyranny.[4]

While this hiero-historical scheme is among the most common symbolic models in early Ismāʿīlī sources, it was left for later figures to clarify what precisely was meant by "*taʾlīf*" (composition). It was the non-Fāṭimid Ismāʿīlī missionaries of the Iranian dioceses of Rayy and Khurāsān such as Abū Ḥātim al-Rāzī (d. 322/934-935) and Abū Yaʿqūb al-Sijistānī (thrived mid fourth/tenth century) who first explained the mechanics of prophecy and its compilation.

Abū Ḥātim al-Rāzī's description bristles with technical terminology meant to maintain God's purity and separation from the material world, while also holding that the speaker-prophet enjoyed a direct connection (*ittiṣāl*) to Him. He wrote that prophecy comes from al-Sābiq, the first of al-aṣlān (the two roots) in the pleroma beyond matter. From al-Sābiq flow the mawādd, the supernal resources, via al-Jārī (the one who flows) to al-Jadd, the first of the angelic triad beneath the two roots. From al-Jadd the mawādd flow to the speaker-prophet, who is *muʾayyad,* divinely "aided" and thus able to receive them. For al-Rāzī these cascading layers of hypostases preserved God's purity while also linking the prophet to Him.[5]

Abū Ḥātim al-Rāzī claimed there were seven nāṭiqs but only three scriptures (*kutub*), the Torah, the Gospels, and the Qurʾān. He explained that the first three nāṭiqs, Adam, Noah, and Abraham, composed drafts of these scriptures while the second triad, Moses, Jesus, and Muḥammad, completed them. The subject arose in the context of the debate among the Iranians as to whether the first speaker-prophet, Adam, compiled a law or worshiped God directly without need of good works. Abū Ḥātim al-Rāzī held the former position, whereas al-Nasafī and al-Sijistānī held the latter.

The Ismāʿīlī missionary Abū Yaʿqūb al-Sijistānī drew liberally from the Neoplatonic philosophical tradition that was popular in the Samanid court life. The philosopher al-Farābī (d. 339/950), with whom the Ismāʿīlīs in the Iranian dioceses were clearly familiar, held that great prophets possessed souls who combined a supreme intellectual faculty with an imaginative faculty with the capacity to imitate the rational faculty. Both these rational and imaginative faculties are so well developed in the prophet that his imaginative faculty is able to express pure abstract intelligibles (*maʿqūlāt*) as "sensible" symbols. Prophecy is thus the soul's capacity to express theoretical, abstract "intelligibles," abstractions that are determined through logic, as "sensibles" (*maḥsūsāt*), which can be appreciated by the senses. Prophets can express these intelligibles through "sensible" symbols. The prophet institutes these symbols into law, which is useful to constrain the rabble and compel them to do good, thereby maintaining a just social order.[6] Al-Sijistānī adapted aspects of this Neoplatonic theory of prophecy. What is most important, he added that the prophet's soul possessed a special faculty, *al-quwwa al-qudsiyya* (the sacred faculty). His scheme attributed to the lawgiver a special linguistic power that allowed him to produce verbal representation of intellectual forms that, in their original state, are beyond language. The Prophet was thus able to translate pure intellectual forms into sublime legislative language.[7] Al-Sijistānī's model thus focuses less on the imaginative faculty and forms, and more on the Prophet's special capacity for language.

These theories of prophecy were part of larger philosophical projects that allowed the Iranian missionaries to debate philosophers in the courts of Rayy for the favor of the viziers there. Early Fāṭimid taʾwīl offered far less theoretical speculation on the metaphysics and mechanics of prophecy than did these figures. However, there are a number of passages on prophecy in Jaʿfar ibn Manṣūr al-Yaman's *Sarāʾir al-nuṭaqāʾ,* and they clearly betray awareness of the concepts of the non-Fāṭimid Ismāʿīlīs in Iran.

The Early Fāṭimids on Prophecy

While the early Fāṭimid missionaries wrote less than the Iranians on the mechanics of prophecy, there are a number of relevant passages scattered in the sources. In *Taʾwīl al-sharīʿa,* a work attributed to al-Qāḍī al-Nuʿmān, the Fāṭimid caliph al-Muʿizz was asked about the status of God's speech when asked to comment on Qurʾān 69:40, "Indeed, it is the speech of a noble messenger." Prima facie the verse is problematic, as it seems to mean that the Qurʾān is the speech of the Prophet, rather than God. Most commentators read the verse as having been revealed with an ellipsis, and that the verse means "the Qurʾān is the speech of God transmitted by a loyal messenger." Al-Muʿizz's interpretation was radically different and delves into the metaphysical status of revelation as both the speech of God and the speech of the Prophet.

> [Al-Muʿizz] said: God sent down light to the heart of Muḥammad as was mentioned in the Qurʾān. The Prophet was not able to send this divine light to the believers, for they are not able to bear it [*iḥtimālu*]. This is a difference between the Prophet and the believers of the *umma.* [The Prophet] produced [*awrada*] the meanings of revelation and light and its prescriptions, rulings, and signs through composed expressions [*alfāẓ*

> *muʾallafa*] and crafted letters composed of understandable, audible writings [*bi-ḥurūf murakkaba, mafhūma masmūʿa*]. When the Prophet ordered [*rakkaba*] these expressions and inserted in them [*ḍammanahā*] meanings that are encompassed by revelation, the Qurʾān was established upon [*mabnī ʿalā*] the light, which is the revelation that had been sent down as the speech of the messenger. Thus the [Qurʾān's] formulation, expressions, and composition is the Prophet's. It is, then, the speech of God, as well as the speech of the Messenger of God, praise be upon him.[8]

God's speech could not possess sounds or letters as these possess matter, of which God had no part. God's speech is pure light; it is described elsewhere in the same source as the "light of intellection." Through the inspiration of God's spirit, the Prophet transforms this divine light into expressions, sounds, and letters. The Prophet shapes God's speech into human language. Thus in its pure, original, immaterial form, the Qurʾān is the speech of God; in its articulated, linguistic expression, it is "the speech of the Messenger." This formulation is similar to that of the Neoplatonic models of prophecy of the non-Fāṭimid Iranian missionaries described above, although free of much of its technical terminology.

In the opening to the story of Adam in the *Sarāʾir*, several passages describe the metaphysics of prophecy. According to Jaʿfar prophecy represents the imprints from the light of origination that descends from the supernal to the material world. While "the generality"—that is, non-Ismāʿīlīs—describe *waḥy* (revelation) as "sound and speech in arranged letters" brought by an angel, those who possess true knowledge know that scripture is beyond conventional human speech.[9] Revelation is

> the imprints [*nuqūsh*] of the simple worlds upon correct intellects and chaste minds [*adhhān fasīḥa*]. . . . This is because in the simple world there is neither voice nor speech with composed letters through which expressions and [verbal] arrangement appeared. Understandable speech and natural discourse is, rather, part of the corporeal, natural world via natures. It is spoken through a faculty which is that support which attaches to it. Then it occurs in its idiom in its corporeal language. This faculty and imaginings which appear to the cogitation of the thinker are called [by the specialists in religion] "angels." They said this and held this opinion from their deficient knowledge of the ḥudūd and of the stations and ranks of the nāṭiqs.[10]

Revelation consists of the "imprints" (nuqūsh) from the supernal, simple worlds on intellects that have been sufficiently refined as to be able to receive these supernal, immaterial traces. Jaʿfar continues:

> Revelation . . . is from the power of the word [*al-kalima*] in its connection to "the stream" [al-jārī]. When intellects are purified and souls refined, spirits are cleared of the turbidities of the world stamped with nature. They connect to the simple world, and then they return to their home, which is the body, and purify it of the filth and turbidities of natures and clean the brain [*damāgh*] of the foul vapors and filthy mixtures. The intellect is purified and glows, and the resource [*mādda*] of the spirit strengthens it. At that point, the impressions [nuqūsh] of the simple world leave their impression on the intellect, just as the impression of a stamp influences what it stamps.[11]

An intellect that has been freed from the filth of materiality "glows" from its connection (ittiṣāl) with al-jārī (the stream) that descends from the first of the two primordial roots. The intellect is predisposed to receive revelation by the mādda (resource), divine sustenance that descends on the speaker-prophet.

Ja'far's use of mawādd and its relationship to al-jārī recalls the conception of the non-Fāṭimid missionary Abū Ḥātim al-Rāzī. According to al-Rāzī, "the Preceder," the first of the two roots, streams (*yajrī*) al-jārī (the stream); the contents of al-jārī is al-mawādd.[12] Ja'far and al-Rāzī are near contemporaries, although al-Rāzī likely composed his works several decades prior to Ja'far. As these concepts are better developed in al-Rāzī's works and he composed these works before Ja'far, it is likely that it was al-Rāzī who first developed this model and that it was later adopted by Ja'far.

Ja'far clarifies that not only speaker-prophets, but also their legatees and Imāms all receive *ta'yīd* and *mawādd*, divine support and resources. These supernal links allow them to serve as bridges for the believers to journey from this world of matter to the supernal world of light.

> By the command of God, the message [*al-risāla*] connected with the first of the two speakers. . . . When, through the command of its Lord, the world of Intellect with its lights within began to shine upon the world of soul, it shone upon that which was below it. So the spheres illuminated the world of body [*jirm*], and they received the command. One attached to the next until it reached the sphere of the moon, and the decrees [*aḥkām*] of that blessed conjunction [*qirān*]. [. . .] So it traveled from the light of the message, like the traveling of the sun's light in the air which emerges in the world of humanity. The condition of the possessors of the supernal mansions and heavenly decrees in bodily forms and human souls, those who have knowledge from the book, became in a good state from that command. They are the Prophets, wāṣīs, Imāms, and deputies [khulafā']. So the light of the message shone on their souls, descending upon them, bestowed unto them.[13]

Through the Command, God's message (*risāla*) is sent from the world of Intellect, which reflects its light on soul. Soul, in turn, bestows it on the sun, moon, and celestial spheres. This light reaches the prophets and the human hierarchy (waṣī, Imām, khalīfa) whose souls are receptive to it.

Elsewhere the sun and moon are invoked as mathals for the speaker-prophet and legatee, for the intellect and soul, and for the Preceder and Follower, the two supernal roots. The symbol of the sun and its rays also appears as a mathal for the nāṭiq and his power of prophecy elsewhere in the *Sarā'ir.*

> When the sun descends, it cools and cannot be seen. Similarly, the speaker-prophet is in the state of power as long as his rays [*shurūq*] continue. When his limit reaches its expiration, and his sun has set, and his power has declined, it is necessary for dissimulation and screening. For it is the entrance of the night and its shade from the light of the day. The light is screened from the people, and they return to the expanse of the moon, which is the sign of the light and the planets.
>
> So too, is it necessary for the Imāms to hide the knowledge of the interior and the ta'wīl that they possess from the pharaohs of the exterior. They extend [this knowledge] to their believing friends, those obedient to them, little by little, under prudent dissimulation and after firm oaths.[14]

Just as the sun declines and its rays weaken, and its light is refracted off the moon and planets after it sets, so too do the rays of light emanating from the speaker-prophet decline when he fades from history. During the speaker-prophet's "night," his rays are concealed; the moon and the planets, symbols for the Speaker-prophet's legatee and the Imāms, come to the fore.

Such passages in works ascribed to Ja'far ibn Manṣūr al-Yaman suggest the following model. The divine light of origination emanates from the God beyond the supernal world of intellect. This light is too subtle and refined to descend into the world of matter. However, from the first of the two roots emanating from God, this divine light streams (jārī) down, leaving impressions (nuqūsh) on the world of matter below that indicate the forms in the supernal world of intellect. At the same time supernal resources (mawādd) connect to the intellects of the speaker-prophet, allowing him to receive the pure, subtle light of intellect and translate it into human speech, signs, and symbols. These mawādd also connect to the legatee and Imāms, allowing them to decode these traces, and share them with the believers in the *da'wa.*

Ja'far's conception of prophecy suggests a metaphysical model which is gnostic in character. Prophets translate the nuqūsh, athār, ishārāt, and rumūz (traces, imprints, indications, and symbols) from the light of intellect in the supernal world into nomoi (laws), scripture, and other sources. Ja'far refers not only to the placement of these signs, but their recovery. The nāṭiq embeds these signs, and the waṣī or Imām retrieves them. Such a model lends itself to a taʾwīl that goes beyond scripture, for the traces from the supernal world can be hidden in different types of sources in the material world. As the taʾwīl of the story of Adam shows, both the placing and collecting of this saving knowledge is closely linked to politics.

The Making of a Speaker-Prophet: The Taʾwīl of the Story of Adam

In the *Sarāʾir* we read that before Adam there were hiero-historical cycles led by beings without matter such as angels and jinn. Adam was the first being created that had both matter and intellect. He was born in the abode of his adversary, a king, who was served by specialists in philosophy and astronomy.[15] At Adam's birth the planets aligned in such a way that they seemed to bow down to him. Based on the planetary conjunctions, the astrologers recognized that Adam "would rule the entire earth according to the divine nomoi (*nawāmīs ilāhīya*), intellectual governances (*tadbīrāt ʿaqlīya*), and the law."[16] They saw that the suzerainty of Adam and his mission would one day encompass all the kings and remain over many hiero-historical cycles.

News of Adam's birth reached the adversary-king, and he recognized that, once grown, Adam presented a threat to his rule, and he attempted to have him killed. Adam's parents fled with Adam to another kingdom on the island of al-Būrān in Ceylon and camped in its gulf, a region rich with water and fruit trees.[17] Aware that the adversary-king was in pursuit, Adam's parents hid him on the island and fled, leaving Adam to be raised by wild animals.

> When his parents were absent, the animals came to his aid and befriended him. They circled around him and took care of him. One of the lionesses of that jungle took pity on him, took charge of his upbringing, and raised him. She suckled him, and he grew and became stronger. Adam continued to go from rank to rank and level to level, until his creation was completed, his state (*amr*) was perfected, and he reached adulthood and merited spiritual deputyship (*khilāfa ruḥānīya*).[18]

One day while on a hunting expedition, a servant of the king came upon Adam. He was astonished by Adam's perfect visage. He brought Adam to the king, and the king marveled at his special, luminous appearance. The king spoke to him, but he did not understand his speech. But the king had Adam join them and complete his rearing, and Adam learned the language of the people.[19]

After his rearing the king of al-Būrān found that Adam had grown more knowledgeable than the angel who had been acting as his ḥujja. The king declared that Adam would replace this angel as his deputy. Referring to Adam and the ḥujja, the king announced, "Verily I will place a deputy for the earth" (Qurʾān 2:30), "the earth" being a mathal for the ḥujja.[20]

Some of the angels doubted whether Adam should be their leader and refused to recognize Adam. God then imparted to Adam secret knowledge of ta'wīl and excluded the angels from this knowledge. Then the angels recognized Adam's superiority. To repent for their previous doubts, the angels circumambulated Adam's throne seven times; this, it is explained, is a mathal for seven requests for secret knowledge from Adam. This angelic act was the basis for the Muslims' ritual circumambulation around the sacred house of the Kaʿba, although this hidden sense is unknown to them.[21]

One of the angels, Iblīs, pretended to recognize Adam's superior rank but secretly plotted against him. God warned Adam not to share secret knowledge with Iblīs. Adam, believing himself the Mahdi, thought that he was capable of making such decisions himself; he countermanded God's command and took Iblīs into his confidence, sharing secret knowledge with him. For this error God cast Adam out of paradise, that is, He ceased to provide him supernal mawādd (resources). When Adam recognized his error, he convened with the senior missionaries and clarified that he now realized he was not the mahdī, but the deputy of the Imām. The special knowledge and supernal resources were then restored to him.[22]

The narrator provides explanations for several of the stories' central figures. The wicked adversary-king in the kingdom in which people practiced philosophy and astrology is a mathal for the head of a competing diocese that did not recognize the rightful Imām. The king of al-Būrān is a mathal for the Imām of the period (Imām al-zamān), and Adam's parents and the lioness who reared him were this Imām's missionaries. In a "ta'wīl of the ta'wīl," the author declares that the Imām of the period was actually the Universal Intellect, and Adam, the Intellect's deputy.

In another interpretation, Jaʿfar provides a different account. Adam was born in the daʿwa of Iblīs, who was a high-ranking dāʿī of the Imām. Adam rose in rank until Iblīs and Adam competed with one another. The issue was raised to the Imām, who was king of the island. When the Imām heard Adam's clear speech, he favored him, choosing him over all the other missionaries. He ordered Iblīs to bow down to him—that is, to recognize that Adam was superior to him in rank. Iblīs refused, and, in a ta'wīl of the Qur'ānic verse in which Iblīs declares that he is made of fire and Adam matter (Qur'ān 7: 11-12), Iblīs declares that despite the Imām's explicit order, that he was of higher rank than Adam. Consequently Iblīs was cut off from the connected resources of the daʿwa, that is, he was removed from paradise, the island in which Adam now ruled. The Imām commanded the rest of the missionaries to be obedient to Adam, and they complied.[23]

After Iblīs had been thrown out of that daʿwa, he made a law for himself based on his own opinion and analogy. Jaʿfar claims that the leading missionaries (ḥudūd) in Iblīs's daʿwa have continued to apply the law based on their opinions "until the present."[24]

Eventually the time came for the Imāmate to be transferred from the Imām to Adam. The "angels"—the ḥudūd of the daʿwa—submitted to Adam, and he became the commander of the time, appointed ḥudūd to serve under him, and went out to subdue his enemy Iblīs and his armies. Adam sought a new dār hijra where he might strengthen his hand. Adam went out from the dār hijra of his father and settled in Yemen, where his power rose. He then went to Mecca, where he established the Kaʿba from the rays of the light of prophecy he emitted. The Imām's ḥujjas, called angels, recognized their rank and submitted to Adam.[25]

When Iblīs realized Adam's power had grown too great for him to challenge him, he changed tactics. He realized that the people had been promised resurrection of the dead (*al-qiyāma*), and he went underground, focusing his sedition on this point. The story goes on to describe how the forces of Adam were continued on through Seth, and the forces of Iblīs through Cain.[26]

In the *Sarāʾir*'s Adam narrative, prophecy is described in terms commonly used by Islamic philosophers in the Greek tradition. In one passage, the "light of origination" (*nūr al-ibdāʿ*) descends from intellect and casts a shadow on the soul, creating the traces of the supernal world in matter. In another, the Imām of the prophet is identified as the Universal Intellect (*al-ʿaql al-kullī*)—the technical term for the first emanation in Neoplatonic cosmology. In a third passage, instead of God, Jaʿfar writes that it is the Universal Intellect who appoints Adam as its deputy (khalīfa) in Qurʾān 2:30.[27] Elsewhere, the author refers to prophecy as divine "indications" (dalāʾil) and "traces" (athār), from the supernal world. These traces are translated into symbols (rumūz) and signs (ishārāt); they are "imprints" (nuqūsh) in the material world.

These philosophical terms were commonly used by Islamic philosophers in the Greek tradition, or philosophically inclined Ismāʿīlīs from the eastern dioceses. However, such terminology is unusual in Fāṭimid sources that were composed in the period of al-Muʿizz li-dīn Allāh (d. 975). Al-Muʿizz is on record as having been against mixing philosophy with taʾwīl. When he granted an audience to an Ismāʿīlī visitor from one of the eastern dioceses, al-Muʿizz responded that the visitor's mix (*takhlīṭ*) of philosophy and religious doctrine "neither taught the discourse of philosophy as its specialists expound it, nor elucidated the religion of God as [the visitor] claimed. The blend [of philosophy and religion]. . . causes seceding from the community (*milla*) and calling for unbelief."[28]

But if al-Muʿizz proscribed this mix of *falsafa* and doctrine, why do we find philosophical language in sources composed by his missionary Jaʿfar? The work of several scholars supplies one plausible explanation. Madelung established that as part of the Fāṭimid caliph al-Muʿizz's effort to expand the empire, he attempted a rapprochement with the missionaries to the east. Toward that end, al-Muʿizz reformed Fāṭimid doctrine by reinstating the status of Muḥammad ibn Ismāʿīl as the awaited redeemer, a central pillar of pre-Fāṭimid and non-Fāṭimid Ismāʿīlīs.[29] Michael Brett has suggested that just as al-Muʿizz reached out to the Iranians by elevating the status of Muḥammad ibn Ismāʿīl, so too did he accept the Iranian missionary al-Sijistānī's Neoplatonism as a basis for Fāṭimid doctrine. For Brett, al-Sijistānī's universalistic Neoplatonic theology served "as a prescription for universal empire" and "became the formula of the caliphate in Egypt."[30] Could it be, then, that al-Muʿizz changed his mind about the mix of philosophy and doctrine, and, in order to appeal to the Iranian missionaries, he commanded his missionaries to include *falsafa* in their taʾwīl?

A close reading of the Adam narrative militates against the explanation that the turn to philosophical terminology was meant to appeal to the Iranians. Specifically, themes in the text suggest that Adam is a veiled reference to the first Fāṭimid Imām ʿAbd Allāh al-Mahdī, that Iblīs is a mathal for Abū ʿAbd Allāh al-Shīʿī, and that the philosopher who leads the wicked island to the east, is a mathal for the Iranian missionaries who had left the Fāṭimid fold. I argue, then, that rather than as a concession to the Iranians, the Adam story is intended as a riposte.

In Jaʿfar's account, Adam was born in the territory of the Imām's adversary, but raised as an acolyte (mustajīb) of the true Imām of the period. The Imām's adversary is the head of an island (ṣāḥib jazīra) whose inhabitants are "experts in philosophy and astronomy."[31]

ʿAbd Allāh, the first Fāṭimid Imām, was born in Khuzestan in Iran, which, from the vantage point of the Fāṭimids, was the center of this "philosophical" styled taʾwīl about which al-Muʿizz complained, and that had been operating for some time. The Ismāʿīlī center in Rayy was likely founded fairly early—before the advent of the Fāṭimids.[32] It would appear that just as Adam is a mathal for the first Fāṭimid Imām ʿAbd Allāh, this island of the "wicked philosophers and astronomers" into which Adam was born refers to one of the Iranian dioceses which rejected the Fāṭimid Imām.

In another taʾwīl, Iblīs is referred to as a missionary who became jealous of Adam when he surpassed him in rank. When the Imām chose Adam as his successor and leader of the daʿwa, Iblīs refused to recognize him and plotted against him. Adam at first trusts Iblīs, but then God discloses to him that Iblīs is plotting against him. The author identifies Iblīs as the ḥujja and one of the leading ḥudūd of the true Imām of the period.

In Fāṭimid historiography, after ʿAbd Allāh was announced as the Mahdī, Abū ʿAbd Allāh al-Shīʿī pretended to support him, but secretly plotted against him with Berber tribesmen. The plot was discovered and Abū ʿAbd Allāh al-Shīʿī was executed.[33] Iblīs' relationship to Adam parallels that of Abū ʿAbd Allāh al-Shīʿī's relationship to ʿAbd Allāh al-Mahdī in Fāṭimid historiography. Iblīs and Abū ʿAbd Allāh al-Shīʿī were both described as the leading missionaries of the period. Out of hubris, both failed to obey the rightful Imām. While Iblīs is not put to death by Adam, we read that he is banished from paradise and "cut off from the daʿwa"—a mathal for "death" in daʿwa parlance. In short, Iblīs is a mathal for Abū ʿAbd Allāh al-Shīʿī, the early Ismāʿīlī missionary who organized a plot against the first Fāṭimid Imām ʿAbd Allāh.[34]

Other themes also draw parallels between the Adam taʾwīl and the Fāṭimid Imāmate's early history. In one taʾwīl, God's command "not to approach the tree" (Qurʾān 7:19-23) is interpreted as a mathal for the Imām's command that Adam should not trust Iblīs with secret knowledge. Adam, however, believed himself to be the Mahdī, and thus capable of making the decision to approach the tree—that is, to trust Iblīs. He thus countermanded God's explicit command. As a result of Adam's misrecognizing his rank, God ceased to provide Adam with supernal mawādd (resources).[35] Adam then recognized his error and convened with the senior ḥudūd (missionaries) to repent of his mistake; he declared that was not the final redeemer, but merely a khalīfa—a deputy of intellect. As a result of Adam's recognition of his true role, God's supernal resources, special knowledge, and divine aid were restored to him. The "light returned to his eyes" and Adam was able to complete his mission and establish a dār hijra in Mecca.

Adam's error and recovery mirrors the story of ʿAbd Allāh, the first Fāṭimid Imām. At the advent of the Fāṭimid caliphs in 909, ʿAbd Allāh was at first declared to be the awaited redeemer who would usher in the End of Days. He erred by trusting Abū ʿAbd Allāh al-Shīʿī, who would betray him. This doctrinal position was later updated by the Fāṭimid caliphs al-Manṣūr and later, al-Muʿizz: ʿAbd Allāh not the final redeemer, but a khalīfa, a deputy.[36] This section of the Adam story constitutes an abbreviated symbolic retelling of this shift in Fāṭimid doctrine.

In another section of the story, Jaʿfar writes that Adam was born during a hiero-historical cycle when the true Imām and his ḥudūd were hidden, for his Imām was the Universal Intellect and the emanations that proceed from it did not possess matter. According to Fāṭimid sacred history, ʿAbd Allāh the Mahdī, too, was born into the movement during a "period of screening" (*dawr al-satr*) when the Imām and his high ranking missionaries led the mission secretly in Syria. And just as Adam was the first speaker-prophet "apparent to the eye," so too was ʿAbd Allāh al-Mahdī the first Fāṭimid Imām who would lead the mission openly, establishing the Fāṭimid Caliphate in North Africa. Late in the taʾwīl, Adam travels to Yemen seeking a *dār hijra* (abode of refuge), while "Iblīs' armies" were said to have risen in India. Yemen was a well-known Fāṭimid stronghold that was a possible site for the Fāṭimid caliphate before it was decided to establish the Fāṭimids in North Africa.[37] And India is a site in which heterodox doctrine was known to have proliferated, prompting an epistle from al-Muʿizz.[38]

Like the development of the Fāṭimid state, Adam's career is presented as a political project. He established a dār hijra in Mecca, appointed a successor, and subdued his enemies. After establishing the dār hijra in Mecca, Adam rises to the rank of nāṭiq. He is then able to fashion the house of the Kaʿba.

> The light stopped at the site of the house, and a tent of red rubies descended from the sky. He commanded for the house to be built based on the ropes of the tent. [Adam] resided in the house all of his life. Then, he looked at the site of the rays of light, and he fashioned a Kaʿba for them. He set the black stone in it as a mathal for his ḥujja, being Eve, who disseminated his knowledge (*ḥawā ʿilmahu*) and wisdom. The angels struck camps around him, and their shading and settling in the desert became an established practice for his offspring. Adam became the house of God and the direction to which prayer is directed for the angels. The angels and believers took to circumambulating its dome, praying to him two prostrations each time they circumambulated, weekly. This became a *sunna* for his offspring and followers and his acolytes until our day, and until this world comes to an end. He who is prevented from prostrating himself to Adam, does not obey him, and aggrandizes himself over him, is a lāḥiq for Iblīs and his forces . . .When his command was strengthened, his ḥujja enabled, and his power at its height, and he had two sons, Cain and Abel, his first corporeal birth of the two came to pass, in which the good and foul were mixed. God commanded to appoint one of the two as his deputy. He then organized the house as a sanctuary, and made it twelve miles from ʿArafat, as a *mathal* for the twelve ḥujjas.[39]

From the divine light of prophecy and Imāmate, Adam established the daʿwa's institutions. The Kaʿba and the black stone are *mathal*s for the speaker-prophet Adam and his ḥujja, Eve. ʿArafat, which is twelve miles from the Kaʿba, is a mathal for the twelve ḥujjas who administer the different islands. Circumambulation and prostration signify obedience to the speaker-prophet and his legatee. Failure to acknowledge them is tantamount to unbelief and serving as an adjunct for Iblīs. The passage, and Jaʿfar's Adam narrative as a whole, links metaphysics and politics.

The Adam narrative is the story of the overcoming of apostasy within the daʿwa wrought by those who failed to accept their true status. By taking up his role as speaker-prophet and deputy for the Universal Intellect, God's resources and support (*mawādd* and *taʾyīd*) allow Adam to institute the divine light of prophecy and Imāmate in symbols and institutions. Those who are not obedient to his authority are condemned as adjuncts for Satan. This period is likened to the establishment of the first Fāṭimid Imām, ʿAbd Allāh who also were tested by renegades who failed to submit to his divinely-guided authority.

After Adam: Speaker-Prophets, Scriptures, and Signs

The stories of the other speaker-prophets in the *Sarāʾir,* Noah, Abraham, Moses, Jesus, and Muḥammad, follow along the same lines as the story of Adam. Each speaker-prophet starts as a missionary, acquires special knowledge, raises a daʿwa on behalf of the Imām of the day, struggles against the adversaries of the period, and eventually ascends to the rank of speaker-prophet when the supernal mawādd descends on him. However, the political circumstances of the respective periods dictated that their careers followed different trajectories.

The second speaker-prophet, Noah, called a daʿwa and was joined by the believers, but his adversaries were strong. When, fearing defeat, Noah's followers joined the camp of his enemies, only eighty remained in Noah's camp and were able to enter the ark built to save them from destruction wrought by the floods. The ark itself encoded secret wisdom. The ark is a mathal for the *daʿwa*—those who joined it were saved; those outside it, drowned in the seas of perdition. The adversaries of the period survived by hanging on the edge of the ark, without fully entering it—perhaps another barb against Ismāʿīlīs who failed to fully enter the daʿwa of the rightly guided Fāṭimid Imām.[40]

The ark was known as the "limit [ḥadd] of respite for the one who waits" [*ḥadd al-faraj al-muntaẓir*]. Specifically the ark's architectural plan encoded the hidden traces of the supernal world, as we see in the following passage.

> The Torah provides immutable proof [*naṣṣahu al-tawrāh*] that the length of the ark was three-hundred cubits, and its width sixty cubits. This is a sign that the daʿwa of the Imāms is not cut until it has reached thirty Imāms, fifteen of whom bring the exterior, and fifteen are missionaries for their interior, proselytizing for who comes to abrogate them, and bring into appearance another law. . . . The "three hundred and sixty cubits" of the length and width of the ark, refers to each Imām having twelve ḥujjas as likenesses of the twelve months. Each month has thirty days. Thus, each ḥujja has thirty missionaries serving in his island. This is three hundred and sixty missionaries and ḥujjas.[41]

The Torah presents proof that the ark encoded the structure of the daʿwa hierarchy. The length and width of the ark encode the numbers of differing ranks of missionaries in the daʿwa. Just as the cubits measuring the length and width of the ark equal 360 units, so too does each Imām possess twelve ḥujjas, each of whom has thirty missionaries, equaling 360 missionaries. (These measurements are consistent with those of Genesis in the Hebrew Bible; as they are not widely attested in Islamic texts, it seems likely that author had a Jewish or Christian source.)

The message of the story of Noah is, once again, the importance of allegiance to the divinely-guided speaker-prophet. When the missionaries and believers abandon Noah, he is unable to compile a dār hijra and scripture, and is forced to encode symbols in the ark. This leads to the loss of the community in the flood.

Abraham was born in a period ruled by the tyrant Nimrod, who ruled according to the movements of the stars. Learning from his astrologers that a figure would be born who was destined to replace him, Nimrod sequestered the women to prevent Abraham's birth, but this plan failed. Abraham's mother reared Abraham in a cave. In the ta'wīl of the story, it is explained that his mother was the missionary who converted him, and his father, Tirakh, was one of the ḥujjas of the Imām. Tirakh reared him in hidden knowledge.

> In his beginning, before the mawādd attached to him and he was established, Abraham was hidden in the law of Noah. This was until he came to have ninety-nine missionaries, among them, thirty reporting missionaries [dāʿī balāgh]. Then "he was circumcised," meaning that his command and secret became apparent. He cut from the law of Noah, and established a new law for himself. His law was the interior of the law of Noah, just as the staff of the penis is under the foreskin, and when the foreskin is cut, the staff appears and becomes apparent.[42]

Abraham's circumcision at the age of ninety-nine is a mathal for his appointment of ninety-nine missionaries. His circumcision alludes to the break with the law of Noah and the instituting of his own, new law. Just as Adam embedded the traces of the supernal in the Kaʿba, and Noah in the ark, so too did Abraham through instituting the rite of circumcision. After overcoming Nimrod, Abraham was able to attract missionaries to his cause; it is this that allowed him to compile a new law. In the story of Abraham, mawādd and political action are directly linked.

During his life Abraham was able to achieve political success and pass on his prophetic and Imāmic legacies to Ismāʿīl and Isaac. Moses's capacity to pass on his legacy is more complicated. After Shuʿayb, his predecessor, bequeaths to him his staff and the light of prophecy, he and his brother Aaron confronted Pharaoh and led his people across the sea to found a dār hijra in Jerusalem. But his followers, jealous of the idols of their neighbors, requested a goddess instead (Qur'ān 7:138). Later, fearful of the giants who dwelt in the promised land (Qur'ān 5:21–22), they refused to enter and asked to return to the land of their adversary, the land of the Copts. In response "Moses forbade them [from returning to] Egypt or [going to] the land of Jerusalem for the rest of their lives, and brought them to the wasteland."[43] Because of his followers' cowardice and disobedience, Moses was unable to found a dār hijra.

After failing to found a dār hijra, Aaron, who had been named as Moses's successor, comes to realize that he will soon die, predeceasing Moses. Aaron's sons' inability to follow instructions of a burnt offering demonstrates that neither is worthy to lead the community. Moses thus appoints Joshua to succeed him and bequeaths the Torah to him. Joshua is to serve as the "deputy-Imām" for the descendants of Aaron, to whom the true teaching would one day return. After deputing Joshua, the narrator, reports that Moses

> extracted [the Torah] from the tablets and surrendered it to him. He gathered the Israelites and had them bear witness to that—that he had installed the legatee after him by the command of God. . . . He then said: "He is cursed who diverges from him, and he is cursed who regresses from this, my utterance. For these are the tablets which God commanded be surrendered to His fundament when they descend to him."
>
> But when Moses was absent [*ghāba*], the leaders [nuqabā'] ignored what Joshua had brought them. They composed this Torah which is in the hands of the Jews which they claimed came from Moses. They changed and embellished what [came] from Joshua, disregarding what Moses and his legatee said . . . and returned to their composing through opinion and analogy.[44]

In Moses's absence the Israelite nuqabā' (leaders) disregarded this book. They composed their own scripture based on their own opinion and analogy.

Ja'far modifies the standard Islamic topos that it was the rabbis who altered the Torah. Rather than the rabbis, he claims that it was the Israelite nuqabā' (leaders), who distorted the Torah according to their opinions and analogies. Ja'far's reference to Moses' "nuqabā'" draws a parallel between the Israelite leaders and the descendants of 'Alī who served under the 'Abbāsid caliphs and were known as nuqabā'. These figures were charged with maintaining the registry of the Prophet's descendants and exposing false claims to the Prophet's lineage.[45] Ja'far's claim that the nuqabā' in the period of Moses distorted the Torah that Moses had compiled and bequeathed to Joshua is, then, meant as a polemic against the corrupt Ṭālibid nuqabā' who served the 'Abbāsid caliph instead of recognizing the rightful Imām.[46]

The story of Jesus and John comprises some twenty-six pages, by far the longest account in the *Sarā'ir.* The unusual character of the material suggests that Ja'far drew from a variety of Christian sources, perhaps from one of the Syrian Christian monasteries proximate to the Fāṭimid leadership in Salamīya.[47]

Jesus was born in Nazareth to Joseph and his mother, "Baydanu" (?). As a child he was adopted by his uncle Judah Saḥr Butta, the head of the academy of the Jews who would teach Jesus the secrets of the Prophets. Judah took Jesus to Antioch, where he was converted by a traveling missionary of the Imām of the period, 'Imrān, a follower of the law of Moses, but who also was familiar with philosophy and knowledge from different schools. Jesus was soon recognized as a prophet by John the Baptist and ascended the ranks of the da'wa of Moses through his direct connection (ittiṣāl) with God. Jesus reformed the law of Moses and battled his Jewish enemies, including Judah Saḥr Butta, who refused to recognize Jesus's legitimacy. He sent missionaries throughout the land to establish a dār hijra but was unable to do so and was thus unable to compose a scripture. Instead Jesus embedded the signs and symbols of true knowledge in Christian symbols and institutions. Judah Saḥr Butta led the party against Jesus and eventually crucified him on the cross. While the patriarch and his followers among the Christians fabricated the four Gospels from their own opinions and analogies and claimed them to be revealed scripture, Jesus's authentic knowledge and legacy was preserved by Simon-Peter, who surrendered it to Clement. A student of Clement hid this teaching, until it eventually found its way to the monk Baḥīraʾ and Zayd ibn ʿUmar, the head of the Arab "island" of the Imām. Muḥammad was a student of Zayd ibn ʿUmar and Baḥīraʾ until he succeeded them as head of the diocese.

The *Sarāʾir* emphasizes several times that Jesus is unable to found a dār hijra, and that this dār hijra was necessary in order to formulate a law. "It was narrated that the traveling of Jesus and his apostles was to seek an abode of refuge [dār hijra] to flee and in which to institute the judgment [*ḥukm*] and justice of God such as the rulings of the divine laws [*aḥkām al-sharāʾiʿ*], . . . the amputating of [the hand of] the thief and lashing the adulterer. . . . He divided his disciples among the islands of the earth, and they continued to wander until God took him up. But he did not found an abode of refuge."[48] Jesus wandered and traveled seeking to found an abode of refuge in order to compile and implement a law. He and his followers were not successful, and this, in turn, led to the formulation of a false scripture propagated by errant disciples.

After the Christ disappeared and his legatee fled, his other disciples

> composed these four gospels in which they compiled the life stories [*siyar*] of the Christ. This was when they did not acquire the [true] Gospel. Therefore, we see them describe what he did, the knowledge and wisdom that he spoke, and the parables [*amthāl*] that he transmitted which we have discussed. They were not able to verify it with him, and he did not bequeath it to them during his lifetime.[49]

When Jesus had disappeared and his legatee, Simon-Peter, had fled, Jesus's other disciples composed four gospels and presented them as scripture. However, these gospels were not authentic scripture that had been compiled by Jesus. Rather they were *siyar,* life stories with the disciples' recollections of his words and mathals.

Jesus is unable to compile a scripture is thus because of historical vicissitudes—his inability to found a dār hijra. Simon, his legatee, does have a book that captures Jesus's actual revelation.

> Simon has the book which agrees with his words, as we said. Its interpretation, he did not divulge to anyone. When it was time for him to transfer it, he delivered it to Aqlīmus [Clement], to the pious servant John the Younger by the command of God. Generation after generation, they continued bequeathing this [book and interpretation] as those preceding them did, until Muḥammad (praise and peace upon him) appeared. The Gospel that descended from the spiritual Father within which is the command and prohibition, revelation and interpretation [ta'wīl], the knowledge of the first and last ones, it was entrusted to its elect [*ahlihi*]. One generation transferred it to the next until it reaches he who will enforce it, it will be bestowed on the one whom God endows with the reaching of its truths.[50]

Jesus's legatee, Simon, hid the authentic scripture and delivered it to his student, Clement, who shared it with "John the Younger." They prevented the dissemination of the source, protecting it until it passed to one who had the capacity to enforce and understand it. This account parallels early Shīʿite views that claim that ʿAlī bequeathed to his progeny the complete version of the Qur'ān.

Unable to compile an abode of refuge and proper scripture, Jesus preserved his teachings in symbols, institutions, and rituals.

> When he [Jesus] had traveled for a long time without finding an abode of refuge to establish in which he could take refuge to battle [his adversaries], he had his disciples adopt the exterior of his law and filled it with mathals [*amthāl madrūba*]. Among them are: the rules [*adāb*] of prayer and what a man approaches in it [prayer], recognizing the three hypostases with which he was crucified in appearance [. . .], the peg of his wisdom hidden away in his cross, the likeness of the sashes that they tighten around their waists, the Eucharist through which they approach him, the limit [ḥadd] of baptism, and of all that wisdom which [these *amthāl*] hold. He administered the oaths in order for them to practice these [rituals], and he excommunicated anyone who abandoned any of them. All this was because he did not have a dār hijra [abode of refuge] in which to take sanctuary.[51]

Such Christological elements as the doctrine of the trinity, rules for prayer, structure of the cross, sashes tied around the waists of the monks, and the Eucharist are mathals for the true teaching of the daʿwa. Jesus resorted to embedding the hidden signs in these symbols and rituals because he failed to establish an abode of refuge in which to establish an "island."

In a remarkable passage, the hierarchy of the church is likened to the ranks of the daʿwa.

> We now return to knowledge of the seven lower ones which He placed to face the seven higher ones. They are from the patriarch to the officiate

> [marsūm].[52] The Patriarch is the speaking one [al-nāṭiq] because the Patriarch sits in the seat of prophecy on a chair, high above the people, reciting the Gospels to them. The archbishop is like the fundament [asās], and the bishop is like the completer [mutimm], the priest is like the proof, and the head is like the missionary undertaking the command of the mission because of the oath administered over them. The deacon is a likeness [mathal] of the permitted one [ma'dhūn], and the officiate for the reporting believer [ma'mūn bāligh] consigned to the da'wa.[53]

The ranks of the church hierarchy are mathals for the ranks of the da'wa. While the Christians are unaware of the supernal sense of their own institutions, Ja'far shows them to be in perfect parallel to the ranks of the da'wa. Through the prism of da'wa knowledge, it is clear that Jesus was able to institute signs of the supernal hierarchy through signs outside the church hierarchy.

The story of Jesus demonstrates how a speaker prophet who is unable to gain political power is able to preserve secret knowledge. The career of the sixth speaker-prophet, Muḥammad, exemplifies the ideal. Muḥammad first became a missionary for the Imām of the period. He was reared in knowledge by five ḥujjas who were in parallel to the supernal pentad of the pleroma.[54] Muḥammad eventually surpassed the Imām of the period in rank and successfully founded a da'wa, attracting a number of converts to the movement—of most importance his wife Khadīja and cousin 'Alī.[55] Like Abraham, Muḥammad appointed four senior missionaries and sent them to spread the mission throughout the world. He established a dār hijra (abode of refuge) in Medina and appointed members of the Anṣār (helpers) as leaders.[56] Eventually the Imām, who led the da'wa from Syria, recognized that Muḥammad had surpassed him in rank and surrendered the mission to him. The divine mawādd were thus transferred to the Prophet.[57] After overcoming his adversaries, the Meccan pagan Abū Jahl and his maternal uncle Abū Lahab, Muḥammad ascended to the rank of speaker-prophet. The stream (al-jārī) conjoined with him from the Preceder, the first of the two roots in the pleroma, and Muḥammad compiled a new law and abrogated the law of Jesus.[58] After he completed his compilation of the external law, his legatee, 'Alī, disclosed its ta'wīl. Ja'far stressed that the religion became complete only when 'Alī' ascended to the status of legatee. The Imāms who descended from 'Alī are also emphasized. Thus the hidden sense of the prophetic tradition that "the Qur'ān was revealed in seven dialects" refers to the legatee, as he is responsible for revealing the Qur'ān's inner sense, and the seven Imāms who follow him.[59]

The career of the speaker-prophet Muḥammad was thus ideal.[60] Ja'far emphasizes that Muḥammad was the first speaker-prophet since Abraham who successfully combined Imāmate and prophethood, having received the light of Imāmate from his forefather Quṣayy, who inherited through his forebear Ismā'īl, and the teachings of the prophets through his missionary teachers.[61]

He successfully makes many converts, founds a dār hijra, compiles a law and scripture, the Qurʾān, and appoints a legatee, ʿAlī, who interprets it. In short he is the paradigmatic speaker-prophet.

The Imām of the period into which Muḥammad was born is identified as Baḥīrāʾ, a figure known in Islamic sources as a Christian monk who saw Muḥammad while he was a youth on a trading mission with his uncle in Syria and recognized that he would become a Prophet. In the *Sarāʾir* Baḥīrāʾs leading missionaries in the "island of the Arabs" are Zayd ibn ʿAmr, a *ḥanīf* (unaffiliated monotheist), and Ubayy ibn Kaʿb, an early convert who is recalled as having his own rescension of a Qurʾānic codex in which Jesus specifically named Muḥammad as his successor.[62] Jaʿfar claims that first Zayd ibn ʿUmar taught Muḥammad the truth of the prophets, waṣīs, and Imāms. The Imām Baḥīrāʾ commanded the Prophet to undertake the mission on behalf of the Messiah (al-masīḥ). When Muḥammad successfully garnered seventy male missionaries and one female from the Tihāma and Ethiopia, Baḥīraʾ surrendered the command to him.[63] Thus the legacy of prophecy that was his bequest from Isaac was transferred to him from a Christian monk, just as Muḥammad had received the legacy of Imāmate originating from Ismāʿīl through his uncle, Abū Ṭālib.

Now, according to the logic of Ismāʿīlī hiero-history, it is perfectly correct for Muḥammad to have been reared in the mission of Jesus, for it is Jesus who was the previous speaker-prophet, and his law was still operative. Still, it is surprising that Jaʿfar's account goes to some length to emphasize that Muḥammad began his career as a disciple of Jesus. In one taʾwīl Jaʿfar mentions that Muḥammad studied with Bahīrāʾ's for twenty years, and that Bahīrāʾ was referred to in the sources as the angel Gabriel. As Gabriel is known in Islam as the angel who transmitted the Qurʾān from God to the Prophet, the interpretation that he was actually a Christian monk is astonishing.

In fact this interpretation of Bahīrāʾ's relationship to the Prophet does have precedent, although not in Islamic sources. From the late eighth century, Christian polemicists reinterpreted the Islamic legend of the monk "Sergius-Bahīrā" for their authors' own purposes. In one such source, the Arabic *Apocalypse of Peter,* the Christian teacher of Muḥammad is presented as a heretic who had been banished from the church, a Christian topos that can be traced back to John of Damascus in the eighth century, who charged that Muḥammad's false teachings were due to his tutoring by an Arian monk.[64] Since the notion that Muḥammad was tutored by a follower of Jesus is unimaginable in Islamic sources, it seems likely that the *Sarāʾir*'s narrative adapted a Christian account of the Baḥīrāʾ legend viewed through the lens of daʿwa knowledge. The legend of Baḥīrāʾ, which began as an Islamic story, has thus come full circle. The question, of course, is the purpose this legend served in Jaʿfar's taʾwīl.

I believe an answer comes in the *Sarāʾir*'s explanation of the patriarch of the period. This passage comes several generations after the passing of Jesus, when

Simon kept the hidden knowledge secret. In this period a wicked patriarch arose who falsely claimed the inheritance of Simon.

> They continued to be cognizant of this until the patriarch [jathālīq] came who claimed the inheritance of Simon and the apostles. . . . The infidels [who believed in him] lorded themselves over the believers [al-muʾminūn] and expelled them. [The true believers] fled to all quarters of the earth when they saw the sunna of the prophet [Jesus] and his legatee had changed, and that his rulings had been tampered with. . . .
>
> This patriarch and his parties were from the progeny of Esau, the enemies of the sons of Jacob, and the enemies of the religious elect [*ahl al-diyānāt*]. The [latter] were the inheritance of the Christ, his deposit, the choice part [*sirr*] of his legatee. They are the progeny of Fāris and therefore, the rest of the community did not deny them and were not jealous of them, for the testament and inheritance was with them. They continued to hide and conceal [themselves] until the command of George, who is Baḥīrāʾ the monk from the progeny of Fāris, was complete.[65]

Baḥīrāʾ arose to counter the wicked adversary of the period, the Christian patriarch who had altered the true teaching of Jesus. Baḥīrāʾ, Jaʿfar explains, became the Imām of the period who carried the true teaching of the speaker-prophet Jesus, as well as past prophets, and bequeathed this knowledge to Muḥammad. The figure of Baḥīrāʾ as a missionary who fights the religious establishment appealed to Jaʿfar, who similarly viewed the daʿwa as in a constant struggle with the scholars. In essence Baḥīra is not truly a Christian, but a "Jesus follower," a figure who held to the true teaching of the speaker-prophet and his legatee in the face of an oppressive Christian establishment.

Conclusion

While in the *Sarāʾir*, the speaker-prophet's primary aim was the composition of a scripture, a process which required divine aid in conjunction with political success. The speaker-prophets Noah, Moses, and Jesus were unable to leave a scriptural legacy because they are unable to found an abode of refuge. Because of this, they are forced to deposit the supernal signs into other forms, such as symbols, rituals, and institutions. It was his successful founding of a mission and safe-haven that allows the speaker-prophet to successfully complete his critical role.

The subtext, of course, is that Jaʿfar's Ismāʿīlī co-sectarians who failed to recognize the Fāṭimid Imām were not merely disloyal, they were apostates. For when they rejected the rightly-guided Imām, they turned against God Himself.

Besides establishing a new law, Jaʿfar wrote that in each cycle, each speaker-prophet abrogated the law that preceded his. But if the laws of the previous prophets have been abrogated, why do we find taʾwīl of Torah and Gospels in

Ismāʿīlī sources? One explanation for this practice can be found in Ismāʿīlism's epistemology: divinely-aided Imāms can recover the supernal traces in these corrupt sources.

A second factor is the doctrinal tenet that at the End of Days, the secrets of all the religions would be disclosed. Jaʿfar writes,

> And it was narrated that he said, "When twelve of this type come," and he pointed to the west (*al-maghrib*), "then, the revealed books will be unfurled, their secrets, revealed, and the religious communities (*umam*) returned to one word that one man will institute. All the communities and religions will join him, and he will unite them in one religion, and institute the rulings and punishments (ḥudūd) mandated by the law."[66]

The prophecy refers to the onset of the Fāṭimids, an extended apocalypse in which the secrets of all past scriptures will be revealed and religions be one under the leadership of the redeemer. It was the project of the missionaries to fulfill this expectation by revealing secrets of past scriptures. For Jaʿfar, the Torah, including passages which were not well known to medieval Muslims, was particularly useful to discuss periods in which no Imām was present.

The Torah's Imāms

CHAPTER 5

Although the Qur'ān was the most important object of ta'wīl, the missionaries also interpreted passages of the Torah and Gospels, sometimes in Hebrew and Syriac.[1] This is quite unusual. To explain it, S. M. Stern speculated that the missionaries composed ta'wīl of Torah to convert Jews.[2] In a previous article, I argued against the claim that Jews were the target of Ismāʿīlī ta'wīl of Torah. In Torah interpretations in the *Sarā'ir al-nuṭaqā'*, many of the missionary's explanatory glosses suggest that his ta'wīl was intended for a Muslim audience, rather than prospective Jewish converts. I speculated that Ismāʿīlī missionaries interpreted material outside the Muslim mainstream in order to provide the believers with the forbidden, hidden knowledge they had long been promised.[3]

Since that publication there has been a great deal of interest in the role of Jewish and Christian sources to frame the Qur'ān. Gabriel Reynolds has argued that there was a "biblical subtext" for the Qur'ān and reads the Qur'ān in light of Christian sources he thinks informed its composition and early understanding.[4] This point has direct relevance for my argument, for if Reynolds is right and Jewish and Christian sources were a subtext for medieval Muslims, then the Ismāʿīlī ta'wīl of Torah and Gospels is not at all unusual.

However, pace Reynolds and others who have attempted to substantiate this thesis, subsequent scholarship has provided little evidence that most early and medieval Muslims were deeply immersed in Jewish and Christian sources. On the contrary, even after Arabic translations of the Hebrew Bible were readily available, it was quite rare for the ʿulamā' to consult them.

After describing the Sunnī and Shīʿite conceptions and use of Torah lore, I argue that the Ismāʿīlī missionaries' ta'wīl of the Torah was distinctive, and that its distinctiveness illuminates aspects of the character of the movement. Rather than using Torah lore to narrate ancient stories of the prophets or explicate passages in the Qur'ān, the Ismāʿīlī missionaries treated the Torah as, like the Qur'ān, revealed scripture and applied ta'wīl to it. A theoretical basis for this practice is that an Imām with access to divine support and mawādd can recover signs of the supernal in a wide variety of objects. This included previously abrogated scriptures such as the Torah, and rituals and institutions of the Jews.

The Torah's stories provided the missionaries with material to rationalize contemporary daʿwa politics. The missionaries showed that questionable appointments of succession—such as al-Muʿizz's appointment of his second son, Nizār—parallel those of the ancient Israelite Imāms. They used this material to polemicize against competing Shīʿite groups who failed to recognize the Fāṭimid Imām after a period of fatra (interregnum), just as the Jews failed to recognize Jesus. And they showed that archaic Israelite and Jewish festivals paralleled those in the contemporary daʿwa. Taʾwīls of the authentic Torah that were available to the believers alone provided the missionaries material to authorize positions using sources unavailable to outsiders.

The Proto-Sunnī ʿUlamāʾ on the Hebrew Bible and the Stories of the Prophets

In academic literature Islamic narratives of the lives of Noah, Abraham, and Moses have at times referred to them as "biblical prophets." But for medieval Muslims these figures were not intrinsically linked to the Bible; they were prophets and historical figures. Scholars had unimpeachable evidence of these prophets' historicity, for in the Qurʾān, God Himself alluded to them. But God commented on these stories without narrating them in their entirety. Even in a story as important as the binding and near-sacrifice of Abraham's son, the identity of the son to be sacrificed is not mentioned in the Qurʾān. The first generations of Muslim storytellers, preachers, and narrators of tradition turned to other sources to fill in the gaps, including traditions of Torah transmitted by Jews and Christians. Proto-Sunnī scholars later adduced this material in their histories and exegesis by attributing reports to "experts in the Torah."

Islamic tradition names several Muslim converts from Judaism such as ʿAbd Allāh ibn Salām (d. 663/664) and Kaʿb al-Aḥbār (d. c. 653) who were known for translating "the Torah" (by which is meant the Hebrew Bible and oral literature) to provide this background material. When they cited these figures and the "Torah narratives" they transmitted, they were not commenting on the Bible as revealed scripture. Rather they were transmitting reports of uncertain reliability to reconstruct the biography of the ancient prophet in question. Muḥammad ibn Isḥāq (d. 767) drew from a source he called "the first scripture" (*al-kitāb al-awwal*), in which he paraphrases biblical passages from Genesis, Deuteronomy, and Isaiah.[5]

The medieval Muslim historians claimed that the reason to transmit stories of the ancient prophets was to provide edification for the Islamic community. Abū Hudhayfa Bishr al-Qurashī's (d. ca. 205/820) *Mubtadaʾ al-dunyā wa-qiṣaṣ al-anbiyāʾ* (The Beginning of This World and the Stories of the Prophets) is among the earliest extant "stories of the prophets" works. Al-Qurashī explained his aim in the work's opening section. "We will narrate to you the stories of the messengers . . . for your benefit. The scholars said that God the Exalted narrated to the Prophet the reports of past prophets and fallen nations as a proof and sign of his favored status, and the favor and lofty place of his community."[6]

Al-Qurashī held that through such stories, God warned Muslims that He would vanquish those who, like the ancient Israelites, turn away from Him. In the Qurʾān God exclaims that past nations had "split up their relations and become factions" (Qurʾān 30:31), an admonition that the communities surrounding Noah, Abraham, Moses, and Jesus failed to heed (Qurʾān 42:14). The Muslim community should remain obedient to the teachings of the Prophet to avoid repeating the errors of past communities. Similar explanations are found in later universal histories and works of stories of the prophets.[7]

These stories of ancient prophets served a number of ideological functions for medieval Muslims. First, they provided a typological reading of history: the narrative of past prophets and communities prefigured the coming of the last Prophet, Muḥammad.[8] Such stories highlighted Muḥammad's special status and warned the Muslim community against repeating the failures of the communities surrounding previous prophets, in particular, the dangers of fissures within the community. For medieval Muslims these ancient tales reflected the evolution of Islam's self-image as well as serving the religious and political agendas of the authors and their patrons.[9] For example a report in the chronicle of the ninth-century historian Ibn ʿAtham al-Kūfī portrays a Jewish Torah interpretation that claims that the Muslim conquest of Palestine was a renewed expression of God's original covenant and Israelite conquest of Canaan.[10] Another report mentions the discovery of scrolls that mention the coming of the Prophet and the Muslim people; this was clearly a triumphalist message to trumpet Islam as God's chosen historical dispensation. The narrator of this "conquest tradition," Kaʿb al-Aḥbār (Kaʿb of the rabbis), was remembered as a Jewish convert to Islam. Uri Rubin calls these figures "Judeo-Muslims," crossover figures whose role was to confirm Islam's status.[11] Such figures amplified and provided historical context for God's warnings transmitted in the Qurʾān. More recently Antoine Borrut has offered complementary claims on the role that the genre universal history served after Islam's second century. Borrut writes that to displace the Umayyad *lieux de mémoire* (sites of memory) and the imminent messianism associated with the ʿAbbāsid revolution, the scholars developed a new Islamic "ʿAbbāsid vulgate," an account of the past that included stories of the ancient prophets. In this explanation stories of the ancient prophets and last Prophet were intended to neutralize messianic expectations associated with prophecy and prophets that no longer served them or the state.[12]

From where precisely these first- and second-century transmitters and exegetes gathered this material has been the subject of research by a number of scholars. Such material mainly consists of paraphrases of biblical passages intermixed with extrabiblical commentary and Qurʾān. Noting the repetition of the same biblical passages in several ninth- and tenth-century scholars, Camilla Adang suggests that there may have been an Arabic *Vorlage* of biblical passages from which scholars such as Ibn Qutayba and Ibn Rabbān drew, and that was perhaps compiled by Ibn al-Layth for the caliph Hārūn al-Rashīd to dispute the Byzantine Empire Constantine VI in the early ninth century.[13] Alternatively it has been shown that Ibn Qutayba drew from a Syriac translation of the Torah into Arabic.[14] Others who have weighed in on the question of the sources for the Torah have noted a number of Syriac pseudo-epigrapha (*The Book of Jubilees,*[15] *The Book of the Cave of Treasures,*[16] and *The Fourth Book of Ezra*[17]) as possible sources. Reports transmitted orally are a likely explanation, although we cannot of course support this except through the claims of the compilers themselves. After the ninth century, Arabic translations of the Bible and Gospels were, in principle, accessible to medieval Muslims, but few seemed to have consulted them.

From the early period until the third/ninth century, there is little evidence that transmitting sources from Jews and Christians was problematic.[18] But it is clear that by the fourth/tenth century this situation had changed. The spread of traditions in which the Prophet signals the inadmissibility of reports narrated on the authority of Jews and Christians shows that *muḥaddith*s (experts in tradition) became increasingly mistrustful of the traditions of Jews and Christians.[19] In his biography of the Prophet, Ibn Hishām excised large sections of Ibn Isḥāq's biography that narrate the history of the ancient prophets.[20] By the fourth/tenth century, the term "*isrāʾīlīyāt*" came to have a strictly negative connotation among Sunnī scholars, for whom it meant corrupt and unreliable traditions that had crept into the Islamic tradition through Jewish and Muslim converts.[21]

After the fourth/tenth century, most Sunnī scholars followed two guiding principles in dealing with traditions transmitted by Jews and Christians. The first is the doctrine of textual corruption or *taḥrīf,* a Qurʾānic concept (Qurʾān 4:46, 5:13, 2:75) amplified by the ʿulamāʾ. Taḥrīf connoted "perverting the language through altering words from their proper meaning, changing words in form, or substituting words or letters for others." It was believed that while the Torah and Gospels had been revealed by God to Moses and Jesus, the original texts that these prophets received had been irreparably corrupted by the tampering of Jews and Christians through the ages and were thus considered extremely problematic. (Shīʿites made this precise charge of the Sunnīs—that like the rabbis, the Sunnī scholars had held back parts of the Qurʾān that alluded to the family of the Prophet.[22] One wonders whether the charge of Judeo-Christian tampering preceded or followed this Shīʿite topos.) Much like a critical modern historian concerned with the fidelity to narrating the past, the fourth/tenth-century historian Ibn al-Miskawayh (d. 421/1030) wrote that after such a long period, it is impossible to reconstruct the narratives of the ancients with any certainty.[23]

The doctrine of taḥrīf was linked to a second principle. Since medieval Muslims held that they could not know which parts of these scriptures were corrupt and which were authentic, they took the position that whatever agreed with the Qurʾān and the sunna (example) of the Prophet Muḥammad may be taken as authentic and whatever was in conflict with them should be disregarded. Effectively this meant that rather than turn to the Torah directly, most ʿulamāʾ depended on their scholarly predecessors for their knowledge of what these sources contained. When a ninth-century author such as ʿUmāra ibn Wathīma al-Qurashī (d. 902) compiled "stories of the prophets" works or Ibn Jarīr al-Ṭabarī reconstructed the lives of the ancient prophets for his universal history, they drew from materials that had long been Islamicized by generations of sermonizers, Qurʾān commentators, and specialists in tradition.[24]

After the ninth century, there were occasions in which Sunnī ʿulamāʾ consulted the Hebrew Bible and Gospels in the hands of the Jews and Christians, but they were usually restricted to a particular genre: theological polemics. One such epistle was composed in the middle of the ninth century by a courtier named Abū Rabīʿ Ibn al-Layth for his patron the ʿAbbāsid caliph Hārūn al-Rashīd (d. 809) to assist the caliph in his deliberations with the Byzantine emperor Constantine VI. In the epistle Ibn al-Layth listed all the biblical passages that predicted the coming of Muḥammad. This practice of listing passages believed to allude to the Prophet was also adopted in the *dalāʾil al-nubūwa* (the proofs of prophethood) genre, as well as other polemical works by well-known scholars such as al-Masʿūdī (d. 956), Abū Ṭāhir al-Maqdisī (thrived mid-tenth century), and ʿAbd al-Jabbār (d. 1025).[25] The Zaydī Imām al-Qāsim ibn Ibrāhīm and the Andalusian jurist Ibn Ḥazm provide other examples of scholars who engaged sources in the hands of Jews in order to refute the authenticity of the Torah.[26]

Aside from these theological polemics and prophecies of the coming of the Prophet alluded to in the Torah and Gospels, it was uncommon for Sunnī ʿulamāʾ after the ninth century to consult texts of the Hebrew Bible directly. To narrate the stories of the ancient prophets and comment on references to prophets mentioned in the Qurʾān, they adduced "Torah lore" that had long been Islamicized in earlier historiography and commentaries. This point has been made recently by Sidney Griffith, where he notes that the formidable historians Abu Jaʿfar al-Ṭabarī (d. 923) and Ibn ʿAsākir (d. 1176) wrote biographies of Jesus with little connection with the canonical Gospels.[27] When we consider that the Qurʾān frequently alludes to figures widely attested in Jewish and Christian sources, that medieval Muslims produced tens of thousands of pages of Qurʾān commentaries where biblical material would be apposite but rarely drew from Jewish and Christian material, and that translations of the Hebrew

Bible and Gospels were readily available, overall I would suggest that medieval Muslim use of sources in the hands of Jews and Christians was rare.

Gabriel Reynolds has spent great energy attempting to show that the "biblical subtext" is necessary to understand the Qurʾān and its interpretation.[28] I would argue that it is precisely the opposite point that needs to be emphasized: what is notable is not early and medieval Muslims' dependence on the Bible and Gospels, but their lack of interest in these sources.

The ʿulamāʾ's independence from Jewish and Christian sources can be explained by their scholastic sensibility. Studies of scholasticism across cultures show that scholastics tend to build on a closed corpus of canonical texts rather than adding texts from outside the tradition.[29] Thus when ninth- and tenth-century ʿulamāʾ transmitted Torah reports they had received from reliable Muslim transmitters and avoided Torah "in the hands of the Jews" by the standards of their scholarly world, this was not lack of rigor, but sensible precaution.

There was at least one notable exception. In his Qurʾān commentary, *al-Naẓm al-durar fī tanāsub al-ayāt wal-suwar,* the Cairene scholar Ibrāhīm ibn ʿUmar al-Biqāʿī (d. 1480) adduced the Torah and Gospels frequently. Walid Saleh shows that al-Biqāʿī consulted Arabic translations of the Bible as well as Jewish and Christian informants. However, al-Biqāʿī's exegesis precipitated controversy, censure, and widespread recrimination precisely because he used these materials. A contemporary scholar, al-Sakhāwī, rebuked al-Biqāʿī's approach in a treatise specifically on this topic, *al-Aṣl fī taḥrīm al-naql min al-tawrāt wal-injīl* (The Source for the Prohibition of Transmitting from the Torah and Gospels), in which he rehearses all the good reasons that the sources in the hands of Jews and Christians are to be avoided. As Griffith has noted, al-Biqāʿī's work was the exception that proves the rule.[30]

Ironically the ʿulamāʾ's reluctance to consult Jewish and Christian sources might have added to its mystique and its role in apocalyptic rhetoric. In his monograph on the role of messianism as a source of ʿAbbāsid caliphal legitimacy, Hayrettin Yücesoy recounts an important use for reference to the ancient scriptures, relics, and prophecies said to emerge from the antediluvian and Israelite traditions. Throughout Islam's first two centuries, both rebels and caliphs' references to such sources could be used to generate messianic enthusiasm. The first ʿAbbāsid caliph al-Mahdī attempted to recover the original sources of the Torah and Gospels, as well as sacred relics such as the Ark of the Covenant. A hidden treasure alluded to in Qurʾān 18 was understood by early exegetes as knowledge kept in ancient books and scriptures. Perhaps based on knowledge gleaned from the Jacobite Patriarch of Antioch, Dionysius of Tell Mahre, the ʿAbbāsid caliph Al-Maʾmūn excavated the pyramids of Cheops to attempt to find ancient libraries from antedeluvian times, perhaps to find Adam's prophetic bequest to his son Seth. For the caliph the revelation of the true nature of these sources carried a messianic valence that served his identity as the Mujaddid, the messianic renewer of the pure faith and guardian of religion.[31] Perhaps the recondite, exotic association with these materials led to it inhabiting a special aura for medieval Muslims.

Shīʿites and Biblical Lore

The Shīʿite use of Israelite lore was more extensive than that of Sunnīs, and Ismāʿīlī taʾwīl is best situated in this context. From an early period, ancient Israelite lore held special significance for them. Since they viewed their Imāms as the rightful rulers deprived of power and aliened from history's victors, they recognized their own plight in the stories of the ancient prophets. Like the ancient prophets, the Shīʿites were the righteous elect awash in a sea of tyranny and iniquity, victims of tyrants who recur in every era. Thus the conflict between Adam, Abel, Seth, and their adversaries (aḍḍād), the devil Iblīs and Cain, became a paradigm for future generations—the wicked, it was expected, usually are successful in gaining worldly power, while true knowledge for salvation lies with the weak, who suffer to follow God's path. Cain and his descendants would become the pharaohs who ruled as tyrants and endeavored to prevent the worship of God. Adam's successor Seth, and his offspring, inherited *ṣuḥūf*, divine scrolls, and special knowledge that they kept secret to protect.[32] These sources were in the possession of the Imāms who, like many of the ancient Israelites prophets, were deprived of power, and whose followers suffered from being a minority in lands ruled by unjust tyrants. For Imāmī Shīʿites, the tradition that the Prophet predicted that "things will happen to my community similar to what happened to the Children of Israel" explained why it was that the errant were dominant while those who boarded God's ship of salvation and allied with the Imāms were weak and disenfranchised.[33]

The work of Kohlberg, Amir-Moezzi, Rubin, and Sindawi show the enormous number of traditions that circulated in Imāmī and later Twelver Shīʿite sources that drew on ancient Israelite prophetic lore to legitimize the Imāms. To adduce just a few: God's true religion is that which has been given to Noah, Abraham, Moses, and Jesus (following Qurʾān 42:13); this is the exclusive religion of the family of the Prophet.[34] Noah's ark paused above Karbala, the site of al-Ḥusayn's future martyrdom.[35] The ark landed on dry land on the tenth day of the month of Muḥarram, the day on which al-Ḥusayn was later martyred in Kufa.[36] Noah was buried in Najaf, the town of ʿAlī's grave. ʿAlī reported that he inherited from Muḥammad complete knowledge of the Torah and Gospels, a statement made while wearing Muḥammad's armor and sword.[37] Muḥammad's sword Dhū al-Faqār was brought to earth by Adam from paradise and was inscribed to ʿAlī.[38] The names of ʿAlī's two sons Ḥasan and al-Ḥusayn are parallel to that of Aaron's sons Shubbar and Shubbayr.[39] The relationship between Muḥammad and ʿAlī as Prophet and waṣī (legatee) was said to parallel that of Adam to Seth, Noah to Shem, Abraham to Isaac, Moses to Aaron (or

Joshua), and Jesus to Peter.[40] The position of the Shīʿites among the Muslims was likened to that of the Israelites under Pharoah in Egypt.[41] In the Twelver tradition, the twelve Imāms are compared to the twelve tribes of Moses, or Jesus's twelve disciples.[42] The martyrdom of al-Ḥusayn was compared to John the Baptist.[43] The scriptures of the Christians, it was believed, described ʿAlī's virtues.[44]

Through recourse to the massive encyclopedia of Shīʿite traditions, al-Majlisī's *Biḥār al-anwār,* these examples could be multiplied indefinitely. They testify to the importance of Israelite lore in Shīʿite identity. It is worth noting that in the period in which Sunnīs restricted recourse to traditions from "the peoples of the book," fourth/tenth-century Shīʿite compilers of traditions such as al-ʿAyyāshī, Pseudo-Masʿūdī, and al-Majlisī were free to adduce such traditions without censor. Although it is unclear precisely when the Imām was widely held to have supernatural status in Imāmī Shīʿism, it is clear that by the late third century—the period when Ismāʿīlism arose—it had long been held that the Imāms inherited books from the ancient prophets and knew Hebrew, Syriac, and Greek and that their specially endowed divine intellect allowed for conversations with angels and past prophets.

While many of these traditions were previously Islamicized, Uri Rubin has shown that Pseudo-Masʿūdī adduced material that shares a common source with the Syriac *The Book of Jubilees,*[45] and Griffith, that Yaʿqūbī drew from the Syriac *Cave of Treasures.*[46] There is evidence that the potency of invoking the ancient Israelites also entered the popular Imāmī imagination. In fourth/tenth-century Kufa, Imāmī Shīʿites possessed amulets that contained secrets that had been transmitted by a Jew who converted during the time of the Prophet who knew the Hebrew names of holy men who descended from Moses and Aaron. In the year 923, the Imāmīs of Kufa used these amulets to protect their homes during the times of the Qarmāṭī invasions.[47]

We know that in Islam's first century, descendants of the Prophet claimed to be prophets in the Israelite tradition. One such figure, al-Mukhtār, claimed that the awaited redeemer Muḥammad ibn al-Ḥanifīya had been predicted in "the scriptures of the first prophets" (*zubūr al-awwalīn*). Al-Mukhtār gave orations in rhymed prose reminiscent of the Qurʾān, suggesting he received revelation. He would be carried into battle on ʿAlī's chair and claimed that the chair was like the *tābūt,* the Israelite Ark of the Covenant; his followers were like the Israelites, and he was like Joshua. In another tradition he is recalled to have claimed that "whatever had happened to the people of the past will happen to this people. The Israelites possessed the *tābūt* (ark) which contained the relics of the family of Moses and Aaron; this [chair] is like the *tābūt.*"[48]

The character of criticism of the Sabaʾīya suggests that it was strongly associated with ancient Israelite symbology. A contemporary Christian, John of Phenek (Bar Penkaya), recognized the use of al-Mukhtār's imagery as apocalyptic.[49] Aʿsha Hamdān (d. 83/702), a south Yemeni tribesman and poet in Kufa who was sympathetic to the Zubayrids, wrote a poem attacking al-Mukhtār's and his followers' "worship of the chair" and their claims that the *sakīna,* the divine indwelling known to have rested in the Israelites' Ark of the Covenant, resided in it. He instead called for fealty to the family of the Prophet and the revelation "contained in the *maṣāḥif* (leaves or books of Qurʾān)."[50] The basis of Aʿsha's criticism is that the militant rebel sect had adopted an Israelite model of prophecy rather than a model focused on the Prophet and written scripture. The case of al-Mukhtār shows that continuation of prophecy employing an ancient Israelite symbolic idiom could carry militant, apocalyptic valence in early Shīʿism.

It is clear that Israelite metaphor played a far greater role among both militant and quietist Imāmī Shīʿites in the earlier period than it did for proto-Sunnīs. And in the third and fourth centuries, when most Sunnī scholars depended on early generations of Islamic scholars for sources of ancient Israelite story, Imāmī scholars consulted Jewish and Christian texts more freely.

Early Shīʿism's identification with Israelite prophets and the Banū Isrāʾīl, and their scholars' openness to looking to the books in the hands of Jews and Christians, provide context for the Ismāʿīlī missionaries' use of this material.

Ismāʿīlī Hiero-history and Torah

The centrality of prophetic history and Torah lore in Ismāʿīlī taʾwīl emerged from the Ismāʿīlī theory of history, scripture, and interpretation. Ismāʿīlīs viewed history schematically, as a series of cycles with well-defined features. Each of the first six cycles was initiated by a speaker-prophet—Adam, Noah, Abraham, Moses, Jesus, and Muhammad—who received revelation, compiled a scripture, and founded a dār hijra, an abode of refuge from which to battle the tyrant who ruled without God's sanction. Each prophet was accompanied by a waṣī (legatee), who succeeded him as leader, and disclosed the secret interpretation of this law. The legatee was succeeded by a series of seven Imāms who led the community and transmitted these secret teachings to their missionaries. After the completion of the era of Muḥammad, the seventh, final cycle is marked by the onset of the End of Days and the Qāʾim (arising one), Muḥammad ibn Ismāʿīl; in this cycle, rather than reveal a new scripture, the Qāʾim will reveal the secret sense of all prior scriptures.

This system of parallels of prophetic cycles emerges from the earliest period of the movement. The Fāṭimids Imāms refined the scheme to accommodate their role as Imām-caliphs. ʿAbd Allāh and his missionaries presented the End of Days as itself an extended era that would be unveiled in phases; during its initial period, the Imāms would rule openly; the resurrection of the dead would come later, when the entire world is under God's rule.[51] In the *Asās al-taʾwīl* (The Foundation of Allegorical Interpretation), al-Nuʿman claimed that in the period of the Prophet Muḥammad, heptads of Imāms would follow one another as in past cycles, but that no new speaker-prophet would be forthcoming. The heptads of Imāms would continue until the arrival of the Qāʾim. This scheme provided a rationale for their rule for an extended period. Thus the cycles of Imāms in various Israelite periods provided material for cycles of Imāms that paralleled the current period.

Like its theory of historical cycles, Ismāʿīlism's conception of revelation, scripture, and interpretations also provided the framework for an epistemology in which ancient scriptures would play a prominent part. For Ismāʿīlīs, prophets had a far greater role in scripture's formation. Because of his direct connection (ittiṣāl) to emanations from God in the pleroma, the speaker-prophet enjoys God's support (taʾyīd). The prophet composed (allafa) revelation as a written scripture whose full meaning is only accessible to the legatee and Imāms; in some sources, the written text is referred to as a "silent book," for it is not accessible without this divinely aided interpreter. The legatee and Imāms received divine support (taʾyīd), which provided access to the hidden meanings that the prophet embedded in scripture.

Such a scheme provides a basis that would encourage taʾwīl of Torah. Since the Imām interpreter received divine support (taʾyīd), issues of the Torah's corruption by Jews and Christians were not problematic. In the words of al-Qāḍī al-Nuʿmān, "The Gospels and Torah are similar to what is in the Qurʾān: there are [in it] mathals, signs, and symbols. The exterior sense requires taʾwīl, which is the hidden knowledge that has been stored away."[52] The Imām could discern those passages that were genuine and held important meaning.

Such a theory of scripture and interpretation allowed for access to Torah materials inaccessible to non-Ismāʿīlī. They used the complexity of Torah tales for a variety of purposes: to show that contemporary rituals echoed those of the ancient prophets, to justify atypical appointments of succession, and to polemicize against competing claimants. Moreover, by offering taʾwīl of Israelite material inaccessible to non Ismāʿīlīs, the missionaries imbued the believers with a sense of kashf, that secrets were being disclosed.

The Daʿwa during the Cycle of Moses

The following relates a series of Torah taʾwīls during the cycle of Moses in the *Sarāʾir al-nuṭaqāʾ*. (The source ascribed it to Jaʿfar b. Manṣūr al-Yaman, but it was likely completed after his lifetime, and so we are uncertain whether it was Jaʿfar or one of his students who compiled it.) The source parallels ancient rituals and stories with those central to the contemporary mission.

As I have discussed, the oath of allegiance is a crucial moment in the life of the believer, the moment when he "is born"—that is, joins the mission. In a passage in the *Sarāʾir,* the author transmits an archaic form of the oath of allegiance set during the period of Moses and Aaron. "Their oaths were on sacred scrolls (*sufūr*) upon which they would swear. There were seven scrolls, and upon each there were seven circles, and upon each circle there was written 'Say: He is God, One' (Qurʾān 112:1)."[53]

In the Mosaic period, believers would take the oath of allegiance on seven scrolls (sufūr) with seven circles upon which is written the Qurʾānic verse testifying that God is one. This reference to an ancient oath mirrored the contemporary oath of allegiance during which the believer formally joins the daʿwa by affirming a written oath recited to him from a book. In the villages and towns in the early fourth/tenth century, when books were still a relatively new technology, the parallel with a Mosaic talisman suggests that the oath was seen to have special power. The seven scrolls with seven circles recall a talisman that was known to be commonly in use in Shīʿite circles from an early period, the magical "seven seals." This was a magical formula in pictographs that the Prophet's cousin ʿAlī was known to have discovered inscribed on a rock. It was reported to be a theurgic representation of *al-ism al-aʿẓm* (the Greatest Name of God).[54]

Another archaic ritual in the period of Moses describes a taʾwīl of the Israelite burnt offerings.

> Moses commanded each one offering a sacrifice to bring two sheep, and to slaughter one and smear its blood on the horn of the other. The other sheep should remain and not be slaughtered until it dies.
>
> He then would take the fat of the slaughtered sheep from its bowels and put it in the altar of sacrifice. With Moses and Aaron present, the doors would then be locked. Fire from the sky would emerge and burn that fat until a hot, musky odor wafted out so that everyone of the city could smell it, and there did not remain a single house of the Israelites but that they could smell that scent. So they scattered out toward the alter-house to know its master, and to be obedient to him. So to them, he was one honored and respected and who received intercession [from God], a paragon of his nation, a companion for the trustworthy. And whoever does not offer his sacrifice would have his home among the ruffians of the people.[55]

The anecdote describes and analyzes an ancient Israelite burnt offering. Although the account does not parallel any biblical passage closely, its emphasis on odor mirrors the "pleasing odor" of the *olah* (whole burnt sacrifice) referred to Leviticus 1:1–7.[56] In this taʾwīl the odor of the burning fat is directed not toward God, but toward the community. It "reaches into every home" to remind the Israelites that they are to obey the one who offers the burnt offering, Moses. The author explains that the ritual sacrifice symbolizes and reinforces a sense of obedience among the community to the legitimacy of the Imām. In what is at heart a functionalist sociological analysis, the interpreter explains that the scent of the burnt offerings binds each individual in the entire community to its leader. He explains that it was meant to bind the community of believers together.

The author of this taʾwīl presents an ethnographic description of an unknown archaic ritual. By "ethnographic" I mean the sense discussed by the anthropologist Robert Redfield. The ethnographic perspective represents the vantage point of an observer who views himself as witnessing an archaic, unchanging "ethnographic present" in remote, primitive sites.[57]

Other taʾwīls of the burnt offerings in the *Sarāʾir* present an archaic demonstration of a crucial point of doctrine: succession. In the following sequence of interpretations, the succession of Moses is used to rationalize problematic moments in Fāṭimid succession of the Imām. In Jaʿfar's account, while Moses was still alive, Aaron became aware that he would soon die, predeceasing his brother. Aaron "received no revelation" to advise him as to which of his three sons should succeed Moses and consulted Moses on the matter. Moses advised Aaron to instruct his two sons to offer a burnt sacrifice—we learn elsewhere in the *Sarāʾir* that a *qurbān* (burnt offering) is a mathal for the acknowledgement of the succession to the rightful Imām.[58] Moses explains that whichever brother offers the sacrifice acts on behalf of his sibling, as his agent, tacitly acknowledging his authority. Thus the brother of the one who performs the burnt offering ceremony would be appointed to succeed Moses as Imām.

Aaron does as Moses instructed and tells his sons that one of the two should offer a burnt sacrifice. While his two sons are deliberating on who would make the offering, "the adversaries," hiero-historical figures who recur in every cycle attempting to foil the mission of truth, intercede. They advise Aaron's sons to make a pact in advance of the ritual: The younger son will administer the oath of allegiance to the elder, who, in turn would agree to bequeath the Imāmate to his young brother, rather than his son, when he dies.[59] The adversaries' plan is thus to meddle with the burnt offering ritual rather than allowing it to reflect God's will.

Aaron's sons adopt the adversaries' suggestion, and the adversaries, who are described as "ahl al-raʾy wal-qiyās"—jurists who depend on their whims—prepare the fire for the brothers. When the older son attempts to make the sacrifice, the sacrificial fire rises, consumes their clothes, and burns them. God then reveals to Aaron that he should tell Moses that rather than appoint either son, Moses should appoint Joshua as an Imām *mustawdiʿ*, a "caretaker Imām," until such time as one of Aaron's descendants is ready to assume the role of Imām. It is thus Joshua, not Aaron, who becomes Moses's legatee, receives the true Torah, and leads the community after Moses's death.

The Imām mustawdiʿ, an Imām who guards the genealogical legacy of the Imāmate for a fixed period, was a useful concept for the Fāṭimids. Madelung shows that it was applied by al-Muʿizz to explain the role of Muḥammad Abū

Shalaghlagh, the first Fāṭimid Imām's uncle.[60] He was thus caretaker of the Imāmate prior to ʿAbd Allāh, thus providing a rationale for both he and ʿAbd Allāh's father, al-Ḥusayn, to be considered legitimate, despite the fact that the latter never was recognized as Imām. Moses's successor, Joshua, is thus placed in a status parallel to that of Muḥammad Abū Shalaghlagh and Aaron in the role of his father, al-Ḥusayn; Joshua holds the Imāmate for the lineage of Aaron until such time as Aaron's progeny are in a position to reclaim it.

The Moses-Joshua succession also mirrors that of the fourth Fāṭimid Imām al-Muʿizz li-dīn Allāh. Al-Muʿizz had appointed his son ʿAbd Allāh to succeed him. However, when ʿAbd Allāh passed away before al-Muʿizz, he then appointed the second son, Nizār. This is contrary to Ismāʿīlism's foundational model; when Jaʿfar al-Ṣādiq's appointed successor, Ismāʿīl, predeceased him, it was his grandson, Muḥammad ibn Ismāʿīl, who was appointed, rather than one of Ismāʿīl's brothers. Al-Muʿizz's departure from this model drove the missionaries to provide parallels in prior historical cycles that paralleled al-Muʿizz's appointment, and the Moses-Joshua case served this end. This point is bolstered by the fact that Moses was the fourth nāṭiq, and al-Muʿizz the fourth Fāṭimid Imām (in the period of disclosure).[61] A similar scheme is found in al-Qāḍī al-Nuʿmān's *al-Risāla al-mudhhiba* where the narrator refers to Joshua as a Mustawdiʿ Imām for the progeny of Aaron.[62] Similarly, in his *Taʾwīl al-zakāt,* Jaʿfar ibn Manṣūr al-Yaman notes five prior cases during which the Imām appointed not one, but two (consecutive) legatees: Abraham (Isaac and Ishmael), Moses (Aaron and Joshua), Muḥammad (Ubayy ibn Kaʿb and ʿAlī), Jaʿfar al-Ṣādiq (Ismāʿīl and Muḥammad ibn Ismāʿīl), and al-Muʿizz (ʿAbd Allāh and Nizār).[63] Such a scheme demonstrated the right of al-Muʿizz to choose two successors.

The reason that such taʾwīls were necessary is suggested by the taʾwīls of Ismāʿīlī missionaries who rejected the Fāṭimids' legitimacy. In his *Kitāb al-Iṣlāḥ,* the (non-Fāṭimid) Ismāʿīlī missionary Abū Ḥātim al-Rāzī presented the period immediately before Moses's Imāmate as a fatra, an interregnum when no rightly guided Imām is extant. In this period the daʿwa of truth was hijacked by an unjust pharaoh, an illegitimate daʿwa leader who deceived the majority of the believers by illegitimately claiming the Imāmate. During this fatra true knowledge rested with Shuʿayb (Jethro), a lead missionary who led the twelve islands in secret. Al-Rāzī criticized an unnamed illegitimate "leader of the daʿwa" who falsely claimed the status of Imām for himself and pulled the majority of the mission to his side. This is a polemical barb directed against the Fāṭimids.[64] Al-Rāzī probably viewed himself in the role of Shuʿayb (Jethro), a leader of the twelve "wings" (lawāḥiq) who administer the daʿwa until the reappearance of the coming Imām.

For the Fāṭimid missionaries who competed with missionaries such as al-Rāzī, legitimizing the succession from one Fāṭimid Imām to the next was thus of great concern. The taʾwīl of the ancient prophets and Israelites provided a vehicle to rationalize the appointment of a Fāṭimid Imām and criticize those who failed to recognize him. This was particularly useful when, for unforeseen reasons, the transfer from Imām to Imām departed from expectation, as in the case of al-Muʿizz.

The preceding taʾwīls were set in the time of Moses and said to be from the Torah but are not closely related to particular passages from the Hebrew Bible. The following taʾwīls interpret passages that the author claims were "still written in the Torah which they [the Jews] have today." In fact the passages are close paraphrases to verses from the Hebrew Bible or Jewish tradition. They thus represent the missionaries treating passages from the Torah as they do the Qurʾān: as revealed scripture.

The following is an interpretation based on Exodus 21:2.

> If one of you takes a slave, then take him as a slave for six years. On the seventh year, he [the slave] who asks for mercy is manumitted, and [from that point] he shall not be designated as property [milk]. If this comes to pass, his owner takes him and puts him on the platform of the door of the house. . . .
>
> [Moses] meant, "the six Imams arising after me are like the masters [*al-mawālī*] of the community; to them, the *umma* are like slaves. When the seventh appears, it is necessary to obey him and abandon the first [the earlier] command; the law is to be undertaken on his [the seventh's] behalf."[65]

This taʾwīl locates the hiero-historical symbolic form that the seventh in the heptad of Imāms is the successor through a paraphrase and interpretation of Exodus 21:2, which stipulates the manumission of a slave in the seventh (Sabbatical) year. The second part of the passage seems to be an allusion to Exodus 21:6, a verse that states that if a slave declares he does not want to be manumitted, the master "takes him to the door or the doorpost and pierces his ear with an awl, thus becoming his slave for life." Since these verses are not among those known to other medieval Muslims, it seems likely that this reflects an interpretation of a Jewish or Christian source.

In addition to providing objects of interpretation for standard symbolic forms such as the six Imāms, the Torah provided material for more complex hiero-historical patterns that were conducive to Fāṭimid apologetics. One such interpretation comes in a verse pertaining to a verse in Leviticus.

> Then he said regarding the second cycle [*al-dawr al-thānī*]: "When you cultivate land, cultivate it for six years, and let it grow wild in the seventh year. Then, the fathers among you are not to cultivate it. Rather, the children [abnāʾ] cultivate it. . . ."[66] [This is because] Jesus did not have a bodily birth because his daʿwa was instituted with apostles. Thus the notables,

> missionaries, and the rest of the people of the daʿwa are the "children" [abnāʾ] of the prophets because they "built it [*banawhā*]."[67]

The missionary interprets a paraphrase of Leviticus 25:3–4, a verse that describes the so-called sabbatical year, the command to let agricultural land go fallow every seven years. In the taʾwīl, the cultivation of the fallow ground by the children alludes to the role of missionaries during the cycle of Jesus who must establish a daʿwa during political instability when no *dār hijra* had been established. The Torah's phrase, "the children who work the land," is a *mathal* for the nuqabāʾ, the leading missionaries, who missionize on behalf of the khulafāʾ, the deputies of God. The missionary draws on the assonance of key-words for the taʾwīl: in the absence of the speaker-prophets, it is the *abnāʾ* (children) who *banaw* (build) the mission. The taʾwīl supports the author's claim that in purely "spiritual" periods such as that of Jesus and Adam, the daʿwa is led by apostles and missionaries rather than by a speaker-prophet himself.[68] Pseudo al-Qāḍī al-Nuʿmān's *al-Risāla al-mudhhiba* also alludes to the seventh year when the ground should be left fallow and the slaves freed as references to periods of "screening" (from the rightly guided Imām). In such periods, every group claims for themselves their own Imām, like "sheep being led to slaughter."[69] Only those who recognize the true Imām will be saved.

A third taʾwīl of Torah in this sequence of interpretations offers another interpretation of a heptad.

> "If one among you dies, then wrap your heads seven days with their [eight] nights." . . . By "death" he meant the death of the rank of Isaac and his progeny. For when their regime [dawla] died, they "wrap their heads" by surrendering to the rightful one, just as nations in the past surrendered leadership to the one to whom it rightfully belonged, as has been mentioned. Thus they covered themselves until the time of the appearance. This is just as in your days [there] is "covering" in your days. This is done by those with knowledge and understanding.[70]
>
> The ignorant and foolish people followed their satans. At some point, their hearts became callous, and they returned to their own views and analogies. They did not know that when seven Imāms and eight deputies [khulafāʾ] of Muḥammad ibn Ismāʿīl had completed, the corporeal command of Muḥammad would be complete, and the spiritual cycle would begin. This is confirmed in the Torah, when it says: "at the End of Days will be sent seven true missionaries," meaning the seven Imāms, and "eight noble Adams," meaning eight illustrious deputies.[71]

In this mourning ritual, the mourner wraps his head for seven days and eight nights. "Death" is a mathal for the end of a period of rule for a particular genealogical line, "wrapping" or "covering the head" refers to the recognition of this transfer, and "seven days and eight nights" refer to the seven Imāms and eight deputies (khulafāʾ) who precede "the appearance" (ẓuhūr) when the secrets behind the laws are disclosed. The "eight nights," the other goes on to explain, refer to the eight corporeal deputies (khulafāʾ) of Muḥammad ibn Ismāʿīl—the Fāṭimid Imāms—after which the spiritual cycle of Muḥammad ibn Ismāʿīl begins. According to Jaʿfar, the Torah's claim that at the End of Days God will send seven true missionaries connotes the seven Imāms, and "the eight noble Adams" connotes the eight caliphs.[72]

The mourning ritual in question is Talmudic, where it is known as *ʾatifat yishmaʿilīm,* "the wrapping of the Ishmaelites."[73] The question at issue was whether while undertaking the traditional Shivaʿ (seven day period of mourning), Jews should cover their faces by wrapping themselves, a practice they associated with the "Ishmaelites" (the term for Arabs in rabbinic parlance.) The issue was discussed by the North African Talmudic commentator Hananel ben Ḥushiʾal (d. 1055 or 1056).[74] As this practice had no reference in the Hebrew Bible and is unlikely to have been learned from a Christian source, it seems likely that its origins were a Jewish informant.

This passage is an example of a practice that recurs in taʾwīl of the Torah and Gospels: the tendency to extend the sense of "Torah" beyond texts to Jewish practices, symbols, rituals, and institutions. The missionaries combined passages of Torah with the practices of the Israelites and Jews and related the hidden meaning behind them.

In another example of this mix of Torah legislation and praxis, in a brief taʾwīl that follows, it is explained that the Qāʾim would be "the fourth from Moses," and then to commemorate these four, Moses legislated four festivals.

> Moses anointed four festivals for his people. They are: ʿĪd Yasuʿ [Christmas?], The Day of Remembrance [ʿĪd al-dhikr—Rosh Hashanah], Passover, and Sukkot [ʿId al-muṣallāt]. By the "Festival of Passover" he meant merely the festival. By the festival of Yasuʿ he meant Jesus, who is the seventh of the aforementioned completers previously mentioned, and who will abrogate his law. By "The Day of Remembrance" [ʿĪd al-dhikr], he meant Muḥammad. He named him this in His book [when He said] "God has sent down unto you a reminder" [Qurʾān 56: 10–11]. . . . The fourth festival is the Qāʾim; it makes plain the palm-branches, all types of fruits, the most splendid clothes, and the recitation, supplication, and imploring of God. . . . Each of these festivals gathers the people of every land. And at the time of the fourth, all will be revealed, as we said.[75]

Moses legislated four festivals, with each festival meant to commemorate a speaker-prophet. Passover was set on behalf of himself, Christmas for Jesus,

Rosh Hashanah for Muḥammad, and Sukkot for the Qāʾim.[76] The author extends the object of interpretation from passages of the Torah to festivals celebrated by Jews and Christians; not just scriptures, but the religious praxes of the peoples of the book now become potential objects of taʾwīl. In consequence, taʾwīl of pre-Islamic scripture blends with ethnographic interpretation of the practices of Jews and Christians. Consider the following description of the Passover Seder in the Sarāʾir.

> In their festival the Jews ate a flatbread, and did not eat food with leaven. They would do this according to the model [sunna] of their forefathers, when they wanted out from Egypt, fleeing, outcasts. Moses had prescribed that for this festival, people of means among them are to take a sheep and slaughter it. They are to carry it on a table and gather the people of the family and the owners of its meat. They should wear binds on their midsections, and put restraints on their necks similar to that of their fathers like their forefathers when they were fleeing from Pharaoh. Then they walk around the table.[77]

The taʾwīl offers an ethnographic description of the festival of the Jewish celebration of Passover. Its elements include the biblical injunctions of the pascal lamb offering and the prohibition of leavened bread, as well as other elements, the wearing of bindings and restraints on their midsections and necks, and the circumambulation around the Passover table, that are not well known.

There are several unusual features of the taʾwīls of Torah discussed thus far. First, the missionaries adduced passages of Torah not known in the Islamic tradition. Second, these interpretations of Torah are not part of Qurʾānic exegesis; rather the focus is on the verses of the Torah itself. The missionaries treated these Torah verses just as they did the Qurʾān: as revealed scripture. Finally, in their interpretations missionaries often blurred Torah taʾwīl with interpretations of rituals, symbols, and festivals that are celebrated by Jews and Christians. Contemporary communities become texts that also reveal the *ḥaqāʾ iq,* the supernal patterns.

Errant Israelites in the Interim (Fatra)

In the story of Judah and Tamar, the missionaries present an exemplum of a fatra, an era in which no rightly guided prophet or Imām is accessible. Abū Ḥātim al-Rāzī criticizes the Fāṭimids as tyrants who exploit periods of fatras to seize power. The following story could be viewed as a response to this sort of polemic.

The story comes nested in a section called "The Story of Joseph" and describes a time in which the Imām was hidden and a judge, Judah, ruled. The biblical story is meant to provide the Fāṭimid perspective on fatra. The Iranian missionariy Abū Ḥātim al-Rāzī held that during a fatra, one of the lawāḥiq, a chief-missionary, is to rule. Jaʿfar b. Manṣūr al-Yaman's story of Judah and Tamar offers another view.

Like some of the passages adduced above, it is likely that the story came to Jaʿfar directly through a Jewish or Christian source, rather than a previously Islamicized account. Unlike much Islamic "Israelite" material, the story of Judah and Tamar is not attested in Islamic chronicles, *Qiṣaṣ* collections, or commentaries. When we consider the content of the story, the reason that early Muslim interpreters did not adopt the story becomes clear.

In the biblical tale, Judah, one of the twelve sons of Jacob and the forefather of the prophet David, is presented in a poor light. He is shown to be corrupt, hypocritical, and incompetent: he breaks the law when it suits him to do so, allows himself to be duped by his daughter-in-law Tamar, and inadvertently commits incest with her. For medieval Muslims guided by the principle of *ʿiṣma* (the infallibility of prophets), these are not the acts of one who sires prophetic offspring. The fifth/eleventh-century Andalusian scholar Ibn Ḥazm (d. 456/1064) found the story so objectionable that in the section of his heresiography that discusses Judaism, he adduced the Judah-Tamar story as a clear indication of the Jewish corruption of the authentic Torah, as well as Jews' general propensity toward vile behavior.[78]

Where did Jaʿfar learn the Judah-Tamar story? If it were a source already circulating in Islamic circles, one possibility is an Arabic translation of *The Book of Jubilees* (which has yet to be discovered) that al-Yaʿqūbī, who wrote in the same period, is known to have adduced. This source does narrate the story of Judah and Tamar. Another possibility is that Jaʿfar learned of the story from an Arabic translation of the Hebrew Bible. Al-Qayrawān was a center for Judeao-Arabic biblical translation and exegesis in this period, so this is certainly a possibility.[79] Since the language differs significantly from both Saʿadya Gaon's and Yefet ben ʿAlī's Arabic translations, our current state of knowledge does not allow us to speculate further on Jaʿfar's source.[80] Another possibility is that Jaʿfar had a Jewish or Christian informant, although this raises the question of how he came to ask about the story, given that it is not well known in Islamic circles.

In Jaʿfar's story we are told that Judah was chief judge in the period of the pharaohs. When Judah married his eldest son to Tamar, the son died before having fathered a child. Tamar, as was her right, demanded her late husband's brother in marriage, but Judah evaded marrying him to her. When Tamar realized that Judah had no intention of marrying Judah's second son to her, she tricked Judah into himself fathering a son with her by posing as a prostitute. When she was convicted of adultery, a crime that carried the punishment of execution by fire, she produced evidence that Judah had fathered her child. She gave birth to two sons, one of whom was destined to beget the lineage of David, Solomon, and the Christ. The following is the translation of the story.[81]

When [the pharaoh] Tāyzūn rose by the command of God, the [Israelite] tribes stirred and called to one another for leadership. But the master of the age was concealed, similar to, as has been stated previously, the concealment of the son of Ismāʿīl, when darkness rose and covered the light, the true reality, and its adherents.

It comes from the Torah that Judah son of Jacob had married a woman who gave birth to three sons. When the oldest son, ʿAyn, had reached manhood, he married a woman called Tamar. When he entered unto her, he died before fathering offspring. [So her brother-in-law Awbān who was the second son, married her and entered upon her and died before producing offspring.[82]] And so Tamar went to demand that his [ʿAyn's] brother Sīlān marry her. But he refused her, for he [Sīlān] was young for marriage.

So she went to Judah in the place where he sat in judgment [*majlis ḥukmihi*]. He was the head of the yeshiva[83] [*mathnīya*] of the Jews [a position] known today as the chief judge [*qāḍī al-quḍāh*] to whom they defer. Their law [ḥukm] from ancient times in the Torah, to which they are bound up to the present, is that when a man dies leaving a wife without a son and he has a brother who has not married, they marry him to her to continue the [late] brother's lineage. If he does not do so, the woman brings him to the courthouse and raises the issue of their marriage. If in the courthouse he declines [to marry her], the woman takes his shoe from his foot, spits on it, and sticks it in his face saying: "This is what comes to him whoever does not maintain his brother's house!" After that, the man becomes known as "The Shoeless One" and his progeny after him are known as "The family of the house of the Shoeless One."

And so Tamar came to the court and demanded that he [Judah] give his son in marriage. In his place of judgment in which she had demanded his son, he affected kindness toward her. He said to her:

"Return to the house of your father and stay in his quarters until Sīlān reaches manhood, and then I will marry you to him, because [if I married you to him now] I fear that what befell his brother will befall him." So Tamar went to her house and wore her robe of mourning. They would wear black for mourning. For this reason, the offspring of al-ʿAbbās adopted it [the color black] in their claim [to rule], out of grief for al-Ḥusayn.

So Tamar sat in her house. When Sīlān grew up, she found that Judah had no intention of marrying her to him, for he was the judge [ḥākim]. The women of the Israelites are not permitted to marry others if the late son had an heir.

So Tamar removed her robe of mourning and donned an ornate robe. She adorned herself, but concealed herself from those who knew her, and went out among the throngs of people. She came to the paths of

Bethlehem that Judah would take, sitting down [waiting] for him but disguising herself from him. She was stunningly beautiful.

One day he passed by and saw her. When she saw him coming, she hurried toward him but turned her face away. When he saw her, his heart became attached to her, and he leaned over her, concealing himself from the people, and said to her: "Let us join in temporary marriage." He did not consider the fact that she was concealed. She covered her face, concealing herself for fear that he would know her. She said to him, "What will you give me for us to join in temporary marriage?"

"I will give you two young sheep," he said.

"Give me something as a deposit," she said.

"And what do you want?" he said.

"More [*akthar*], I mean [*yaʿnī*]. Your ring, your staff, and your *maʿbūla,*" she said.[84] He agreed to pay her price.

She went with him to the place, and he entered it at night. He spent the night with her and she didn't leave that place until she had become pregnant.

In the morning Judah passed by his house and called to one of his students. He ordered him to take two young sheep and bring them to her. He described to him the place in which she was staying, and ordered him to take her the payment [and retrieve his deposit].

So the man went to the place and asked about her, but no one was able to give information on her. He said to those who were in the area, "Where is the prostitute [*mutamattiʿa*] who used to stay here?" The people of the place swore that they knew no one of that description in this area. So he returned to Judah and informed him.

"Perhaps she has changed what she had earlier demanded," Judah said. So he increased [the payment] to a third sheep. The messenger returned and continued persisting with questions and a thorough search, but did not find anyone with information on her. So he returned and told Judah, but Judah neglected the matter.

After time had passed, the pregnant woman's child began showing and her affair become known to people until word of it reached Judah's associates. They came to him and informed him of Tamar's state, that she had fallen into sin, and so he [Judah] ordered that she be thrown into the fire. They came and brought her out of her house. When she was outside, she said to them, "Bring me to the courthouse to stand before the judge." But they refused. When she saw what had befallen her, she sent one of her relatives to bring the deposit, and told him of her story with [Judah]. The messenger then came and testified to what she had said and brought the evidence. When [Judah] saw the deposit, he lowered his head and said:

> "She has told the truth in what she has said, for I am the father. I know that she did this when I would not marry her to Sīlān."
>
> When it was the time for her to give birth, the midwife sat in her seat as Tamar's labor commenced. She was pregnant with twins. Then, the hand of one of the twins emerged. So the midwife took it and wrapped it. [. . .] The interpretation of this in Arabic is [*tafsīruhā bil-ʿarabīya*] "Come out!" Not long after that, following the praised hand, the other [hand] returned the two of them, and delayed them, and then the other hand came forward. The midwife said at that point, "You will die, my children!" And so he was named "Ṣāḥib al-qarrayn." The other was named "Zurūḥ"; its interpretation in Arabic [*tafsīruhā bil-ʿarabīya*] is "eastern" [*mashriq*].
>
> As for "Sāḥib," he is the source of David, Solomon, and the Christ, and those who came after Solomon. And there have been no trials on the friends of God as severe as those which the practitioners of legal reasoning and analogy [*aṣḥāb al-raʾy wal-qiyās*] afflicted upon them, with their charges that the prophets [rusul] lied, and rejection of the legatees [waṣīs], and the establishment of Pharaonic rule. But the legatees held fast to the heritage of the prophets. And while Pharaohs arose, people composed works with their legal theory and opinions "trying to extinguish the light of God" in what they composed and in their speech, "but God refuses but to perfect His light, despite the hatred of the unbelievers" [Qur'ān 9:34].

The plot of Jaʿfar's version is similar to that of Genesis 38, although, even shorn of the interpretive glosses, it is certainly not identical to it. In the Bible Judah is described as the eldest brother and the leader of the brothers, but not as a "judge" as he is in Jaʿfar's version. The biblical version narrates that before denying Tamar his third son, Judah first marries her to his second son, whom God destroys after he spills his semen on the ground instead of going unto Tamar; this plot point is absent from Jaʿfar's telling. Finally, Tamar plays a more prominent role in Jaʿfar's version. The narration provides a detailed description of her plans, intentions, and deeds.[85]

Jaʿfar's version begins by paralleling the Israelites during their captivity in Egypt with the Ismāʿīlīs during the concealment of their seventh Imām, Muḥammad ibn Ismāʿīl, the final speaker-prophet and guided redeemer (al-Mahdī) in Ismāʿīlī cyclical metahistory. The narrator then describes the political situation of the Jews under the pharaoh. "When [the pharaoh] Tāyzūn rose by the command of God, the [Israelite] tribes stirred and called to one another for leadership. But the master of the age was concealed, similar to, as has been stated previously, the concealment of the son of Ismāʿīl, when darkness rose and covered the light, the true reality, and its adherents. . . . He [Judah] was the head of the yeshiva of the Jews, [a position] known today as the chief judge (qāḍī al-quḍāh) to whom they defer."

History unfurls in cycles (adwār), with a cycle of darkness and concealment (satr) alternating with a cycle of light and public disclosure (kashf). This story took place in a period of pharaonic darkness in which the Master of the Age (Ṣāḥib al-zamān) was hidden, and the Israelites were without the guiding presence of a divinely appointed speaker-prophet (nāṭiq) or legatee. The story is set in a period known as a "fatra," a period in which no divinely guided Imām is available. This period thus parallels the period before the advent of the Fāṭimids.

In this period of darkness, the Israelites were led by a chief judge, Judah, under the pharaoh's suzerainty. The story juxtaposes two parallel fatras: the Pharoah and the qāḍī (judge) Judah being one, and the ʿAbbāsid caliph and the Islamic Aṣḥab al-raʾy wal-qiyās (unjust jurists) as the other. The link between the Pharaonic and Islamic periods is made explicit in the story's denouement: Judah's oppression of the righteous is said to prefigure trials brought against his speaker-prophet progeny.

> As for "Ṣāḥib," he is the source of David, Solomon, and the Christ, and those who came after Solomon. And there have been no trials on the friends of God as severe as those which the jurists [*aṣḥāb al-raʾy wal-qiyās*] afflicted upon them, with their charges that the prophets [rusul] lied, and their rejection of the legatees, and the establishment of Pharaonic rule. But the legatees held fast to the heritage of the prophets. And while Pharaohs arose, people composed works with their legal theory and opinions "trying to extinguish the light of God" in what they composed and in their speech, "but God refuses but to perfect His light, despite the hatred of the unbelievers" [Qur'ān 9:34].

Just as Judah's legalism was used to oppress Tamar against God's will, so too the corrupt Muslim jurists, the aṣḥāb al-raʾy wal-qiyās, applied false jurisprudence to oppress the legatees and prophets in future generations. The ʿAbbāsid caliph, a figurehead for the dynastic rulers in much of the central and Eastern Islamic lands in the fourth/tenth century and the enemy of the Ismāʿīlī Fāṭimid caliphate, appointed and patronized judges in this period. The phrase "and while the Pharaohs ruled, people wrote books on legal theory" equates the later Sunnī and Imāmī fuqahāʾ (jurists) with Judah and implicates Islamic jurists in complying with the unjust, dark rule of the pharaoh-caliphs.[86] Some Imāmī scholars in this period were indeed in the employ of the caliphate; al-Sharīf al-Murtaḍa wrote a treatise justifying working with the ʿAbbāsids.[87]

The stranglehold of the corrupt chief judge was broken by Tamar. She understood that it was God's plan for her to continue Judah's lineage and acted to accomplish this using covert means. Tamar came to this realization after she was sent to her mother's house by Judah. "So Tamar went to her house and wore her robe of mourning. They would wear black for mourning. For this reason, the offspring of al-ʿAbbās adopted it [the color black] in their claim, out of grief for al-Ḥusayn. Thus Tamar sat in her house. When Sīlān grew up, she found that Judah had no intention of marrying her to him, for he was the judge [ḥākim]. . . . So Tamar removed her robe of mourning and donned an ornate robe." While obeying Judah's command, Tamar followed the custom of the pharaonic ʿAbbāsids (the children of al-ʿAbbās) and wore black. But she soon recognized her true destiny, removed her oppressive ʿAbbāsid robe, and disguised herself in a beautiful gown to fulfill her divine mission. Just as many divinely guided Imāms, legatees, and missionaries had done for the Fāṭimid mission in times in which "the adversary" was powerful, Tamar worked in concealment on behalf of the mission.

When Judah propositioned Tamar, he asked her to join him in *mutʿa* or "temporary marriage." While Imāmī and Ismāʿīlī law were similar, one of the crucial differences was precisely the status of mutʿa, which is permitted by Imāmī legal scholars but proscribed by the foremost Ismāʿīlī legal scholar al-Qāḍī al-Nuʿmān. Here Judah is presented as an Imāmī Shīʿite.[88] Judah's servant reinforces this by using the word *mutamattiʿa,* a word derived from "mutʿa" for the word prostitute.[89] The narrator thus associates the Imāmī rite of temporary marriage with prostitution. Imāmī scholars would have been particularly sensitive to this charge, for they were known to denigrate other groups as "children of adultery" or "bastards" *(awlād zināʾ*) and were less lenient than other legal schools on the status of children born of a prostitute.[90] The story polemicizes against Imāmī jurists who were known to accommodate the ʿAbbāsid caliph in the period.[91]

Tamar is not the only heroine in the story. In the climactic birth scene in which the twins struggle for power, the midwife took an active role in the birth of Tamar and Judah's twins. She knew which one of the twins was divinely chosen and wrapped the praised one's hand, designating him as the rightful heir. When the firstborn was held back by the brother who attempted to steal his birthrite, the story recalls the injustice wrought when the sixth Imām Jaʿfar al-Ṣādiq's son Ismāʿīl was wrongfully deprived of his rightful legacy by the younger son Mūsā. The midwife's actions ensured the rightful place of the progenitor of the prophetic line of David and the Messiah.

At several points in the narrative, the narrator emphasizes the story's alien quality. In the following passage, the narrator describes Judah's position and the workings of the law. "He was the head of the Jews [a position] known today as the chief judge (qāḍī al-quḍāh) to whom they defer. Their law (ḥukm) from ancient times in the Torah, which they are bound to until the present, is that when a man dies leaving a wife without a son and he has a brother who has not married, they marry him to her to continue the [late] brother's lineage." Explanations are related in the third person: "their" system of law still binds "them" until the present day—the "they" referring to the Jewish descendants of the Israelites, a substantial community in tenth-century Qayrawān near the

Fāṭimid capital.[92] The use of the third person in these glosses accentuates the distance between the characters in the historical narrative and the tale's audience. Levirate marriage, an ancient Near Eastern institution that the Israelites shared with prior cults, was problematic even for medieval Jewish sages. Nothing like it was ever incorporated into Islamic law, and it most likely sounded odd to fourth/tenth-century Muslims.

The Levirate marriage's alien quality is emphasized with a short anecdote explaining what would come about if the surviving brother fails to fulfill the rite of *Yibbum* (Levirate marriage) and marry his late brother's wife.

> If he does not do so, the woman brings him to the courthouse and raises the issue of their marriage. If in the courthouse he declines [to marry her], the woman takes his shoe from his foot, spits on it, and sticks it in his face saying: 'This is what comes to him who doesn't maintain his brother's house!' After that the man becomes known as 'The Shoeless One,' and his progeny after him are known as the 'The family of the house of the Shoeless One.'

This colorful digression, a paraphrase of Deuteronomy 25: 7–10, does nothing to advance the narrative. For the purposes of understanding the story, the audience merely needed to know of Levirate marriage. This aside must have sounded exotic to its fourth/tenth-century audience.

In several places in the text, the narrator "explains [a word's meaning] in Arabic" (*tafsīruhā bil-ʿarabīya*), an odd way of providing a gloss. For example the name Zurūḥ (from the Hebrew root *zarcha,* "east") is "translated in Arabic" (*tafsīruhā bil-ʿarabīya*) as "eastern" (*mashriq*).[93] The narrator draws attention to the fact that the story was not originally written in Arabic, again emphasizing that this is a foreign source unfamiliar to medieval Muslims.

I would suggest that like the aside to the Yibbum, these explanatory glosses served a greater role than merely aiding the audience's understanding of the story. By alluding to the fact that the text was not originally in Arabic, the narrator accentuated its exotic, alien quality.

During this fatra it was two women, Tamar and her midwife, who overcame the pharaonic-jurist tyranny to ensure that the prophetic lineage of the future prophets was sustained. The midwife represented the symbolic matriarch of the legatees while Tamar was foremother of the speaker-prophets David and Jesus. There is evidence that women were not infrequently cast in a symbolic role as Ismāʿīlī dāʿīs in Jaʿfar's corpus.[94] Perhaps since women such as Tamar and her midwife must express their power through covert rather than public means, the Ismāʿīlīs identified their future divine guides with these figures.

The story of Judah polemicizes against Shīʿites who are in league with an illegitimate suzerain. Jurists require the presence of a rightly guided Imām to dispense justice. This anti-Imāmī polemic showed Ismāʿīlīs the deficiencies of other Shīʿite doctrinal positions.

As in the taʾwīl of verses described above, this taʾwīl of the story of Judah and Tamar offers an ideological component articulated in sources that the text itself presents as foreign and obscure. While Abū Ḥātim al-Rāzī defended and normalized an extended period of fatra, in the story of Judah and Tamar, we see a far darker presentation in which those who carry the truth are forced into darkness because of the lack of divinely guided leadership. In a polemic against the Iranian dioceses who claim authority without the guidance of Imāms, the story shows that during fatras, true believers go under cover. The Israelite narratives afforded the missionary material to convey the message that in the true Torah lie crucial messages that warn against following those who attempt to guide without recourse to an Imām.

The identification of the believers with the Israelites and their modern descendants allowed for some highly unconventional taʾwīl of Qurʾānic passages. In a taʾwīl in the fifth treatise of *Kitāb al-kashf* (The Book of Disclosure), an anonymous sage instructs his student by revealing to him the secret meaning of several Qurʾānic verses that pertain to the comportment of the missionaries and their approach to proselytizing. The sage explains Qurʾān 29:46, "Do not debate with the people of the book unless it is in [a way] that is better," a verse that is conventionally understood to refer to debate with Jews and Christians.

> Do you know the meaning of "dispute" [*jadal*]? Its meaning [refers to] what the believers say when they gather in multiple daʿwas. One says, "This is my father—meaning 'father' in knowledge, and he is better than your father, and my mission is better than your mission." While that one says, "My father is better than your father." But all the fathers (peace be upon them) call to God, the Almighty! So it is not permitted for anyone to slander anyone whom the Imām (peace be upon him) had put in a rank, through the grace of God, the Almighty, for he did not set him there as a debater or transgressor.
>
> God the Almighty said, "Do not dispute with the people of the book unless it is in [a way] that is better." You and those like you are the people of the book. For you have learned that "the clear book with no defect" [Qurʾān 20:108] is the Imām (may the praises of God be upon him and his family) who recognize him in his time. It is not permissible for you to dispute the people of the book, for perhaps one with whom you dispute knows more than you; you may only . . . when knowledge [*fāʾida*] is requested of you. And be extremely cautious about disclosing anything that is with you, for one who is less than you might turn to unbelief. Do not be other than a humble questioner. Guard against distorting any knowledge, and be on your guard when it is requested.[95]

"The book" in the Qurʾānic verse referring to ahl al-kitāb (people of the book) refers to the Imām—book is frequently a mathal for "Imām." Thus the Qurʾanic prohibition against disputing with "people of the book" is taken to apply to those within the daʿwa.

With missionaries working independently in semi-independent covert cells of believers who sowed the mission in secret,[96] it is likely that different formulations of doctrine abounded. It is easy to imagine why a prohibition against disputation among the missionaries would be necessary. In this passage the experience of the believers, including disputation within the ranks, is made part of the fabric of a living hiero-history.

Conclusion

While the status of Israelite material had been established by several generations of Shīʿites, for Ismāʿīlī missionaries it took on still greater importance. The missionaries used passages that they found in Jewish sources to show their symmetry with contemporary doctrine and dispute Imāmīs and Ismāʿīlīs who rejected the Fāṭimid Imām's legitimacy. The believers were taught the hidden sense of the true Torah, a source to which their leaders alone had access. They were taught that ancient rites and rituals paralleled rituals that they had themselves participated in such as the oath of allegiance.

In particular, it was Torah lore on lesser figures such as Judah and Tamar that was particularly useful for missionaries such as Jaʿfar. Such lengthy narratives that were not well known to medieval Muslims provided material to identify parallels with the Fāṭimid present or recent past that might appear problematic. Such unknown Torah tales provided a fresh and varied symbolic palette for missionaries to paint their imaginal world in the polemic hues that suited the moment.

Epilogue

After the End of Days—From Imminent to Immanent Apocalypticism

During the first century after the rise of Ismāʿīlism, Ismāʿīlī taʾwīl was produced by a sectarian socio-political movement. Similar to other genres of esoterica produced in sectarian milieus, these teachings call on their audience to inhabit an ideational "second world." Taʾwīl's repetition of secret symbols, schema, and "logics" precipitated a break from the old cognitive world, bound its community of believers together, and provided content to the claim that they alone enjoyed access to special, saving knowledge. This is reflected in the language of the sources. The acolyte's conversion to the movement is described as his or her "birth"; he is then spiritually "circumcised" and "suckled" on special knowledge. Like similar esoteric, sectarian genres such as *Pesher* by the communities at Qumran, the symbolic world which taʾwīl evoked dramatically differed from that of those outside the movement.

But, unlike the sectarians at Qumran, the Ismāʿīlī daʿwa was not just a sect; the daʿwa served a vital role in the founding of an empire. Similar historical constellations show that the path that the Fāṭimid Imāms and missionaries chose was far from inevitable.

Like the rise of the Fāṭimids, so too the ʿAbbāsid revolution began with Shīʿite missionaries in the hinterlands proselytizing for a redeemer from a descendent of ʿAlī who would usher in the End of Days. But after assuming power the ʿAbbāsid caliphs assassinated the top missionaries, viewing them as a potential threat to their legitimacy. The ʿAbbāsids changed the source of their legitimacy and lineage and replaced chiliasm with patronage of largely Sunnī ʿulamāʾ.[1] Under Shāh Ismāʿīl the Safavids also arose on the backs of a messianic, millenarian movement that declared their leader as a divinely guided Imām before later retreating to a Shīʿite legalist position.[2] Like the Safavids the Ottomans, too, arose based in part on realizing messianic expectations. Yavus Sultan Selīm (r. 1512–20) was believed to be *muʾayyad min Allāh* (aided by God) and the Ṣāḥib qirān (master of the conjunction). Selīm's military accomplishments, as well as the early reforms initiated by Sülaymān, were framed within an apocalyptic setting. But they, too, would retreat to a traditional Sunnī posture in the latter half of his rule.[3]

Apocalypticism and imperialism were productively joined in the case of Christianity and the Roman Empire of late antiquity.[4] Finding a rhetoric that suited both church and empire seems to have taken time, for long after Constantine, Christian authors such as Andrew of Caesarea (thrived mid-sixth century) continued to emphasize the impermanence of this world and the inevitable downfall of all earthly rulers—doctrines unsuitable for an imperial religion.[5] Thus when Kosmas Indikopleustes (thrived sixth century) privileged the role of the Roman Empire in Christ's Second Coming, this represented a major shift in what was possible for a Christian theologian to claim. In *The Christian Topography,* Kosmas argued that through the empire, the Gospel was now reaching the whole world. The Second Coming was still expected, and, according to Kosmas, the empire had a crucial role to play. He held that the Roman Empire echoed the Kingdom of Heaven on earth: Constantinople was the New Jerusalem, and the Christian calendar, public liturgy, cult of saints, and divine *epiphaneiai* (signs of the divine appearance) all served to assimilate the heavenly and earthly kingdoms.[6]

From these historical examples, it is apparent that after the founding of the empire, there were a number of courses that the Fāṭimids could pursue. They could, like the ʿAbbāsids or Ottomans, dramatically turn from the millenarian ethos and missionaries that brought them to power and tack toward the ʿulamāʾ. Or, like the Byzantines, they could adapt their followers' apocalyptic rhetoric to state ceremony and ritual, bringing it squarely into public life. The Fāṭimids charted a different path. They supported the daʿwa, and the Imām was its symbolic head; he continued to play a crucial symbolic role as the infallible link to God who had access to the law's inner sense. However, this role as Imām was distinct from his role as head of state. Thus after the founding and spread of the Fāṭimid state, the Imām assumed two roles. He was the leader of an empire; and he was the source of salvation and head of the daʿwa of the true believers.

This issue of the relationship between daʿwa and dawla, between mission and state, was crucial for the missionaries. Most historians have described the founding of the state as a victory for the daʿwa and have suggested that the Imāms' two roles as head of state and mission were complementary. I have argued against this view. Patricia Crone has pointed out that Ismāʿīlī doctrine required a symbolic Imām, but had no real need for a state.[7] I would take this claim one step further: From the perspective of the Ismāʿīlī missionaries and their concern for the mission, the rise of the state provided a challenge. The Fāṭimid Imām may have been both the head of state and daʿwa, but there is evidence that these two roles frequently chafed. As "commander of the faithful," the Fāṭimid Imāms presented an irenic Shīʿite position that drew on their genealogical legitimacy as descendants of the family of the Prophet. Unlike the Safavids, who would compel the populations under their rule to implement their interpretation of Islam, there seems to have been little missionizing in the lands under Fāṭimid control. This was not, as has often been repeated, because of the "tolerance" of the Fāṭimid Imām toward religious difference ("tolerance," at least as it is understood in the Enlightenment tradition of John Locke, has, as the medieval Iberianist Robert Burns said, as much place in the Middle Ages as a Toyota Corolla).[8] As Najam Haider has suggested, this absence of missionizing close to the locale of the Imām more likely resulted from the Fāṭimids' awareness that the supernatural capacities of the Imām reported by the missionaries could not easily survive the scrutiny of a great many converts near the capital.[9] The attempted revolt of the leading missionary Abū ʿAbd Allāh al-Shīʿī against the first Fāṭimid Imām demonstrated that the believers' close proximity to the Imām served neither state nor daʿwa. Putting some distance between Imām as savoir and Imām as emperor served both mission and state well. From the perspective of the missionaries, the political victory of the Fāṭimids was a threat to the millenarian, revolutionary ethos that gave rise to the mission in the first place. Historians have tended to present the role of Ismāʿīlism as a tool for the state, but, from the vantage point of the missionaries, the observe is more likely the case: the state was a tool for the salvation of the believers.

The solution of the missionaries to this doctrinal problem was to shift from an imminent, militant, apocalypticism to what John Hall refers to as an apocalypticism of an immanent, "other worldly" type.[10] The sense that the world would end in the near future was replaced by a focus on gaining access to the divine, secret knowledge that led the believer to salvation. When the Fāṭimids provided interpretations of the Torah, Gospels, and practices of the Jews and Christians, they fulfilled the expectation that at the End of Days, the secrets behind all religions would be revealed—a theme in early Ismāʿīlī sources such as the *Kitāb al-kashf*.[11] Through the sequestering and unveiling of this secret knowledge, the Fāṭimid missionaries maintained a sense of the apocalyptic. Such an approach sustained the ethos of distinctiveness that was crucial to maintaining the mission, but also would not upset the state. This interpretation could be called "apocalyptic interpretation."

This is not to say that the Fāṭimid missionaries who composed taʾwīl were divorced from politics. But it was politics of the ecclesiastic type intended to rebut the leaders of non-Fāṭimid Ismāʿīlī dioceses. The missionaries could have merely pointed to the unfortunate end of the mission of Rayy and the execution of Abū Ḥātim al-Rāzī, or the antinomian debacle in Baḥrayn to argue their case. But they did so, instead, through taʾwīl of stories of the ancient prophets. Throughout taʾwīl, the hidden sense of the stories, signs, and scriptures of the ancient prophets reinforced the theme that recognition of the daʿwa on behalf of the true Imāms represented reality in its purest form, and was crucial for salvation. By internalizing the themes and logics that underlie these sources, the believer came to recognize this divine scheme, and acknowledging his or her role as a believer was a part of it.

At the end of the *Sarāʾir*, Jaʿfar ibn Manṣūr al-Yaman addresses the Shīʿites directly.

> Do you and we not agree that there must be a pure, impeccable Imām who knows what humankind needs? Who gathers the commandments, erects His religion, guards the people of truth? Who is known by His name, and His genealogy in every age and time? Who is from the family of the Messenger, who does not need humanity, but whom humanity needs in the commands of their religion and their world, in what is allowed for them and prohibited to them, and the ordinances and judgments of them, and to maintain justice among them, just as was done by the prophets, legatees, and Imāms who have passed in the bygone centuries which we have mentioned?[12]

Jaʿfar goes on to compare Shīʾite sects such as the Nuṣayrīs and Imāmīs with Christians and Jews who failed to recognize the Imām of the age. For the missionaries, it was their Imām's salvific role for the believers with which they were ultimately concerned. Subsequent history, and the vibrancy of a great many Ismāʿīlī communities after the end of the Fāṭimid caliphate in 1171, show that the daʿwa, and the Imām as symbolic head, would prove more durable than the state over the long term.

In his classic article on literary and religious rhetoric, Wolfhart Heinrichs identifies four figures that represent the most influential types of intellectual training that had developed by the fourth/tenth century: the faqīh (jurist and religious scholar), adīb (littérateur), ḥakīm (philosopher-scientist), and faqīr (mystic).[13] I claim that the dāʿī, the missionary on behalf of a rightly guided Imām, represents a fifth type, one linked variously to esotericism, allegory, messianism, and social action. Such missionaries, and the esoteric knowledge that they disseminated, have been extremely durable fixtures in Islamic history. They contributed to the ʿAbbāsid, Fāṭimid, and Safavid revolutions and to the success of a great many religious groups, the Nuṣayrīs, Imāmīs, Ismāʿīlīs, Nuqtavīs, Nurbakshīs, and Ḥurūfīs, to name a few.[14] It is understandable that in presenting Islam's intellectual heritage, modern scholars have gravitated to the ʿulamāʾ, the quietist scholars of Islam. We are more like them. But there is considerable evidence that politically active dāʿīs and the esoteric knowledge they disseminated have made a significant impact on the history of Islam.

APPENDIX

Abbreviated Titles of Dated Sources Used in Chapter 3, "Rearing"

Pre-Fāṭimid Sources

ʿĀlim = pseudo-Jaʿfar ibn Manṣūr al-Yaman, *Kitāb al-ʿālim wal-ghulām. The Master and the Disciple: An Early Islamic Spiritual Dialogue.* Edited and translated by James Morris. London: I. B. Tauris, 2001.

Kashf = Pseudo-Jaʿfar ibn Manṣūr al-Yaman, *Kitāb al-kashf*, Edited by Mustafa Ghalib. Beirut: Dār al-Andalus, 1404/1984.

Rushd = Ibn Ḥawshab, *Kitāb al-rushd wal-hidāya.* Edited by Kāmil Ḥusayn. In *Collectanea,* edited by Wladimir Ivanow. Vol. 1. Ismaili Society Series A, no. 2. Leiden: Published for the Ismaili Society by E.J. Brill, 1948.

Taʾwīl al-ḥurūf I = *Kitāb risālat taʾwīl al-ḥurūf al-muʿjama.* "Fragments relatifs à la doctrine des Ismaélis." Edited by S. Guyard. *Notices et Extraits* 22 (1874): 177–428.

Fāṭimid Sources

Abū ʿĪsā al-Murshid = "The Earliest Cosmological Doctrines of Ismāʿīlism." In *Studies in Early Ismāʿīlism,* ed. S. M. Stern, 3–29. Jerusalem: Magnes Press, Hebrew University, 1983.

Asās = al-Qāḍī al-Nuʿmān, *Kitāb asās al-Taʾwīl.* Beirut: Manshūrāt dār al-thiqāfa, 1960.

Fatarāt = Jaʿfar ibn Manṣūr al-Yaman. David Hollenberg, "Pre-Kirmānian Fāṭimid doctrine: A Critical Edition and Translation of the Prologue of the Kitāb al-fatarāt wal-qirānāt. *Le Muséon* 122 (2009): 155–202

Kitāb al-farāʾid= Jaʿfar b. Manṣūr al-Yaman, *Kitāb al-farāʾid wa-ḥudūd al-dīn.* London: Institute of Ismaili Studies manuscript collection, Ms. 928.

Mudhhiba = Pseudo-al-Qāḍī al-Nuʿmān, *al-Risāla al-mudhhiba.* Edited by Ārif Tāmir. Beirut: Dār al-masīra, 1988.

Nisāʾ= Jaʿfar b. Manṣūr al-Yaman, *Taʾwīl sūrat al-nisāʾ.* London: Institute of Ismaili Studies manuscript collection, Ms. 1103.

Ridāʿ = Jaʿfar b. Manṣūr al-Yaman, *Kitāb al-riḍāʿ fī al-bāṭin.* London: Institute of Ismaili Studies manuscript collection, Ms. 167.

Sarāʾir = Jaʿfar ibn Manṣūr al-Yaman, *Sarāʾir wa-asrār al-nuṭaqāʾ.* Edited by Mustafā Ghālib. Beirut: Dār al-Andalus, 1984.

Shawāhid = Jaʿfar b. Manṣūr al-Yaman, *al-Shawāhid wal-bayān fī ithbāt maqām amīr al-muʾminīn wal-aʾimma*. London: Institute of Ismaili Studies manuscript collection, Ms. 734.

Taʾwīl al-ḥurūf II = Jaʿfar ibn Manṣūr al-Yaman, *Risālat taʾwīl ḥurūf al-muʿjam*. London: Institute of Ismaili Studies manuscript collection, Ms. 1209.

Zakāt = Jaʿfar ibn Manṣūr al-Yaman, *Kitāb taʾwīl al-zakāt;* published under the title *Al-Riḍā fī al-bāṭin taʾwīl al-zakāt al-maʿrifa fī tafsīr al-Qurʾān wal-tanbīh ʿalā al-taʾwīl*. Edited by Ḥusām Khaddūr. Salamīya, Syria: Dār al-ghadīr, 2008.

Non-Fāṭimid Sources

Iftikhār =Abū Yaʿqūb al-Sijistānī, *Kitāb al-Iftikhār*. Edited by Ismail K. Poonawala. Bayrūt: Dār al-Gharb al-Islāmī, 2000.

Iṣlāḥ = Abū Ḥātim al-Rāzī, *Kitāb al-Iṣlāḥ*. Edited by Aḥmad ibn Ḥamdān, Mahdī Muḥaqqiq, Shin Nomoto, Ḥasan Mīnūchihr, and Jalāl al-Dīn Mujtabavī. Tihrān: Mu'assasah-'i Muṭāla'āt-i Islāmī, Dānishgāh-i Tihrān, 1998.

Ithbāt = Abū Yaʿqūb al-Sijistānī, *Kitāb Ithbāt al-nubūʾāt*. Edited by ʿĀrif Tāmir. Beirut: al-Maṭbaʿah al-Kāthūlīkīyah, 1966.

Maḥṣūl = al-Nasafī, as excerpted in Ḥamīd al-Dīn Aḥmad ibn ʿAbd Allāh Kirmānī, *Kitāb al-Riyāḍ fī al-ḥukm bayna al-sādayn ṣāḥibāy al-iṣlāḥ wa-al-nuṣra*. Edited by ʿĀrif Tāmir. Bayrūt: Dār al-Thaqāfah, 1960.

Yanābiʿ = Abū Yaʿqūb al-Sijistānī, *Kitāb al-yanābiʿ. The Wellsprings of Wisdom: A Study of Abū Yaʿqūb Al-Sijistānī's Kitāb Al-Yanābīʿ; Including a Complete English Translation with Commentary and Notes on the Arabic Text*. Edited and translated by Paul E. Walker. Salt Lake City: University of Utah Press, 1994.

NOTES

Preface

1. The most important analyses are that of Bar-Asher, "Outlines"; Poonawala, "Ismāʿīlī *ta'wīl,*" 199–205; and EI[2], s.v. "ta'wīl" (Ismail Poonawala). For an important discussion of Ṭayyibi taʾwīl, see Traboulsi, "The Ṭayyibī Ismāʿīlīs," 75–193. Steigerwald briefly describes the history of Ismāʿīlī taʾwīl from its origins to the present. Her section on early Ismāʿīlī taʾwīl is to be used with caution, but her discussion of Alamūt, Ginānic, and modern exegesis are all useful. Steigerwald, "Ismāʿīlī taʾwīl," 386–400. For a broader discussion of the use of taʾwīl in the Islamicate history of religions, see Wasserstrom, *Between Muslim and Jew,* 136–66.

2. *Taʾwīl sūrat al-nisāʾ,* IIS Ms. 1103, 23 (of the signatures).

3. For a discussion of the sociology of secrecy and concealment among sectarians, and the seminal role of the sociologist Georg Simmel in this history, see Stroumsa, *Secrecy and Concealment,* xiii–xxiv.

4. "Imaginal" is a term applied by Henry Corbin to describe the immaterial forms accessible to the imaginative faculty (*khayāl*), as opposed to the sensory and rational world. Corbin, *Mundus Imaginalis,* 1–2.

5. Hollenberg, *Interpretation after the End of Days,* 58–59.

6. Wilson, *The Social Dimensions of Sectarianism,* 46–68. Stark and Bainbridge, *The Future of Religion,* 134–37.

7. Bader, "When Prophecy Passes Unnoticed," 126–28. Bader notes that sects that maintain "socially costly" commitments are more likely to successfully maintain themselves when prophecy fails.

8. Karamustafa, *God's Unruly Friends.*

9. Jokiranta, *Social Identity and Sectarianism;* Pyysiäinen, "Holy Book—a Treasury of the Incomprehensible."

10. Luhrmann, *When God Talks Back,* 372–75.

11. Cassirer, *The Philosophy of Symbolic Forms.*

12. Cassirer, *The Philosophy of Symbolic Forms,* 217.

13. Georg Simmel conceived of the esoteric as representing "a second world." Simmel, *The Sociology,* 330. Cited by Thomas, *The "Mysteries,"* 39.

CHAPTER 1
Competing Islands of Salvation

1. Daftary, *The Ismailis*, 137.

2. Brett, *The Rise of the Fatimids*, 218.

3. Sanders, *Ritual, Politics, and the City*, 50–52.

4. Bierman, *Writing Signs*, 60–99.

5. It is perhaps with the climactic political valence of revolution in mind that al-Mujāhid understands thunder in the Qur'ān as alluding to the *daʿwat al-ḥaqq*. Mujāhid ibn Jabr, *Tafsīr Mujāhid*, 492.

6. Mālik ibn Anas, *al-Muwaṭṭā'*, 1:212.

7. *Tafsīr Mujāhid*, 2:492.

8. One source preserves a sense of the word that fell out of usage in which *daʿwa* connotes a "pact" or "confederacy" between tribes. Al-Munqarī, *Waqaʿat Ṣiffīn*, 529.

9. Muḥammad ibn Iṣḥāq's (d.151/767) history, *al-Mubtadaʿ al-mabʿath wal-maghāzī*, survives in later recensions. See *Sīrat Ibn Isḥāq al-musammā bi-Kitāb al-mubtada'*, 162.

10. Mālik ibn Anas, *al-Mudawwana*, 179. In the contemporary Islamic world, daʿwa also connotes calling on non-Muslims to convert to Islam, although in a completely demilitarized sense.

11. Ḍirār ibn ʿAmr, *Kitāb al-taḥrīsh*, 90–91.

12. Ḍirār ibn ʿAmr, *Kitāb al-taḥrīsh*, 90–91.

13. This view is found in the early transmitter Muḥammad ibn Sirīn, *Kitāb Tafsīr al-aḥlām*, 470.

14. Madelung, *Der Imām al-Qāsim ibn Ibrahim*, 144, 188. Crone, *God's Rule*, 104. For the history of the Ismāʿīlī-Zaydī conflict in Yemen during the third/ninth and fourth/tenth centuries, see Gochenour, "The Penetration of Zaydi Islam," 70–71.

15. Halm, *The Empire of the Mahdī*, 159 citing Nuʿaym ibn Ḥammād, *al-Fitan*.

16. The *Bayānīya*, the followers of Bayān ibn Samʿān (executed 737), are known as the first group to introduce both the notion of continued prophecy and inspired, symbolic interpretation into Shīʿism. Tucker, *Mahdis and Millenarians*, 34–51.

17. Bayhom-Daou, "The Second-Century Šīʿite Ġulāt"; Bayhom-Daou "The Imam's Knowledge." Anthony, *The Caliph and the Heretic*, 79, 149–51.

18. Bayhom-Daou, "The Second-Century Šīʿite *Ġulāt*," 18.

19. Bayhom-Daou, "The Second-Century Šīʿite *Ġulāt*," 18–19.

20. Hodgson, "How Did the Early Shīʿa Become Sectarian?," 1–13.

21. Wilson, *The Social Dimensions of Sectarianism*. Chris Bader notes that sects that maintain "socially costly" commitments are more likely to be successful. Bader, "When Prophecy Passes Unnoticed," 126–28.

22. Stark and Bainbridge, *The Future of Religion*, 124.

23. Melchert, *The Formation*, xiv–xv.

24. El-Shamsy, "The Social Construction of Orthodoxy."

25. Stewart, *Islamic Legal Orthodoxy*, 67.

26. al-Naysābūrī, *al-Risāla al-mūjaza*, 7 (Arabic Text).

27. On the process through which the Ismāʿīlīs were anathematized, see Daftary, *The Assassin Legends*, 6–7.

28. Barth, *Ethnic Groups and Boundaries*, 10–11.

29. Faivre, "Renaissance Hermeticism," 119–20.

30. EI^2, s.v. "al-Mukhtar" (Gerard Hawting). In some sources al-Mukhtār claimed the role of prophet or awaited Mahdī (redeemer) for himself. Ibn Qutayba, *Ta'wīl mukhtalif al-hadith,* 1:73.

31. Corbin, *The History of Islamic Philosophy,* 191. See also Daftary, *Ismailis in Medieval Muslim Societies,* 51–52.

32. Daftary, *The Ismāʿīlīs,* 93.

33. Halm, *The Empire of the Mahdī,* 16.

34. Halm, *The Empire of the Mahdī,* 34.

35. Halm, *The Empire of the Mahdī,* 6.

36. Halm, *The Empire of the Mahdī,* 23. The ultimate source for this is likely Ibn Rizām. A forgery falsely imputed to the Ismāʿīlis by their enemies, "Book of Highest Initiation," starts with the advice to a missionary targeting Shīʿites. While the work mixes authentic knowledge of Ismāʿīlism with fiction, Stern and Halm have argued that the claim that the missionaries focused on Twelver towns is likely to have been accurate.

37. For the Samanid converts, see Crone and Treadwell, "A New Text," 52–58. Halm, *The Empire of the Mahdī,* 35.

38. Madelung, "The Religions Policy," 97–98.

39. Ismāʿīlī sources such as Sīrat Ibn Ḥawshab present early converts as spiritually distraught young men. See al-Nuʿmān's *Risālat Iftitāḥ al-daʿwa,* 33–53.

40. Halm, *The Empire of the Mahdī,* 31.

41. Crone and Treadwell, "A New Text," 52–58.

42. Madelung and Walker, "The *Kitāb al-rusūm,*" 104.

43. Halm, *The Empire of the Mahdī,* 47.

44. Halm, *The Empire of the Mahdī,* 48.

45. Halm, *The Empire of the Mahdī,* 27.

46. The mix of the divinely inspired book and seditious movements is not new to Islamic North Africa. The Banū Māwaṭant tribe claimed a prophet to whom was revealed God's speech in their tribal language in the eighth century. Halm, *The Empire of the Mahdī,* 172.

47. Halm, *The Empire of the Mahdī,* 72, citing al-Ṭabarī, *Taʾrīkh,* 3:2224, and al-Naysabūrī, *Istitār,* 99.

48. Halm, "The Isma'ili Oath of Allegiance," 98.

49. al-Maqrīzī, *Khiṭaṭ,* 1:391.

50. Toorawa, *Ibn Abī Ṭāhir Ṭayfūr,* 9–10.

51. Ibn al-Haytham reported that he also borrowed other books on Imāmī jurisprudence. Madelung and Walker, *The Advent of the Fatimids,* 115, 152.

52. Goody, *The Logic of Writing,* 17.

53. Bayhom-Daou, "Hishām ibn al-Ḥākim"; Bayhom-Daou, "The Imam's Knowledge," 197.

54. Halm, *The Empire of the Mahdī,* 48–49.

55. Madelung, "Das Imamat," 46–47.

56. Madelung, "Das Imamat," 45. The description of the Ismāʿīlīs given by Ibn Rizām (who was, in all likelihood, himself a former Ismāʿīlī) was first related by the sharīf Akhū Muḥsin from Kufa in the early fourth/tenth century. It is this "Akhū Muḥsin

from Ibn Rizām" report that is repeated in many later chronicles. For full references, see Halm, *The Empire of the Mahdī,* 423, 425.

57. The pair Kūnī and Qadar are also referred to as the aṣlān ("two roots") and al-Sābiq and al-Tālī (the preceder and the follower). Halm, *Kosmologie,* 116–17.

58. These three hypostases are identified with the three angels Gabriel, Michael, and Serafel. Halm, *Kosmologie,* 116. Jaʿfar ibn Manṣūr al-Yaman, *Sarāʾir,* 25-26.

59. Stern, "The Earliest Cosmological Doctrines of Ismāʿīlism." For the classical late antique Gnostics, the "acts of the drama" are described by Layton, *The Gnostic Scriptures,* 13–15. Steven Wasserstrom attributes Henri Corbin as having coined the phrase "the prologue in heaven" for this phenomenon. Wasserstrom, "The Moving Finger Writes," 17.

60. Halm connects the apportioning of the seven letters to the speaker-prophets in the *Kitāb al-kashf* to the Kūnī-Qadar myth nested in Abū ʿĪsā's treatise. Halm, "The Cosmology of the Pre-Fatimid Ismāʿīliyya," 78–79.

61. In some sources the term *mutimm* was applied to all the Imāms following the nāṭiq. Hamdānī, "Evolution of the Organisational Structure," 101.

62. In the Kitāb al-fatarāt, Adam's waṣī is identified as Seth (rather than Abel), and Moses's waṣī is Joshua (rather than Aaron). Lists of the names of the heptads of Imāms derived from the Bible or other Christian or Jewish sources, and those of the "adversaries" of each nāṭiq, are detailed in later sources, but it is impossible to know whether such details were schematized prior to the Fāṭimid period; see Halm, Kosmologie, 32–36. In his analysis of the lists of biblical figures in Imāmī fourth/tenth century Shīʿite sources, Uri Rubin has suggested that the details of the names of the lesser-known biblical prophets and their wives may have entered the Shīʿite tradition through *The Book of Jubilees.* Rubin, "Prophets and Progenitors," 56–57.

63. Janowitz et al., "Cults," 219. Melton, "Perspective."

64. Halm, *The Empire of the Mahdī,* 54.

65. Halm, *The Empire of the Mahdī,* 53 citing al-Nuʿmān, *Iftitāḥ,* 46.

66. Halm, *Empire of the Mahdī,* 56.

67. Halm, *The Empire of the Mahdī,* 106, 123.

68. McAuliffe, *The Encyclopedia of the Quran,* s.v. "Apocalypse."

69. That the missionaries used such images to propagate the mission can be inferred by their allegoresis in later sources. See, for example, a ta'wīl of the two blows of the trumpet in Jaʿfar ibn Manṣūr al-Yaman, *Sarāʾir,* 25.

70. Madelung, "Apocalyptic Prophecies."

71. Festinger, *When Prophecy Fails,* 3–32.

72. Bader, "When Prophecy Passes Unnoticed," 126–28.

73. This section of the account departs from Halm, *The Empire of the Mahdī,* and follows the historical reconstruction by Madelung in EI^2, s.v. "Qarmaṭi."

74. Crone and Treadwell, "A New Text," 61.

75. Crone and Treadwell, "A New Text," 52.

76. Halm, *Kosmologie,* 75–80.

77. Madelung and Walker, "The *Kitāb al-rusūm wal-izdiwāj,*" 104–8.

78. The best discussion of the Ismāʿīlī dāʿī al-Nasafī's impact on the Samanid court is Treadwell, "The Political History of the Samanid State," 186–210.

79. Authors whose work is not extant include Abū Saʿīd al-Shaʿrānī (in Iraq), Khalaf and Ghiyāth (in Northern Iran), al-Ḥusayn al-Marwazī (in Khurāsān), and Ibn Ḥammād (in Mosul); see Walker, *Abū Yaʿqūb al-Sijistānī*, 16–17. ʿAbd al-Jabbār mentioned that the missionaries Abū l-Qāsim ʿĪsā ibn Mūsā and the brothers Abū Muslim and Abū Barak ibn Ḥammād of Mosul preserved the legacy of ʿAbdān. Madelung writes that they ascribed their works to him and applied a philosophical approach to doctrine; see Madelung, "Das Imamat," 108. Madelung and Walker have recently published a text form the ʿAbdān circle. Madelung and Walker, "The *Kitāb al-rusūm*," 103–4.

80. Crone and Treadwell, "A New Text," 37–67. Abū Ḥātim al-Rāzī's assertive tone in *al-Iṣlāḥ* leads me to suspect that he considered himself the khalīfa of his period.

81. Al-Sijistānī wrote that the intellectual (*ʿaqlī*) laws would never be abrogated, but that the conventional (*waḍʿī*) laws would be abrogated by the people little by little, not by the Qāʾim. When the Qāʾim returned, there would be no laws left to abrogate. Madelung, "Das Imamat," 108.

82. Walker, *Early Philosophical Shīʿism*, 21–24.

83. Madelung, "Das Imamat," 102–12.

84. Halm, *The Empire of the Mahdī*, 147–48.

85. Halm, *The Empire of the Mahdī*, 159.

86. Stern, "Cairo as the Centre of the Ismāʿīlī movement," 235.

87. Halm, *The Empire of the Mahdī*, 162.

88. Madelung, "Das Imamat," 87–102.

89. Madelung, "A treatise on the Imamate," 71–77.

90. Halm, *The Fāṭimids and their Traditions*, 47–48.

91. Bierman, *Writing Signs*; Sanders, *Ritual, Politics, and the City.*

92. Halm, *The Fāṭimids and their Traditions*, 26–28.

93. Madelung, "A treatise on the Imamate," 70.

94. Poonawala, "Al-Qāḍī al-Nuʿmān and Ismāʿīlī jurisprudence," 121; 128. Madelung, "The Sources of Ismaili Law," 29–40.

95. Sanders, *Ritual, Politics, and the City*, 50-52.

96. Bierman, *Writing Signs*, 62.

97. Blair, "Floriated Kufic and the Fatimids," 108–13.

98. Bloom, *Arts of the City Victorious*, 87.

99. Sanders, *Ritual, Politics, and the City*, 91.

100. Merchant, "'And the Word of your Lords,'" 106.

101. Michael Bates, unpublished notes on Fāṭimid coinage shared with author July 15, 2001.

102. Merchant, "'And the Word of your Lords,'" 112; 116.

103. Ibid., 117–18.

104. Madelung, "Das Imamat," 87-101.

105. al-Maqrīzī, *Ittiʿāẓ al-ḥunafāʾ*, 133.

106. Madelung, "The Religious Policy," 101.

107. Madelung, "A treatise on the Imamate," 77.

108. Madelung, "The Religious policy of the Fatimids," 101–2.

109. Walker, *Ḥamīd al-Dīn al-Kirmānī*, 16–24.

110. Madelung, "Das Imamat," 120–27.

111. Madelung, "Das Imamat," 118–19.

112. Mark R. Cohen, *Jewish Self-Government*, 55.

113. Haider, *Shīʿī Islam*, 119.

114. Shafique Virani traces the political and communal legitimacy of the Nizārī Imāmate to between the thirteenth and fifteenth centuries. Virani, *The Ismāʿīlīs in the Middle Ages.*

115. Haider, *Shīʿī Islam*, 122; Daftary, *The Ismailis*, 453, 467; Virani, *The Ismailis in the Middle Ages*, 139–48.

116. For a celebratory but informative presentation of the Aga Khans in the contemporary period, see Poor, *Authority without Territory.*

117. Qutbuddin, "History of the Da'udi Bohra Tayyibis," 297–330.

118. Abbas Hamdani and Ismaili Poonawala, "A Manifesto on Behalf of the Bohra Community Signed by Two Internationally Recognized Bohra Scholars," last modified January 31, 2014. http://dawoodi-bohras.com/news/2045/107/A-Manifesto-on-behalf-of-the-Dawoodi-Bohra-Community/d.pdb_detail_article_comment/.

CHAPTER 2
Ismāʿīlī Taʾwīl and Daʿwa Literature

1. Fudge, *Qurʾānic Hermeneutics*, 6–7, 12–24. The literature on tafsīr as a genre is extensive. See, most recently, Bauer, *Aims, Methods, and Contexts of Qur'anic Exegesis.* In her contribution to the volume, Bauer surveys the introductions to nine classical tafsīrs to describe the authors' stated aims for writing tafsīr. She finds that the exegetes do not state their aims for the importance of the genre, and at least one author, Fakhr al-Dīn al-Rāzī, relegates it to a status below that of genres in the fields of *uṣūl* (principles). Bauer, "Justifying the Genre," 39–66.

2. Saleh, *The Formation of the Classical Tafsīr Tradition*, 8–15.

3. de Blois, *Arabic, Persian and Gujarati Manuscripts*, xxx.

4. al-Suyūṭī, *Kitāb al-itqān*, 115–17.

5. al-Ṭabarī, *Jāmiʿ al-bayān ʿan ta'wīl al-Qurʾān;* al-Maturīdī, *Taʾwīlat ahl al-sunna*; Maḥmūd ibn Ḥamza al-Kirmānī, *Gharāʾib al-tafsīr wa-ʿajāʾib al-taʾwīl.*

6. EI^{2}, s.v. "ta'wīl" (Ismail K. Poonawala). Another type of allegorical interpretation in this period was that of al-Tustarī (d. 896), who composed mystical, allegorical Qur'ān commentaries that claimed to relate the text's *bāṭin* or hidden sense. Thus for al-Tustarī taʾwīl served to illuminate the individual's self and achieve an awareness of his heart. Böwering, *The Mystical Vision of Existence*, 146–47.

7. Kinberg, *A Lexicon of al-Farrāʾ's* Terminology, 40–43 (Arabic text).

8. The exponents of another theological school in the fourth/tenth century, the Central Asian Māturīdīs, applied ta'wīl only to those verses of the Qurʾān that were believed to be *mutashābih* ("multivalent" according to the Māturīdī understanding). Götz, "Māturīdī and His *Kitāb ta'wīlāt al-Qur'ān*," 181–214.

9. Abrahamov, *Anthropomorphism and Interpretation of the Qur'ān*, 4–5.

10. For examples, see al-Suyūṭī, *al-Itqān*, 115–17.

11. Al-Zamakhsharī, *al-Kashshāf*, 1:388.

12. al-Qummī, *Tafsīr al-Qummī*, 96.

13. Tucker, *Mahdis and Millenarians*, 37.

14. Tucker, "Rebels and Gnostics," 40. Wasserstrom, "The Moving Finger Writes," 1–29.

15. An example of an argument to establish the provenance and date of early Shīʿite heresies is Asatryan, "Heresy and Rationalism in Early Islam."

16. Bar-Asher, *Scripture and Exegesis*, 91.

17. Bar-Asher, *Scripture and Exegesis*, 96.

18. Bar-Asher, *Scripture and Exegesis*, 73–86.

19. Bar-Asher, *Scripture and Exegesis*, 101–24.

20. For a list of these scholars' many publications on Ismāʿīlī doctrine, see Daftary, *Ismaili Literature: A Bibliography.*

21. Poonawala, "Ismāʿīlī *ta'wīl* of the Qur'ān."

22. al-Sijistānī, *Kitāb al-Maqālīd*, 236–44.

23. al-Fekki, *Al-Taʾwīl*, 69–70.

24. Ebstein, *Mysticism and Philosophy in Al-Andalus*, 231–38.

25. Bar-Asher, "Outlines."

26. Daniel De Smet makes this point in his important recent article on prudent dissimulation and the esoteric interpretation of fasting under al-Ḥākim. De Smet, "La taqiyya et le jeûne du Ramadan," 357–86.

27. al-Nuʿmān, *Kitāb asās al-ta'wīl*, 69.

28. Halm, *Empire*, 375.

29. Corbin, *The History of Islamic Philosophy*, 191.

30. Hollenberg, "Neoplatonism in Pre-Kirmānīan Fāṭimid Doctrine," 159–202.

31. Madelung, "Das Imamat," 87–102.

32. Hamdani and de Blois, "A Re-examination."

33. Stern, "The Earliest Cosmological Doctrines of Ismāʿīlism"; Halm, "The Cosmology of the Pre-Fatimid Ismāʿīliyya," 78–79.

34. Paul Walker, personal communication, November 2008.

35. Hollenberg, "Interpretation after the End of Days," 51–66.

36. Poonawala's *Biobibliography* is informed by two medieval chrestomathies compiled in Yemen, al-Ḥārithī's (d. 584/1188) *Majmūʿ al-tarbiya* and al-Bharūchī's (d. 939/1533) *Kitāb al-Azhār*. Ismāʿīl ibn ʿAbd al-Rasūl al-Majdūʿ's *Fihrist*, a work compiled in the eighteenth century, was the basis for Ivanow's *A Guide to Ismaili Literature* (1923). Poonawala, *Biobibliography*, xi.

37. Daftary, *Ismaili Literature*, 122.

38. Strothman, *Kitāb al-kashf.*

39. Jaʿfar ibn Manṣūr al-Yaman, *Kitāb al-Kashf.*

40. Poonawala, *Biobibliography*, 73.

41. Guyard, "Fragments relatifs á la doctrine des ismaélis."

42. Cortese, *Arabic Ismaili Manuscripts*, 168.

43. de Blois, *Arabic, Persian and Gujarati Manuscripts*, 6–7.

44. Morris, *The Master and the Disciple*, 24–25.

45. Ḥusayn, *Collectanea of the Ismaili Society.*

46. The word *ḥudūd* can connote punishments specified by God in the Qurʾān or the ranks of the daʿwa religious hierarchy. I suspect it is a pun. I thank Ismail K. Poonawala for pointing this out. He prefers the latter translation. Ismail K. Poonawala, personal communication, January 2, 2015.

47. Cortese, *Arabic Ismaili Manuscripts,* 64–65.

48. Ibid., 65.

49. Ibid., 65.

50. Gacek, *Catalogue of Arabic Manuscripts,* vol. 1, 42.

51. Poonawala, *Biobibliography,* 73.

52. Madelung, "Das Imamat," 101–2.

53. Cortese, *Arabic Ismaili Manuscripts,* 170. Gacek, *Catalogue of Arabic Manuscripts,* 1:118.

54. Poonawala, *Biobiobliography,* 72.

55. Jaʿfar ibn Manṣūr al-Yaman, *al-Riḍāʿ fī al-bāṭin,* ed. Hussām Khaddūr.

56. Cortese, *Arabic Ismaili Manuscripts,* 186.

57. Gacek, *Catalogue of Arabic Manuscripts,* 1:129.

58. Cortese, *Arabic Ismaili Manuscripts,* 185.

59. Cortese, *Arabic Ismaili Manuscripts,* 69.

60. Gacek, *Catalogue of Arabic Manuscripts,* 1:48.

61. Poonawala, *Biobibliography,* 73.

62. Ivanow, *Ismaili Tradition concerning the Rise of the Fatimids,* 18–19.

63. de Blois, *Arabic, Persian and Gujarati Manuscripts,* 10.

64. Jaʿfar ibn Manṣūr al-Yaman, *Sarāʾir.*

65. Cortese, *Arabic Ismaili Manuscripts,* 159.

66. Gacek, *Catalogue of Arabic Manuscripts,* 1:117.

67. Cortese, *Arabic Ismaili Manuscripts,* 24–25.

68. Gacek, *Catalogue of Arabic Manuscripts,* 1:11.

69. Gacek, *Catalogue of Arabic Manuscripts,* 1:11.

70. Gacek, *Catalogue of Arabic Manuscripts,* 1:11.

71. Poonawala, *Biobibliography,* xiv.

72. Cortese, *Arabic Ismaili Manuscripts,* 168.

73. Gacek, *Catalogue of Arabic Manuscripts,* 118.

74. Halm, "Zur Datierung," 101–5.

75. Hollenberg, "Neoplatonism in Pre-Kirmānian Fāṭimid Doctrine," 159–202.

76. Madelung, "Das Imamat," 84.

77. al-Nuʿmān, *Asās al-Taʾwīl.*

78. Cortese, *Arabic Ismaili Manuscripts,* 22.

79. de Blois, *Arabic, Persian and Gujarati Manuscripts,* 39.

80. Poonawla, *Biobiobliography,* 63–64.

81. De Smet, "The *Risāla al-mudhhiba,*" 309–42.

82. Pseudo al-Qāḍī al-Nuʿmān, *Al-Risāla al-mudhhiba,* edited by Ārif Tāmir.

83. The most plausible explanation for this is that the supernatural claims made of the Imām were easier to maintain far from where he actually resided. Haider, *Shīʿī Islam,* 123–44.

84. Poonawala, "Ismāʿīlī Manuscripts," 221. Poonawala cites al-Maqrīzī, *Ittiʿāz al-ḥunafāʾ,* 393.

85. Poonawala, "Ismāʿīlī Manuscripts," 224–25.

86. The scholar ʿAlī ibn Saʿīd al-Ḥusayn ibn ʿAlī al-Yaʿbūrī al-Ḥamdānī was invited by the thirty-ninth dāʿī muṭlaq Wajīh al-Dīn (d. 1754), continuing the process of the transfer of manuscripts from Yemen to India. Poonawala, "Ismāʿīlī Manuscripts," 225–27.

87. de Blois, *Arabic, Persian and Gujarati Manuscripts,* xvi.
88. Daftary, *Fifty Years in the East,* 191.
89. Ismail K. Poonawala, personal communication, January 3, 2014.

CHAPTER 3
Rearing

1. Stern, "The Early Ismāʿīlī Missionaries in North-West Persia," 59.

2. Other conversion accounts in Ismāʿīlī sources include the conversion of Nāṣiri-I Khusraw, in Ivanow, *Nasiri-Khusraw and Ismailism,* 22–24. Two accounts in non-Ismāʿīlī sources are the conversion of Ḥamdān Qarmat, in Thābit ibn Sinān, *Taʾrīkh akhbār al-qarāmiṭa,* 96–97, and the conversion of ʿAlī ibn al-Faḍl in Muḥammad ibn Mālik al-Yamānī, *Kashf asrār al-bāṭinīya,* 21–23.

3. Ibn Ḥawshab's autobiography survives in fragments in several later works, most important among them being al-Qāḍī al-Nuʿmān's *Risālat Iftitāh al-dawla,* 33–53.

4. Halm, "Die Sīrat ibn Haušab." The fullest account is that of the Ṭayyibi author Idrīs, *ʿUyun al-akhbār,* 4:396. See also al-Nuʿmān, *Iftitāḥ,* 35–36.

5. al-Nuʿmān, *Risālat iftitāḥ al-daʿwa,* 9.

6. Stern, "The Early Ismāʿīlī Missionaries in North-West Persia," 57.

7. al-Nuʿmān, *Iftitāḥ,* 10.

8. al-Zamaksharī, *al-Kashshāf,* 2:741. We do have contemporary Muʿtazilite interpretations of other verses with similar views. For example see Abū Bakr al-Aṣamm's comment on Qurʾān 2:7, *God has sealed their hearing and their hearts.* Abū Bakr al-Aṣamm, *Tafsīr,* 33.

9. Morris, *The Master and the Disciple,* 68.

10. Thābit ibn Sinān, *Taʾrīkh akhbār al-qarāmiṭa,* 96.

11. Luhrmann, "The Magic of Secrecy," 161. Herdt, "Secret Societies and Secret Collectives."

12. Thomas, *The "Mysteries,"* 37.

13. Urban, "The Torment of Secrecy," 210. Stroumsa and Kippenberg, *Secrecy and Concealment,* xiii–xxiv. Erickson, "Secret Societies and Social Structure."

14. In the Qurʾān the word ʿahd can connote an historical covenant between humans and God, a legal agreement, or a pact among believers. Qurʾān 17:34, 23:8, 70:32. EI², s.v. "*ʿAhd*" (Joseph Schacht).

15. The missionary Aḥmad al-Naysabūrī (thrived late fourth/tenth century) refers to this fast before an initiate is administered the oath. Halm, "The Isma'ili Oath of Allegiance," 93. In ta'wīl fasting signifies "maintaining silence," Jaʿfar ibn Manṣūr al-Yaman, *Sarāʾir,* 212.

16. Halm, "The Isma'ili Oath of Allegiance," 91.

17. A full Arabic version of the Arabic oath has yet to be published. There is a manuscript in the Fyzee collection entitled *Khutbat ʿahd al-rijāl wa-khuṭbat ʿahd al-nisāʾ.* The title suggests a version of the oath for men, and a version for women. To the best of my knowledge, this manuscript has never been investigated. Goriawala, *A descriptive catalogue,* 128.

18. Halm, "The Ismaili Oath of Allegiance," 94.

19. Halm, "The Ismaili Oath of Allegiance," 96.

20. Halm, *The Empire of the Mahdī,* 43, citing al-Nuʿmān, *Iftitāḥ,* 69.

21. Halm, *The Empire of the Mahdī*, 44, citing al-Nuʿmān, *Iftitāḥ*, 70.
22. Morris, *The Master and the Disciple*, 118.
23. Jaʿfar ibn Manṣūr al-Yaman, *Sarāʾir*, 22.
24. Jaʿfar ibn Manṣūr al-Yaman, *Kitāb al-ridāʿ fī al-bāṭin*, 113.
25. Ibn Rizām writes that "they collected everything they had in one single place, and in this way they all became equal, and no one surpassed his comrade and brother through possessions of any kind. . . . It signified to them that they had no need of possessions at all." Halm, *The Empire of the Mahdī*, 48–49.
26. Jaʿfar ibn Manṣūr al-Yaman, *Taʾwīl sūrat al-nisāʾ*, 23; Jaʿfar ibn Manṣūr al-Yaman, *Sarāʾir*, 67; Jaʿfar ibn Manṣūr al-Yaman, *Risālat taʾwīl ḥurūf al-muʿjam* (IIS Ms. 1209), 6b. Abū Ḥātim al-Rāzī, *Kitāb al-Iṣlāh*, 185; Abū ʿĪsā al-Murshid's treatise was published by Stern, "The Earliest Cosmological Doctrines of Ismāʿīlism," 17; al-Nuʿmān, *Asās al-taʾwīl*, 302.
27. al-Nuʿmān, *Risālat iftitāḥ al-daʿwa*, 9.
28. Nuckolls, "Cognitive Anthropology."
29. Insights drawn on cognition in neuroscience and the social scientific fields of psychology and linguistics have recently been applied by anthropologists, literary critics, and, most important for our purposes, text analysis of ancient and late antique textual traditions. For one summary of this literature, see Luhrmann, *When God Talks Back*, 280–81.
30. "Repetition priming" has been shown to be reflected in nonexplicit memory—the ability to name pictures or words more quickly than new pictures. Tulving and Schacter, "Priming and Human Memory Systems."
31. Schacter and Buckner, "Priming and the Brain," 185–95. Tulving and Schacter, "Priming and Human Memory Systems"; Cave, "Very Long-Lasting Priming in Picture Naming."
32. Jokiranta, *Social Identity and Sectarianism*; Pyysiäinen, "Holy Book—a Treasury of the Incomprehensible."
33. Robbins, "Conceptual Blending."
34. Luhrmann, *When God Talks Back*, 132–56.
35. Cassirer, *The Philosophy of Symbolic Forms*, 217.
36. Nuckolls, "Cognitive Anthropology."
37. Jaʿfar ibn Manṣūr al-Yaman, *Kitāb al-shawāhid*, 13.
38. Jaʿfar ibn Manṣūr al-Yaman, *Kitāb al-shawāhid*, 14–15.
39. Jaʿfar ibn Manṣūr al-Yaman, *Kitāb al-shawāhid*, 15–16.
40. Jaʿfar ibn Manṣūr al-Yaman, *Kitāb al-shawāhid*, 17.
41. Jaʿfar ibn Manṣūr al-Yaman, *Kitāb al-shawāhid*, 17.
42. For full references to the abbreviated titles used below according to period and Fāṭimid or Fāṭimid provenance, see the appendix.
43. *Asās*, 83; *Iftikhār*, 112. *Iṣlāḥ*, 77, 142.
44. *Fatarāt*, 174; *Asrār*, 60; *Iṣlāḥ*, 206–10.
45. *Sarāʾir*, 81–82; *Mudhhiba*, cited by Halm, *Kosmologie*, 140; *Iftikhār*, 140; *Maqālid*, 245; *Asās*, 70.
46. *Sarāʾir*, 104; *Nisāʾ*, 24; *Islāḥ*, 224.
47. *Islāḥ*, 14; *Sarāʾir*, 181; ʿĀlim, 22; *Shawāhid*, 13; *Taʾwīl al-ḥurūf II*, 5a.
48. *Sarāʾir*, 4; *Nisāʾ*, 4; *Asās*, 68; *Shawāhid*, 15.

49. *Sarāʾir*, 92; *Zakāt*, 55; *Nisāʾ*, 23, *Maqālīd*, 99; *Asās*, 104.
50. *Zakāt*, 55–56; *Sarāʾir*, 26; *Asās*, 97; *Yanābiʿ*, 147; *Mudhhiba*, 34; *Islāḥ*, 288.
51. *Sarāʾir*, 29; *Farāʾid*, 139; *Nisāʾ*, 10, *Mudhhiba*, 54; *Asās*, 59; *Yanābiʿ*, 171.
52. *Islāḥ*, 27–28; *Fatarāt*, par. 26; *Zakāt*, 127; *Asās*, 83; *Shawāhid*, 8.
53. *Zakāt*, 54; *Sarāʾir*, 83; *Asās*, 363; *Yanābiʿ*, 124; *Taʾwīl al-ḥurūf I*, 21.
54. *Nisāʾ*, 2; *Zakāt*, 17; *Fatarāt*, 168; *al-Maḥsūl* (*Kitāb al-riyāḍ*), 227–28; *Zakāt*, 54.
55. *Zakāt*, 138; *Ridāʿ*, 94; *Sarāʾir*, 17; *Islāḥ*, 27–28; *Maḥsūl*, 227; *Fatarāt*, 167; *Mudhhiba*, 60; *Yanābiʿ*, 130.
56. *Sarāʾir*, 24; Abu ʿIsa al-Murshid, 16; *Mudhhiba*, 61; *Yanābiʿ*, 169; *Iṣlāḥ*, 110–20.
57. *Sarāʾir*, 22; *Maqālīd*, 339; *Fatarāt*, 200; *Yanābiʿ*, 170, *Farāʾid*, 3.
58. *Yanābiʿ* 166; *Iṣlāḥ*, 297; *Sarāʾir*, 90.
59. *Asās*, 44; *Yanābiʿ*, 97–98; *Iṣlāḥ*, 23; *Fatarāt*, 167; *Zakāt*, 62; *Mudhhiba*, 68.
60. *Shawāhid*, 35–36; *Asās*, 51; *Zakāt*, 158.
61. *Mudhhiba*, 71; *Farāʾid*, 49; *Fatarāt*, 190; *Taʾwīl al-ḥurūf I, 21; Fatarāt, 170.*
62. *Mudhhiba*, 44; *Ithbāt*, 18; *Fatarāt*, 168; *Iṣlāḥ*, 266.
63. *Mudhhiba*, 70; *Yanābiʿ*, 154; *Iṣlāḥ*, 3; *Taʾwīl al-ḥurūf I*, 25.
64. *Mudhhiba*, 86; *Yanābiʿ*, 181–83; *Iṣlāḥ*, 121.
65. *Iṣlāḥ*, 326; *Asrār*, 189; *Zakāt*, 85.
66. *Iṣlāḥ*, 128; *Fatarāt*, 170; *Taʾwīl al-ḥurūf I*, 21.
67. *Nisāʾ*, 177; *Riḍāʿ*, 75; *Yanābiʿ*, 158.
68. *Mudhhiba*, 71; *Iṣlāḥ*, 103; *Nisāʾ*, 56.
69. *Nisāʾ*, 23; *Taʾwīl al-ḥurūf II*, 1; *Sarāʾir*, 24; *Iṣlāḥ*, 136; *Asās*, 312.
70. *Taʾwīl al-ḥurūf II*, 2; *Nisāʾ*, 155.
71. *Sarāʾir*, 189; *Iṣlāḥ*, 121.
72. *Nisāʾ*, 23; *Sarāʾir*, 62.
73. *Nisāʾ*, 3; *Zakāt*, 156; *Fatarāt*, 177; *Taʾwīl al-ḥurūf II*, 16.
74. *Nisāʾ*, 19; *Zakāt*, 66.
75. *Taʾwīl al-ḥurūf II*, 3.
76. *Zakāt*, 58.
77. *Zakāt*, 58.
78. *Zakāt*, 10; *Nisāʾ*, 41.
79. *Farāʾid*, 26; *Zakāt*, 154; *Iṣlāḥ*, 300.
80. *Asās*, 63; Iṣlāḥ, 278; *Taʾwīl al-ḥurūf I*, 24.
81. *Mudhhiba*, 84; *Sarāʾir*, 193; *Iṣlāḥ*, 312.
82. *Asās*, 45; *Iṣlāḥ*, 247; *Ithbāt*, 182, *Nisāʾ* 58; *Sarāʾir*, 197.
83. *Taʾwīl al-ḥurūf II*, 10a; *Taʾwīl al-ḥurūf I*, 24.
84. *Iṣlāḥ*, 60–61; *Kashf*, 57.
85. *Taʾwīl al-ḥurūf II*, 10a.
86. *Sarāʾir*, 176; *Nisāʾ* 185; *Ridāʿ*, 94; *Taʾwīl al-ḥurūf II*, 13.
87. *Riḍāʿ*, 25; *Nisāʾ*, 43; *Fatarāt*, 172; *ʿĀlim*, 49; *Taʾwīl al-ḥurūf* I, 21.
88. *Kashf*, 30; *Iṣlāḥ*, 237.
89. *Ridāʿ* 41; *Asās*, 41; *Taʾwīl al-ḥurūf II*, 11b.
90. *Sarāʾir*, 85; *Mudhhiba*, 60; *Iṣlāḥ*, 158.
91. *Asās*, 361; *Iṣlāḥ*, 191–2; *Sarāʾir*, 65.
92. *Ithbāt*, 182; *Nisāʾ*, 35.
93. *Asās*, 23; *Nisāʾ*, 23, 113; Zakat, 55; *Fatarāt*, par. 15; *Ithbāt*, 168.

94. *Iṣlāḥ*, 215 (adducing al-Nasafī); *Ithbāt*, 168; *Nisāʾ*, 17.

95. *Nisāʾ*, 23; *Riḍāʿ*, 55; *Fatarāt*, par. 10; *Asās*, 99, *Iṣlāḥ*, 135–36; *Mudhhiba*, 43; *Taʾwīl al-ḥurūf II*, 18.

96. *Iṣlāḥ*, 149–50; *Sarāʾir*, 70–711.

97. *Nisāʾ*, 23; *Sarāʾir*, 67; *Iṣlāḥ*, 185; Abū ʿIsā al-Murshid, 17; *Asās*, 302; *Taʾwīl al-ḥurūf II*, 6b.

98. *Nisāʾ*, 23; *Iṣlāḥ*, 236.

99. *Riḍāʿ*, 113; *Nisāʾ*, 23.

100. *Zakāt*, 66; *Riḍāʿ*, 55; *Sarāʾir*, 23.

101. *Fatarāt*, 155; *Zakāt*, 55.

102. *Asās* 64; *Iṣlāḥ*, 117–18.

103. *Kashf*, 165; *Iṣlāḥ*, 119.

104. *Asās*, 125; *Nisāʾ*, 38.

105. *Mudhhiba*, 85; *Asās* 29.

106. *Asās* 46; *Rushd*, 198; *Iṣlāḥ*, 14; *Nisāʾ*, 17.

107. *Riḍāʿ*, 83; *Zakāt*, 26; *Sarāʾir*, 83; *Asās*, 345; *Mudhhiba*, 84, *Iṣlāḥ*, 268–69; *Nisāʾ*, 58.

108. *Sarāʾir*, 32; *Iṣlāḥ*, 193; *Nisāʾ*, 43.

109. *Riḍāʿ*. 99; *Asās*, 51.

110. *Nisāʾ*, 66; *Zakāt*, 159; *Taʾwīl al-ḥurūf I*, 25.

111. *Riḍāʿ*, 32b; *Asās*, 347, *Mudhhiba*, 32, 84; *Zakāt*, 55; *Taʾwīl al-ḥurūf I*, 23.

112. *Asās*, 33; *Yanābiʿ*, 125; *Iftikhār*, 47.

113. *Nisāʾ*, 52; *Sarāʾir*, 200.

114. *Asās*, 70; *Sarāʾir*, 217.

115. *Nisāʾ*, 66; *Iṣlāḥ*, 275.

116. *Sarāʾir*, 216; *Fatarāt*, 172.

117. *Asās*, 40; *Iṣlāḥ*, 137; *Nisāʾ*, 57.

118. *Shawāhid*, 88; *Sarāʾir*, 43; *Fatarāt*, 177.

119. *Asās*, 54; *Mudhhiba*, 71; *Farāʾid*, 17; *Ithbāt*, 168; *Fatarāt*, 177.

120. *Asās*, 67; *Mudhhiba*, 87; *Iṣlāḥ*, 287; *Sarāʾir*, 233.

121. *Asās*, 116; *Shawāhid*, 12–13, *Nisāʾ*, 11; *Sarāʾir*, 129.

122. *Nisāʾ*, 83–84; *Sarāʾir*, 206.

123. *Asās*, 88; *Sarāʾir*, 208.

124. *Asās*, 351; *Sarāʾir*, 233; *Nisāʾ*, 35.

125. *Sarāʾir*, 237; *Asās*, 146.

126. al-Fekki, *Al-Taʾwīl*, 69–70.

127. Rowson, "Cant and Argot in Cairo Colloquial Arabic," 19.

128. Bar-Asher, "Outlines," 292.

129. Ivry, "The Utilization of Allegory," 155–57.

130. Burkert, *Lore and Science in Ancient Pythagoreanism*, 42.

131. I thank the historian of science Malcolm Wilson of the University of Oregon for his extremely cogent explanations of Pythagorean theory.

132. Madelung and Walker, "The *Kitāb al-rusūm wal-izdiwāj*," 108.

133. Robbins, "Conceptual Blending," 15, 192.

134. al-Nuʿmān, *Kitāb asās al-taʾwīl*, 82.

135. al-Nuʿmān, *Kitāb asās al-taʾwīl*, 79.

136. al-Nuʿmān, *Kitāb asās al-taʾwīl*, 76–79.

137. al-Nu‘mān, *Kitāb asās al-ta’wīl*, 83.
138. al-Nu‘mān, *Kitāb asās al-ta’wīl*, 83.
139. al-Nu‘mān, *Kitāb asās al-ta’wīl*, 85–86.
140. al-Nu‘mān, *Asās al-ta’wīl*, cited by Bar-Asher, "Outlines," 269.
141. Ja‘far ibn Manṣūr al-Yaman, *Ta’wīl surat al-nisā’*, 20.
142. Ja‘far ibn Manṣūr al-Yaman, *Kitāb al-ridā‘ fī al-bāṭin*, 113.
143. al-Majlisī, *Biḥar al-anwār*, vol. 78, 61.
144. Ja‘far b. Manṣūr al-Yaman, *Kitāb al-ridā‘ fī al-bāṭin*, 118.
145. Ja‘far ibn Manṣūr al-Yaman, *Ta’wīl sūrat al-nisā’*, 23.
146. al-Nu‘mān, *Asās al-ta’wīl*, 52.
147. Ja‘far ibn Manṣūr al-Yaman, *Kitāb al-ridā‘ fī al-bāṭin*, 55.
148. Ja‘far ibn Manṣūr al-Yaman, *Ta’wīl sūrat al-nisā’*, 23.
149. Stern, "The Earliest Cosmological Doctrines of Ismā‘īlism," 9.
150. Halm, "The Cosmology of the Pre-Fatimid Ismā‘īliyya," 78–79; Pseudo-Appolonius, *Sirr al-khalīqa*, 89; Walker, *Early Philosophical Shi'ism*, 84. For more parallels on the primordial entities of *irāda* and *amr* in theological sources, see van Ess, *Theologie und Gesellschaft*, 4:445–59.
151. Abū Ya‘qūb al-Sijistānī, *Kitāb al-yanābi‘*, 125.
152. al-Nu‘mān, *Kitāb asās al-ta’wīl*, 39. In light of al-Qāḍī Nu‘mān's conservative interpretation, it is noteworthy that al-Sijistānī's chapter on the *shahāda* in the introduction to his *Ithbāt al-nubūwāt* was omitted from all extant manuscripts. It seems likely that his interpretation fell out of favor with the Fāṭimids. See also Sijistānī, *Kitāb al-iftikhār*, 47–56. Abū Ḥātim al-Rāzī also offered an interpretation of the formula in *Kitāb al-iṣlāḥ*. De Smet, *La Quiétude de l'intellect*, 388. Halm, *The Empire of the Mahdī*, 53–57, 63–64, 217–18.
153. "He or she" is not merely rhetorical. As Halm notes, women were included in the early Fāṭimid sessions of learning. Halm, *The Fatimids and Their Traditions of Learning*, 103.
154. Ja‘far ibn Manṣūr al-Yaman, *Sarā’ir*, 29.
155. al-Ghazālī, *al-Mustaẓhirī*, 52.
156. Ibn Ḥamzah, *Mishkāt al-anwār*, 11.
157. Ja‘far ibn Manṣūr al-Yaman, *Sarā’ir*, 214. De Smet and Van Reeth, "Les citations bibliques," 147–60.
158. Hollenberg, "Neoplatonism in Pre-Kirmānīan Fāṭimid Doctrine," 191.
159. Plato, *Timaeus*, 526. The apologist Justin Martyr (fl. second century) referred to the "two bands" as a reference to the cross in his *First Apology*. During the fourth/tenth century, an Arabic translation of the Timaeus by Ibn al-Biṭrīq was known to be circulating among Christians scholastics. The well-known Christian philosopher Yaḥyā ibn ‘Adī al-Takrītī (d. 363/974) wrote a commentary on it, and perhaps it is in this form that it reached the Ismā‘īlī missionaries. Ibn al-Nadīm, *al-Fihrist*, 256. Ḥunayn ibn Isḥāq's translation of part of the "Synopsis of the Platonic Dialogues" by Galen that recounts parts of the *Timaeus* has been published in Kraus, *Galeni Compendium Timaei Platonis*. Also fragments of Galen's medical commentary on the *Timaeus* have survived. See Larrain, *Galens Kommentar zu Platons Timaios*. See also D'Ancona, "The *Timaeus*' Model for Creation and Providence." I thank Sasha Treiger for these references.

160. Tottoli, *Biblical Prophets in the Qur'an*, 39–42.

161. Goldziher, "The Attitude of Orthodox," 185–215. In the fifth/eleventh and sixth/twelfth centuries, among certain Sunnī and Twelver scholars, falsafa and Greek science was admissible in Qur'ānic exegesis. See Morrison, "The Portrayal of Nature in a Medieval Qur'an Commentary," 115–37. However, in the fourth/tenth century, this impulse seems to have been restricted to Ismāʿīlī missionaries. In this sense Ismāʿīlī taʾwīl could be seen as the avant-garde of Islamic exegesis.

162. EI², s.v. "Ṣalīb."

163. Thomas, *The "Mysteries."*

164. Maurice Bloch, "Astrology and Writing," 295–97.

CHAPTER 4
Beyond the Qurʾān

1. Günthur, "Muhammad, an Illiterate Prophet," 3–4.

2. Günthur, "Muhammad, an Illiterate Prophet," 1–26.

3. al-Zuhri, *Tahdhīb* , 296–97, cited by Comerro, *Les traditions sur la constitution du muṣḥaf de ʿUthmān*, 11.

4. Pseudo-Jaʿfar ibn Manṣūr al-Yaman, *Kitāb al-kashf*, 89. There were, however, variations in the lists of the waṣīs accompanying the speaker-prophets. And there were rare discrepancies in the list of nāṭiqs. For example in the first treatise of the *Kitāb al-kashf*, Adam is omitted. This agrees with al-Qummī's description and most likely describes the pre-Fāṭimid list of speaker-prophets. *Kitāb al-kashf*, 24. Madelung, "Das Imamat," 47. In Abū Ḥātim al-Rāzī's *Kitāb al-zīna*, David is added as a speaker-prophet, making Muḥammad ibn 'Abd Allāh the seventh speaker-prophet. Hamdani, "Evolution of the Organisational Structure," 101.

5. Abū Ḥātim al-Rāzī, *Kitāb al-Iṣlāḥ*, 120–21. Discussed by Nomoto, "Early Ismāʿīlī Thought on Prophecy," 223.

6. Crone and Treadwell, "A New Text," 59–60.

7. Walker, *Early Philosophical Shi'ism*, 117–23.

8. I thank Dr. Nadia Eboo Jamal for providing me with her draft of the critical edition for *Taʾwīl al-sharīʿa* ascribed to al-Qāḍī al-Nuʿmān. Her critical edition of this work is forthcoming. The translation is my own.

9. Jaʿfar ibn Manṣūr al-Yaman, *Sarāʾir*, 25.

10. Jaʿfar ibn Manṣūr al-Yaman, *Sarāʾir*, 25.

11. Jaʿfar ibn Manṣūr al-Yaman, *Sarāʾir*, 24.

12. Nomoto, "Early Ismāʿīlī Thought on Prophecy," 198–99.

13. Hollenberg, "Neoplatonism in Pre-Kirmānīan Fāṭimid Doctrine," 201.

14. Jaʿfar ibn Manṣūr al-Yaman, *Sarāʾir*, 63–64.

15. Jaʿfar ibn Manṣūr al-Yaman, *Sarāʾir*, 27.

16. Jaʿfar ibn Manṣūr al-Yaman, *Sarāʾir*, 28.

17. Jaʿfar ibn Manṣūr al-Yaman, *Sarāʾir*, 28.

18. Jaʿfar ibn Manṣūr al-Yaman, *Sarāʾir*, 29.

19. The pronouns in the source make it ambiguous as to whether it was Adam or the king who learned the language of the people. Jaʿfar ibn Manṣūr al-Yaman, *Sarāʾir*, 32.

20. Jaʿfar ibn Manṣūr al-Yaman, *Sarāʾir*, 29.

21. Jaʿfar ibn Manṣūr al-Yaman, *Sarāʾir*, 30.
22. Jaʿfar ibn Manṣūr al-Yaman, *Sarāʾir*, 34.
23. Jaʿfar ibn Manṣūr al-Yaman, *Sarāʾir*, 33.
24. Jaʿfar ibn Manṣūr al-Yaman, *Sarāʾir*, 34.
25. Jaʿfar ibn Manṣūr al-Yaman, *Sarāʾir*, 38–39.
26. Jaʿfar ibn Manṣūr al-Yaman, *Sarāʾir*, 44–47.
27. Jaʿfar ibn Manṣūr al-Yaman, *Sarāʾir*, 29. "This is the speech of the Imām of the time who is the Qāʾim to the people of his period, the [. . .] for God would erect him and put him in place, so he was named 'God' as he came by the deed of God."
28. al-Nuʿmān, *Kitāb al-majālis*, 374.
29. Madelung, "Das Imamat," 87–101.
30. Michael Brett, *The Rise of the Fatimids*, 218.
31. Jaʿfar ibn Manṣūr al-Yaman, *Sarāʾir*, 32.
32. Crone and Treadwell, "A New Text," 61–63.
33. Halm, *The Empire of the Mahdī*, 168.
34. Halm, *The Empire of the Mahdī*, 159–68.
35. Jaʿfar ibn Manṣūr al-Yaman, *Sarāʾir*, 35.
36. Madelung, "Das Imamat," 95-101.
37. Jiwa, "The Initial Destination," 50-63.
38. S. M. Stern, "Ismāʿīlī Propaganda in Sind," 179–80.
39. Jaʿfar ibn Manṣūr al-Yaman, *Sarāʾir*, 41.
40. Jaʿfar ibn Manṣūr al-Yaman, *Sarāʾir*, 56–65.
41. Jaʿfar ibn Manṣūr al-Yaman, *Sarāʾir*, 59.
42. Jaʿfar ibn Manṣūr al-Yaman, *Sarāʾir*, 69–70.
43. Jaʿfar ibn Manṣūr al-Yaman, *Sarāʾir*, 170.
44. Jaʿfar ibn Manṣūr al-Yaman, *Sarāʾir*, 173.
45. *EI*[2], s.v. "nakīb al-ashrāf."
46. The crypto-Ismāʿīlī Shahrastānī provides a similar account in his discussion of the collection of the Qurāʾn. He claims that the descendants of Aaron maintained the tablets of the Torah, which remains extant and with the Imāms today; the Torah in the hands of the Jews was altered. Mayer, *Keys to the Arcana*, 75.
47. I am currently completing an analysis of the Jesus story in the *Sarāʾir* entitled "A Gnostic Islamic Jesus: Jaʿfar ibn Manṣūr al-Yaman's Story of John and Jesus in His *Sarāʾir al-nuṭaqāʾ*." This article will show that in addition to the numerous passages from the Synoptic Gospels, there are parallels with passages from "The Infancy Gospel of Thomas," "The Second Treatise of the Great Seth," "The Apocalypse of Peter," "The Gospel of Truth," "The Gospel of Thomas," and "The Pseudo-Clementines." For discussions of these sources, see Layton, *The Gnostic Scriptures*.
48. Jaʿfar ibn Manṣūr al-Yaman, *Sarāʾir*, 205.
49. Jaʿfar ibn Manṣūr al-Yaman, *Sarāʾir*, 227.
50. Jaʿfar ibn Manṣūr al-Yaman, *Sarāʾir*, 227.
51. Jaʿfar ibn Manṣūr al-Yaman, *Sarāʾir*, 213.
52. Corriente, *A Dictionary of Andalusi Arabic*, s.v. "*marsūm*."
53. Jaʿfar ibn Manṣūr al-Yaman, *Sarāʾir*, 214.
54. Jaʿfar ibn Manṣūr al-Yaman, *Sarāʾir*, 83–84.
55. Jaʿfar ibn Manṣūr al-Yaman, *Sarāʾir*, 85.

56. Ja'far ibn Manṣūr al-Yaman, *Sarā'ir*, 233–34.
57. Ja'far ibn Manṣūr al-Yaman, *Sarā'ir*, 234.
58. Ja'far ibn Manṣūr al-Yaman, *Sarā'ir*, 236.
59. Ja'far ibn Manṣūr al-Yaman, *Sarā'ir*, 88. The "seven dialects" (*ḥurūf*) tradition is well attested. See al-Bukhārī, *Ṣaḥīḥ*, 6:184; al-Shāfi'ī, *al-Sunan*, 172; and al-Tirmidhī, *al-Jāmi' al-ṣaḥīḥ*, 5:194.
60. My account combines two sections of the source; the first, *Sarā'ir*, 80–89, focuses on the Prophet's legacy from Ismā'īl through the Prophet's Arab forebears; the second, *Sarā'ir*, 229–40, describes his prophetic inheritance passed from Isaac through the teaching of the companion of the Prophet Zayd ibn 'Amr. In the *Sarā'ir* Zayd is called a missionary of Baḥīrā'.
61. Ja'far ibn Manṣūr al-Yaman, *Sarā'ir*, 79–80.
62. Ja'far ibn Manṣūr al-Yaman, *Sarā'ir*, 229. EI², s.v. "'Isā" (G. C. Anawati).
63. Ja'far ibn Manṣūr al-Yaman, *Sarā'ir*, 234.
64. Roggema, *The Legend of Sergius Baḥīrā*, 167.
65. Ja'far ibn Manṣūr al-Yaman, *Sarā'ir*, 228.
66. Ja'far ibn Manṣūr al-Yaman, *Sarā'ir*, 237.

CHAPTER 5
The Torah's Imāms

1. Kraus, "Hebräische und syrische Zitate," 243–63. De Smet and van Reeth, "Les citations bibliques," 147–60. Walker, *Master of the Age*, 25.
2. Stern, "Fatimid Propaganda," 257–88. Building on the work of Stern, Steven Wasserstrom suggested that Ismā'īlī ta'wīl's "Judaizing tendency" demonstrates ta'wīl's role in interconfessional discourse. Wasserstrom also links Ismā'īlī ta'wīl to the pseudoepigraphic *Sefer ha-Yetsirah* (Hebrew) and other Jewish sources. Wasserstrom, *Between Muslim and Jew*, 129–33.
3. Hollenberg, "Disorobing Judges with Veiled Truths."
4. Reynolds, *The Qur'an and Its Biblical Subtext.*
5. Adang, *Muslim Writers on Judaism*, 114.
6. al-Qurashī, *Mubtada' al-dunyā wa-qiṣaṣ al-anbiyā'*, 5v.
7. Abū Isḥāq al-Tha'labī adds that such stories provide evidence of the Prophet Muḥammad's status as messenger-prophet (rasūl) who received a law and was a model for piety. The trials and failures of past communities is a warning to Muslims. al-Tha'ālabī, *'Arā'is al-majālis*, 2–3.
8. Wasserstrom, *Between Muslim and Jew*, 59–60. Rubin, *Between Bible and Qur'ān*, 17–19.
9. Rubin, *Between Bible and Qur'ān*, 1.
10. Rubin, *Between Bible and Qur'ān*, 17–19.
11. Rubin, *Between Bible and Qur'ān*, 19.
12. Borrut argues that this was part of a larger 'Abbāsid project to formulate a new "*vulgate historgraphique*" to displace Umayyad *lieux de mémoire* (sites of memory) with newly formulated 'Abbāsid ones. Borrut, *Entre mémoire et pouvoir*, 179–224. For the theoretical discussion of sites of memory, see Nora, "Between Memory and History," 7–12. I thank Sarah Savant for these references.
13. Adang, *Muslim Writers on Judaism*, 111.

14. Schmidtke, "The Muslim Reception of Biblical Materials."
15. Rubin, "Prophets and Progenitors," 58n109.
16. Griffith, *The Bible in Arabic,* 184.
17. Lazarus-Yafeh, *Intertwined Worlds,* 50–74.
18. In the late ninth century, the word *isrā'īlīyāt* could still be used in a neutral sense by the Ṣūfī scholar Muḥammad ibn ʿAlīya al-Ḥarithī (d. 286/899); see all-Ḥarithī, *Quwat al-qulūb fī muʿālajat al-maḥbūb,* 106, 166, 206.
19. Kister, "Ḥaddithū," 223.
20. Tottoli, *Biblical Prophets in the Qur'ān,* 130.
21. Tottoli, "Origin and Use of the Term *Isrā'īliyyāt,*" 193–201. Tottoli cites Goldziher's claim that the first use of the term *isrā'īliyyāt* was by al-Masʿūdī (d. 956) in *Murūdh al-dhahab.*
22. Kohlberg and Amir-Moezzi, *Revelation and Falsification,* 24–29.
23. Ibn al-Miskawayhi, *Kitāb tajārib al-umam,* 1:49.
24. On al-Qurashī and 'Umāra ibn Wathīma, see Tottoli, *Biblical Prophets,* 143–46.
25. Lazarus-Yafeh, *Intertwined Worlds,* 19–49.
26. Griffith, *The Bible in Arabic,* 180–81, 198–99.
27. Griffith, *The Bible in Arabic,* 201–2.
28. Reynolds, *The Qur'an and Its Biblical Subtext,* 2.
29. Cabezón, *Scholasticism,* 237.
30. Saleh, *In Defense of the Bible,* 21–36. Griffith, *The Bible in Arabic,* 96.
31. Yücesoy, *Messianic Beliefs and Imperial politics,* 97–134.
32. Kohlberg, "Some Shīʿī Views," 41–43.
33. Rubin, "Apocalypse and Authority," 38.
34. Rubin, "Prophets and Progenitors," 46, citing *Biḥār al-anwār,* 23, 366.
35. Sindawi, "Noah and Noah's Ark," 32.
36. Sindawi, "Noah and Noah's Ark," 34, citing Muḥammad ibn Kulaynī, *al-Kāfī,* 8:281.
37. Rubin, "Prophets and Progenitors," 46.
38. Rubin, "Prophets and Progenitors," 47.
39. Rubin, "Prophets and Progenitors," 52, citing Kister "Ḥaddithū," 223.
40. Rubin, "Prophets and Progenitors," 53.
41. Rubin, "Prophets and Progenitors," 53 citing Kister, "Ḥaddithū," 233.
42. Rubin, "Prophets and Progenitors," 54, citing Pseudo-Masʿūdī, *Ithbāt al-waṣīya,* 259.
43. Rubin, "Prophets and Progenitors," 54.
44. Kister, "Ḥaddathū," 225.
45. Rubin, "Prophets and Progenitors," 58n109.
46. Griffith, *The Bible in Arabic,* 184.
47. Friedman, "Kūfa Is Better," 219.
48. Rubin, "Prophets and Progenitors," 63.
49. EI^2, s.v. "Al-Mukhtār."
50. Rubin, "Prophets and Progenitors," 63.
51. Madelung, "Das Imamat," 82.
52. al-Nuʿman, *Kitāb asās al-ta'wīl,* 69.
53. Jaʿfar ibn Manṣūr al-Yaman, *Sarā'ir,* 172.

54. Anawati, "Le Nom Supreme de Dieu (ism Allāh al-aʿẓam)," 29.

55. Jaʿfar ibn Manṣūr al-Yaman, *Sarāʾir*, 171–72.

56. Eberhart, "A Neglected Feature of Sacrifice," 490. For an account of the rabbinic amplification of scent and sacrifice, see Green, *The Aroma of Righteousness*.

57. Redfield et al., *The Ethnographic Moment*, vii.

58. Jaʿfar ibn Manṣūr al-Yaman, *Sarāʾir*, 49.

59. Jaʿfar ibn Manṣūr al-Yaman, *Sarāʾir*, 171.

60. Hajnal, "On the History of the Ismaili Hidden Imams," 101–16. Madelung, "Das Imamat," 98.

61. Madelung, "Das Imamat," 100–102.

62. Pseudo al-Nuʿmān, *al-Risāla al-Mudhhiba*, 81.

63. Madelung, "Das Imamat," 96–99.

64. Abū Ḥātim al-Rāzī, *Kitāb al-Iṣlāḥ*, 312. Nomoto, "Early Ismāʿīlī Thought on Prophecy," 345.

65. Jaʿfar ibn Manṣūr al-Yaman, *Sarā'ir*, 174.

66. Emending Ghālib, *Sarāʾir*, 174 to IIS Ms. 738 *thumma lam yazraʿhā al-abāʾ minka bal al-abnāʾ yazraʿūnahā.*

67. Jaʿfar ibn Manṣūr al-Yaman, *Sarā'ir*, 174.

68. Before the spiritual cycle of Jesus, the author claims that Moses clarified that the progeny of Isaac is to cease "cultivating the ground." This refers to the termination of the status of the genealogical line of Isaac after the Messiah. This is most likely intended to explain the transfer in genealogical line from Isaac to Ismāʿīl, and eventually, the Prophet Muhammad.

69. Pseudo al-Nuʿmān, *al-Risāla al-mudhhiba*, 44.

70. Jaʿfar ibn Manṣūr al-Yaman, *Sarāʾir*, 175.

71. Jaʿfar ibn Manṣūr al-Yaman, *Sarāʾir*, 175.

72. Jaʿfar ibn Manṣūr al-Yaman, *Sarāʾir*, 175.

73. *The Babylonian Talmud, Moed Katan, Part Three*, 24a.

74. *Hananel ben Ḥushi'el*, 59. I thank Sol Cohen of the Center for Advanced Judaic Studies for this reference.

75. Jaʿfar ibn Manṣūr al-Yaman, *Sarāʾir*, 176.

76. It is worth noting that Sukkot carries messianic associations in postexilic Judaism. *The Jewish Encyclopaedia*, s.v. "*Sukkot*."

77. Jaʿfar ibn Manṣūr al-Yaman, *Sarāʾir*, 202.

78. "God forbid that Moses and Aaron, David and Solomon would come from such births, and this is what necessarily proves that this [Bible] was subject to the innovations of a heretic [*zindīq*] who made fun of religion." Lazarus-Yafeh, *Intertwined Worlds*, 146–47. After relating the Judah and Tamar story, Ibn Ḥazm exclaims that if this and other immoral behavior was customary among the children of Israel, their whole genealogy would be full of illegitimate children (Lazarus-Yafeh, *Intertwined Worlds*, 34, 40). Esther Mann writes that late antique and medieval Jewish interpreters of the Judah and Tamar story were distressed by Judah's deeds and went to considerable length to rehabilitate him. She describes two different interpretive traditions: Hellenistic Jewish sources presented Judah as "a warrior king [with a] tragic weakness for women," while the Aramaic sources "develop the characters of Tamar and Judah as positive exemplars of moral behavior under duress." Mann, *Judah and Tamar*, 2.

79. Gil, *Jews in Islamic Countries*, 364.

80. Sa'adia, *Targum*, 4–8. The Karaite translation that is extent is that of Yefet ben 'Alī. It has yet to be edited. For a manuscript of Yefet's translation, see British Library, Ms. OR 2462 folio 72b.

81. The translation is based on Ghālib's edition. I have noted where I have emended the text in light of readings in manuscripts made available by the Institute of Ismaili Studies.

82. This line is missing from Ghālib's edition but is included in IIS Ms. 239, 57.

83. Emending Ghālib, *mabnīya* to *mathnīya*. I thank Mark Cohen for this suggestion.

84. I have not been able to find this word in this precise form. *Ma'būl* is the passive participle of *'abala*, to repel; a *ma'bal* is an instrument that cuts trees; an *a'bal* is a white or black stone. Lane, *An Arabic-English Lexicon*, s.v. "abala."

85. It is worth noting that the names of the characters in the extant manuscripts of the *Asrār* vary considerably. "Sīlān" and "Judā" become "Shīlān" and "Judhā" in IIS Ms. 239, while the heroine Tamar is called "Yamārah" in the Ghālib edition. The divergence in the heroine Tamar's name indicates that the story was not well known among the Ismā'īlīs copying the manuscript. Since the earliest extant manuscript was copied in the late nineteenth century, it is impossible to establish when and where these alterations first emerged. Also telling is that the Judeo-Arabic word for yeshiva, *mathnīya*, has been miscopied as "mabnīya." The presence of a Judeo-Arabic word in the source is further evidence of a Jewish oral source.

86. The term *aṣḥāb al-ra'y wal-qiyās*, elsewhere in the *qiyāsīya* ("analogists"), refers to corrupt jurists of any period. More immediately they may refer to Mālikī jurists with whom the Ismā'īlīs were in conflict in North Africa in the middle of the tenth century. Madelung has shown that Ismā'īlī-Mālikī hostilities may have been in part fueled by family feuds that pre-dated the Ismā'īlī presence in the Maghreb, and were fought along Ḥanafī-Mālikī lines prior to the Fāṭimid da'wa. Wilfred Madelung, "The Religions Policy of the Fatimids," 97–104.

87. Madelung, "A Treatise of the Sharīf al-Murtaḍā," 18–31.

88. Mut'a was proscribed in Zaydī law, and thus Ismā'īlī law follows Zaydī law on this point. Madelung, "The Sources of Ismā'īlī Law," 29–40.

89. The same word, *mutamatti'*, is used by the Jerusalem Karaite exegete Yefet ibn 'Alī in his translation of Genesis. British Library Ms. OR 2462, folio 72b. Sa'adia Gaon refers to Judah as a *mumta'a*. Dourenbourg, 60. David Freidenrich's claim that this may have explicitly referred to temporary marriage is interesting, but the fact that this is a standard word for prostitute in North African middle Arabic militates against the certainty of his reading that Sa'adiah used the term in order to lessen Judah's crime from prostitution to temporary marriage. David M. Freidenreich, "The Use of Islamic Sources in Sa'adiah Gaon's 'Tafsir,'" 369. Corriente, *A Dictionary of Andalusi Arabic*, s.v. "muta'."

90. Since there was a metaphysical counterpart to procreation, Imāmī Shī'ites believed that one should avoid immoral women such as prostitutes. Kohlberg, *Belief and Law*, 244.

91. Al-Sharīf al-Murtaḍā adduced the example of Joseph in the Qur'ān, who accepted the office of the unjust al-'Azīz by "bearing witness on his own integrity by

saying, 'Set me over the stores of the land. I am indeed heedful, knowledgeable' (Qur'ān 12:55)." Madelung, "A Treatise of the Sharīf al-Murtaḍā," 25.

92. In Qayrawān, the North African capital of the Aghlabids before the rise of the Fāṭimids and the Jewish center of the region, the center of Jewish life and authority was the synagogue in which the seat of judgment, the *bayt dīn*, was often located. Ben-Sasson, "The Emergence of the Qayrawān Jewish Community," 5–7.

93. I have not found this interpretation in the medieval Jewish exegetical tradition and suspect it is the Ismāʿīlī missionary's interpretation. M. Cohen, *Mikra'ot Gedolot Part II.*

94. There are obscure references to a "lesser and greater Eve" and "lesser and greater Fāṭima" scattered in works such as Jaʿfar's *Kitāb al-kashf.* See also Bauer, "Spiritual Hierarchy," 29–46.

95. *Kitāb al-kashf*, 115.

96. Halm, *The Empire of the Mahdī*, 22–43.

Epilogue

1. Zaman, *Religion and Politics under the Early 'Abbāsids*, 34–48. Jaʿfar ibn Manṣūr al-Yaman's account of al-Maʾmūn's brief turn toward the family of the prophet to succeed him as caliph suggests that the Fāṭimid missionaries were quite aware of these events. Jaʿfar ibn Manṣūr al-Yaman, *Sarāʾir*, 250.

2. Mazzaoui, *The Origins of the Ṣafawids*, 1–27.

3. Fleisher, "The Lawgiver as Messiah," 160–74.

4. Shoemaker, "The Reign of God Has Come," 514–58.

5. Paul Magdalino has argued that Andrew believed that the Roman Empire was not just a sign of the coming of the Antichrist before the End of Days, but its embodiment. Magdalino, "The History of the Future and Its Uses," 10–11.

6. McGinn, *Visions of the End*, 15.

7. Crone, *God's Rule*, 214.

8. John Burns, University of California Los Angeles, personal communication, December 1995.

9. Haider, *Shīʿī Islam*, 130-131.

10. Hall, *Apocalypse Observed*, 8–11.

11. Ghālib, *Kitāb al-kashf*, 108.

12. Jaʿfar ibn Manṣūr al-Yaman, *Sarāʾir*, 242.

13. Heinrichs, "Contacts between Scriptural Hermeneutics and Literary Theory," 253–44.

14. Bashir, *Messianic Hopes and Mystical Visions*, 165–77. Babayan, *Mystics, Monarchs, and Messiahs*, 57–108; Mir-Kasimov, *Words of Power.*

BIBLIOGRAPHY

Primary Sources

Abū Maʿshar, Jaʿfar b. Muḥammad b. ʿUmar al-Balkhī. *The Abbreviation of the Introduction to Astrology together with the Medieval Latin Translation of Adelard of Bath.* Edited and translated by Charles Burnett, Keiji Yamomoto, and Michio Yano. Leiden: E. J. Brill, 1994.

al-ʿĀmirī, Abū l-Ḥasan. *Kitāb al-Amad ʿalā l-abad.* Edited and translated by Everett K. Rowson as *A Muslim Philosopher on the Soul and Its Fate: Al-ʿĀmirī's Kitāb al-Amad ʿalā l-abad.* New Haven, Conn.: American Oriental Society, 1988.

——. *Rasāʾil Abī Ḥasan al-ʿĀmirī wa-shadharātuhu al-falsafīya.* Edited by Sahbān Khalīfāt. Amman: Jordan University, 1988.

Pseudo-Ammonius. *Die Doxographie des Pseudo-Ammonius: Ein Beitrag zur neuplatonischen Überlieferung im Islam.* Edited by Ulrich Rudolph. Wiesbaden: Steiner, 1989.

[Pseudo-] Appolonius. *Sirr al-khalīqa.* Edited by Ursula Weisser. Aleppo: Institute for the History of Arabic Science, University of Aleppo, 1979.

Aristotle. *De Generatione et Corruptione.* Translated by C. J. F. Williams. Oxford: Oxford University Press, 1982.

Al-Aṣamm, Abū Bakr. *Tafsīr Abī Bakr al-Aṣamm.* Edited by ʿAbd al-Raḥmān b. Kaysān et al. Bayrūt. Dār al-kutub al-ʿilmīyah, 2007.

The Babylonian Talmud, Moed Katan, Part Three. London: Soncino Press, 1960.

al-Baghdādī, Abū Ṭāhir. *al-Farq bayn al-firaq.* Cairo: Nashr al-thaqāfa al-Islamīya, 1948.

al-Bīrūnī, Abū l-Rayḥān Muḥammad b. Aḥmad al-Khawarizmī. *al-Āthār al-bāqīya ʿan al-qurūn al-khālīya.* Edited by Edward Sachau. Leipzig: F. A. Brockhaus, 1923.

Bukhārī, Muḥammad ibn Ismāʿīl. *Ṣaḥīḥ al-Imām al-Bukhārī.* Edited by Muḥammad Zuhayr ibn Nāṣir Nāṣir. Bayrūt: Dār Ṭawq al-Najāh, 2001.

al-Bustī, Abū l-Qāsim. *Min kashf asrār al-bāṭinīya wa-ghawar madhhabihi.* Manuscript, Griffini Collection. Ambrosiana, Milan, no. 41.

al-Fārābī, Abū Naṣr. *Al-Fārābī on the Perfect State.* Abū Naṣr al-Fārābī's *Mabādīʾ ārāʾ ahl al-madīna al-fāḍila.* Edited and translated by Richard Walzer. Oxford: Clarendon, 1985.

——. *Al-Farabi's Commentary and Short Treatise on Aristotle's* De Interpretatione. Translated by F. W. Zimmermann. London: Oxford University Press, 1981.

——. *Kitāb al-milla wa-nuṣūṣ ukhrā.* Edited by Muhsin Mahdi. Beirut: Dār al-mashriq, 1968.

Festugière, André Jean. *Hermetisme et mystique paienne.* Paris: Aubier-Montaignem, 1967.

Ghazālī. *al-Mustaẓhirī fī faḍā'iḥ al-bāṭiniya: Aw faḍā'iḥ al-bāṭinīya wa-faḍā'il al-mustaẓhiriya.* Edited by ʿAbd al-Raḥmān Badawī. Paris: Dār Biblīyūn, 2006.

Ḥamza ibn ʿAlī. *Al-Risāla al-munaffaḍa ilā l-qāḍī.* In *Chrestomathie arabe,* edited by A. I. Sylvestere de Sacy, vol. 2. Paris: De l'imprimerie Impériale, 1826.

al-Ḥarithī, Muḥammad ibn ʿAlīya. *Quwat al-qulūb fī muʿālajat al-maḥbūb wa-waṣf ṭarīq al-murıd ilā maqām al-tawḥīd.* Edited by ʿĀṣim Ibrāhīm al-Kiyālī. Beirut: Dār al-kutub al-ʿilmīya, 2005.

Ḥushi'el, Hananel ben Perushe. *Rabenu Ḥanan'el bar Ḥushi'el: la-Talmud: Yo. l. 'a. p. kitve-yad ve-ḥibure ha-rishonimi.* Edited by David Metsger and Gershom ben Judah. Jerusalem: Mekhon "Lev śameaḥ," 1995.

Iamblichus. *De Anima.* Edited and translated by John F. Finamore and John M. Dillon. Leiden: E. J. Brill, 2002.

——. *De mysteriis.* Edited by Emma C. Clarke, John M. Dillon, and Jackson P. Hershbell. Atlanta: Society of Biblical Literature, 2003.

Ibn ʿAmr, Ḍirār. *Kitāb al-tahrīsh.* Edited by Husayn Khānsū and Muhammad Kaskīn. Istanbul: Dār al-irshād, 2014.

Ibn Bābawayhi. *Man lā yaḥḍuruhu al-faqī.* Qum: Muʿassasat al-nashr al-islāmī, 1992.

Ibn al-Dawādārī, Abū Bakr ibn 'Abd Allāh. *Kanz al-durar wa-jāmi' al-ghurar.* Edited by Bernard Radtke. al-Qāhira: Qism al-Dirāsāt al-Islāmīya, al-maʿhd al-almānī lil-āthār bi-al-Qāhirah, 1960.

Ibn al-Furāt, Muḥammad ibn 'Abd al-Raḥim. *Tārīkh ibn al-Furāt.* Edited by Ḥasan Muḥammad Shammā'. Baṣrah: Maṭba'at Ḥaddād, 1967.

Ibn Ḥamzah, Yaḥyā. *Mishkāt al-anwār al-hādimah li-qawā'id al-Bāṭinīyah al-ashrār.* Edited by Muhammad al-Sayyid al-Jalaynad. Cairo: al-Dār al-Fikr al-Ḥadīth lil-Ṭibā'ah wa-al-Nashr, 1983.

Ibn Ḥawshab, *Kitāb al-rushd wal-hidāya,* edited by Kāmil Ḥusayn. In *Collectanea,* edited by Wladimir Ivanow. Vol. 1. Ismaili Society Series A, no. 2. Leiden: Published for the Ismaili Society by E.J. Brill, 1948.

Ibn al-Haytham, Abū 'Abd Allāh Ja'far b. Aḥmad al-Aswad. *Kitāb al-munāzarāt.* In *The Advent of the Fāṭimids: A Contemporary Shī'ite Witness.* Edited and translated by Wilferd Madelung and Paul E. Walker. London: I. B. Tauris, 2000.

Ibn Isḥāq, Muḥammad. *Sīrat Ibn Isḥāq al-musammā bi-Kitāb al-mubtada' wal-mabʿath wal-maghāzī.* Edited by Muḥammad Hamidullah. Rabāṭ: Maʿhad al-dirāsāt wal-abḥāth lil-taʿrīb, 1976.

Ibn Jabr, Mujāhid. *Tafsīr Mujāhid.* Beirut: al-Manshūrāt al-ʿilmīyah, 1977.

Ibn al-Jawzī, Abū l-Faraj. *Tablīs Iblīs.* Beirut: Dār al-waʿī al-ʿarabī, n.d.

Ibn Khaldūn. *Histoire des Berbères et des dynasties musulmanes de l'Afrique Septentrionale par Abou-Zeid Abd-er-Rahman ibn-Mohammed ibn Khaldoun: Texte arabe.* Algiers: Imprimerie du gouvernement, 1847–51.

Ibn al-Nadīm, Muḥammad ibn Abī Yaʿqūb. *al-Fihrist.* Beirut: Maktaba khayyāṭ, 1966.

Ibn al-Qiftī, ʿAlī b. Yūsuf. *Taʾrīkh al-ḥukamāʾ*. Edited by Julius Lippert. Leipzig: Dieterich'sche Verlagsbuchhandlung, 1903.

Ibn Qutayba. *Kitāb al-ma'arif.* Beirut: Dār al-kutub al-'ilmīya, 1987.

——. *Taʾwīl mukhtalif al-hadith.* Edited by Muhammad Najjār. Beirut: Dar al-jīl, 1973.

Ibn Sīnā, al-Ḥusayn b. ʿAbd Allāh. *Aḥwāl al-nafs: Risāla fī l-nafs wa-baqāʾihā wa-maʿādihā li-shaykh al-raʾīs.* Edited by Aḥmad Fuʾād al-Ahwānī. Cairo: Dār iḥyāʾ al-kutub al-ʿarabīya, 1952.

Ibn Sinān, Thābit. *Taʾrīkh akhbār al-qarāmiṭa.* Edited by S. Zakkār Beirut: 1971.

Ibn Sirīn, Muḥammad. *Kitāb Tafsīr al-aḥlām, al-musammā, Muntakhab al-kalām fī tafsīr al-aḥlām.* Vol. 1. Edited by Riḥāb 'Akkāwī. Beirut: Dār al-Ḥarf al-ʿArabī, 2000.

Ibn al-Ṭayyib, Abū al-Faraj ʿAbd Allāh. *Commentaire sur la Genèse.* Edited by J. C. J. Sanders. Louvain: Universitatis Catholicae Lovaniensis, 1967.

Ibn al-Ṭayyib, Abū al-Faraj ʿAbd Allāh. *Proclus' Commentary on the Pythagorean Golden Verses.* Edited and translated by Neil Linley. Buffalo: State University of New York at Buffalo Press, 1984.

Idrīs b. al-Ḥasan b. 'Abd Allāh b. al-Walīd, 'Imād al-Dīn. *'Uyūn al-akhbār wa-funūn al-āthār.* Vols. 1–6, ed. Muṣṭafā Ghālib. Beirut: Dār al-Andalus, 1973–78. Edited by Muḥammad al-Ya'lāwī as *Ta'rīkh al-khulafāʾ al-Fāṭimīyūn bi-l-Maghrib.* Beirut: Dār al-Gharb al-Islāmī, 1985.

Ikhwān al-Ṣafāʾ. *Rasāʾil ikhwān al-ṣāfāʾ.* 4 vols. Beirut: Dar Sader, 1999.

Israeli, Isaac. *The Book of Definitions. The Book of Substances. The Mantua Text. The Book of Elements. The Book on Spirit and Soul.* In *Isaac Israeli: A Neoplatonic Philosopher of the Early Tenth Century, His Works Translated with Comments and on Outline of His Philosophy.* Translated by Alexander Altmann and S. M. Stern. London: Oxford University Press, 1958.

Jaʿfar b. Manṣūr al-Yaman, Abū al-Qāsim. *Kitāb al-ʿālim wal-ghulām.* In *The Master and the Disciple: An Early Islamic Spiritual Dialogue,* ed. and trans. James Winston Morris, 2–95. London: I. B. Tauris in association with the Institute of Ismaili Studies, 2001.

——. *Kitāb al-farā'id wa-ḥudūd al-dīn.* Ms. 520. Library of the Institute of Ismā'īlī Studies, London.

——. *Kitāb al-fatarāt wal-qirānāt.* David Hollenberg, "Pre-Kirmānian Fāṭimid doctrine: A Critical Edition and Translation of the Prologue of the Kitāb al-fatarāt wal-qirānāt." *Le Muséon* 122 (2009): 155–202.

——. *Kitāb al-kashf.* Edited by Mustafa Ghalib. Beirut: Dār al-Andalus, 1404/1984.

——. *Kitāb al-riḍāʿ fī al-bāṭin.* Ms. 167. Library of the Institute of Ismā'īlī Studies, London.

——. *Kitāb al-shawāhid wal-bayān.* Ms. 734. Library of the Institute of Ismā'īlī Studies, London.

——. *Kitāb taʾwīl al-zakāt.* Ms. 1028. Library of the Institute of Ismā'īlī Studies, London.

——. *Sarāʾir wa-asrār al-nuṭaqāʾ.* Edited by Muṣṭafā Ghālib. Beirut: Dār al-Andalus, 1404/1984.

——. *Taʾwīl sūrat al-nisāʾ.* Ms. 1103. Library of the Institute of Ismā'īlī Studies, London.

Al-Jawdharī, Abū 'Alī Manṣūr al-Azīzī. *Sīrat ustādh Jawdhar.* Edited by Muḥammad Kāmil Ḥusayn and Muḥammad 'Abd al-Hādī Sh'īra. Cairo: Dar al-Fikr al-'Arabī, 1954.

Justin Martyr. *First Apology.* Translated by Thomas B. Falls. Washington, D.C.: Catholic University of America Press, 1948.

Kalām fī maḥd al-khayr. Edited by ʿAbd al-Rāḥmān al-Badawī. In *al-Aflūṭūnīya al-muḥdatha ʿind al-ʿarab.* Cairo: Maktabat al-nahḍa al-miṣrīya, 1955.

al-Kindī, Yaʿqūb b. Iṣḥāq. *Rasāʾil al-Kindī al-falsafīya.* Edited by Muḥammad ʿAbd al-Hādī Abū Rayda. Cairo: Dār al-fikr al-islāmī, 1950.

al-Kirmānī, Ḥamīd al-Dīn. *Kitāb al-riyāḍ fī l-ḥukm bayna al-ṣādayn ṣāḥibay al-Iṣlāḥ wal-Nuṣra.* Edited by ʿĀrif Tāmir. Beirut: Dār al-thaqāfa, 1960.

——. *Rāḥat al-ʿaql.* Edited by Muḥammad Muṣṭafá Ḥilmī. al-Qāhirah: Dār al-Fikr al-ʿArabī, 1953.

al-Kirmānī, Maḥmūd b. Ḥamza. *Gharāʾib al-tafsīr wa-ʿajāʾib al-taʾwīl.* Jeddah: Dār al-qibla lil-thaqāfa al-islāmīya, 1988.

Mālik ibn Anas, *al-Muwaṭṭāʾ.* Edited by Muḥammad Fuʾād ʿAbd al-Bāqī. Cairo: Dār iḥyāʾ al-kutub al-ʿarabīya, 1951.

al-Maqrīzī, Aḥmad ibn ʿAlī. *Ittiʾāz al-ḥunafā bi-akhbār al-aʾimma al-fāṭimīyīn al-khulafāʾ.* Cairo: Muʾassasat Dār at-Taḥrīr liṭ-Ṭabʿ wa-ʾn-Našr, n.d.

——. *Khiṭaṭ al-Maqrīzī.* Edited by Muḥammad Muṣtafā Ziyādah. al-Qāhirah: Dār al-Taḥrīr lil-ṭabʿ wa-al-Nashr, 1967.

[Pseudo-] Masʿūdī. *Ithbāt al-waṣīya.* Najaf: al-Maktaba al-murtaḍawīya, al-Maṭbaʿa al-Ḥaydarīya, n.d.

al-Māturīdī, Muḥammad ibn Muḥammad Abū l-Manṣūr. *Kitāb al-tawḥīd.* Beirut: Dār al-mashriq, 1970.

——. *Tafsīr al-Māturīdī al-musammā Taʾwīlat ahl al-*sunna. Cairo: Lajnat al-Qurʾān wa-al-Sunnah, 1971.

Ibn Miskawayh, Aḥmad b. Muḥammad. *al-Fawz al-Aṣghar.* Edited by Ṣāliḥ ʿAḍīma and Roger Arnaldez. Paris: al-Dār al-ʿarabīya li-l-kitāb, 1987.

——. *Kitāb tajārib al-umam.* Vol. 1. Edited by H. F. Amedroz and D. S. Margoliouth. Cairo: Dār al-Kitab al-Islāmī, 1965.

al-Munqārī, Naṣr ibn Muzāḥim ibn Siyār. *Waqaʿat Ṣiffīn.* Cairo: al-Muʾassassah al-ʿarabīya al-ḥadīthāh, 1962.

al-Naysabūrī, Aḥmad b. Ibrāhīm. *Istitār al-imām wa-tafarruq al-duʿat fīl-jazāʾir li-ṭalabihī.* Edited by W. Ivanow. *Bulletin of the Faculty of Arts, University of Egypt.* Cairo: 1936.

——. *al-Risāla al-mūjaza al-kāfīya fī ādāb al-duʿāt.* Translated by Verena Klemm and Paul Walker as *A Code of Conduct: A Treatise on the Etiquette of the Fatimid Ismaili Mission.* London: I. B. Tauris in association with the Institute of Ismaili Studies, 2011.

Niẓām al-Mulk, Ḥasan b. ʿAlī. *Siyāsatnāmeh.* Edited by Charles Schefer, Moḥammad ebn ʿAbdolvahâb Qazvini, and Morteẓâ Modarresi Čâhârdehi. Tehran: Zavvâr, 1965.

Nuʿaym b. Ḥammād. *al-Fitan.* Edited by Muḥammad b. ʿAyyādī Ibn ʿAbd al-Ḥalīm. Cairo: Maktabat al-ṣafā, 2003.

Pseudo al-Nuʿmān. *al-Risāla al-mudhhiba.* Edited by Ārif Tāmir. Beirut: Dār al-masīra, 1988.

al-Nuʿmān b. Muḥammad b. Manṣūr al-Tamīmī al-Qayrawānī al-Maghribī, al-Qāḍī Abū Ḥanīfa. *Iftitāḥ al-daʿwa.* Edited by Wadad al-Qadi. Beirut: Dār al-Thaqāfa.

——. *Ikhtilāf uṣūl al-madhāhib.* Edited by Musṭafā Ghālib. Beirut: Dār al-Andalūs, 1393/1973.

——. *Kitāb asās al-ta'wīl.* Edited by 'Ārif Tāmir. Beirut: Dār al-thaqāfa, 1960.

——. *Kitāb al-himma fī ādāb atbā' al-a'imma.* Edited by Musṭafā Ghālib. Beirut: Dār wa-maktabat al-hilāl, 1979.

——. *Kitāb al-majālis wa-l-musāyarāt.* 2d ed. Edited by al-Ḥabib al-Faqī, Ibrāhīm Shabbūḥ, and Muḥammad al-Yaʿlāwī. Beirut: Dār al-gharb al-islāmī, 1997.

——. *Ta'wīl da'ā'im al-islām.* 3 vols. Edited by Muhammad Ḥasan al-A'ẓamī. Cairo: Dār al-Ma'ārif. 1967–72.

Plato. *Timaeus.* Translated by Benjamin Jowett. Indianapolis: Bobbs-Merrill, 1949.

[Arabo-] Plotinus. *The Theology of Aristotle.* In *al-Aflatūnīya al-muḥdatha ʿinda l-ʿarab.* Edited by ʿAbd al-Rāḥmān al-Badawī. Cairo: Maktabat al-nahḍa al-miṣrīya, 1955. English translation by G. Lewis in Paul Henry and Hans Rudolf Schwyze, *Plotini Opera,* vol. 2: *Enneades IV–V;* Plotiniana Arabica ad codicum fidem anglice vertit G. Lewis. Paris: Desclée de Brouwer, 1959.

Proclus. *The Commentaries of Proclus on the Timaeus of Plato.* Translated by Thomas Taylor. London: Chthonios Books, 1988.

Qummī, Muḥammad. ʿAlī b. Ibrāhīm, *Tafsīr al-Qummī.* Vol. 1. al-Najaf: Maktabat al-Hudā, 1967.

al-Qurashī, Isḥāq b. Bishr. *Mubtadaʾ al-dunyā wa-qiṣaṣ al-anbīyāʾ.* Bodleian Library, Oxford. Ms. Huntingdon 388.

al-Rāzī, Abū Ḥātim. *Aʿlām al-nubūwah.* Edited by Salāḥ al-Ṣāwī and Ghulām Riḍā A'vānī. Tehran: Imperial Iranian Academy of Philosophy, 1977.

——. *Kitāb al-Iṣlāḥ.* Edited by Ḥasan Mīnūchir and Mahdī Muḥaqqiq. Tehran: Institute of Islamic Studies, 1998.

——. *Kitāb al-zīnā.* Edited by Ḥusayn b. Fayḍ Allāh al-Hamdānī. Sana'a: Markaz al-dirāsāt wa-l-buḥūth al-yamanī, 1994.

al-Rāzī, Fakhr al-dīn Muḥammad b. ʿUmar. *al-Sirr al-maktūm fī asrār al-nujūm.* Cairo: Maṭbaʿ al-hajarīya, n.d.

Sa'adia ben Joseph. *Targum Sefer Mishle u-veuro bi-leshon 'Aravit.* Edited by Joseph Derenbourg and Mayer Lambert. Paris: E. Leru, 1981.

al-Shāfiʿī, Muḥammad ibn Idrīs. *al-Sunan al-ma'thūrah.* Edited by ʿAbd al-Muʿṭī Amīn Qalʿajī, and Aḥmad ibn Muḥammad Ṭaḥāwī. Bayrūt: Dār al Ma'rifah, 1986

al-Shahrastānī, Muḥammad b. ʿAbd al-Karīm. *Kitāb al-milal wa-l-niḥal.* Edited by William Cureton. Piscataway, N.J.: Gorgias Press, 2002.

——. *Kitāb al-Muṣāraʿa.* Edited and translated by Wilferd Madelung and Toby Mayer as *Struggling with the Philosopher: A Refutation of Avicenna's Metaphysics.* London: I. B. Tauris in association with the Institute of Ismaili Studies, 2001.

al-Sijistānī, Abū Sulaymān. *Ṣīwān al-ḥikma wa-thalāth rasāʾil.* Edited by ʿAbd al-Raḥmān al-Badawī. Tehran: Bunyād-i farhang-i, 1974.

al-Sijistānī, Abū Yaʿqūb. *Ithbāt al-nubūwāt.* Edited by 'Ārif Tāmir. Beirut: al-Maṭba'a al-kāthūlīkīya, 1966.

——. *Kitāb al-iftikhār.* Edited by Ismail K. Poonawala. Beirut: Dār al-gharb al-islāmī, 2000.

——. *Kitāb al-Maqālīd al-malkūtīya.* Edited by Ismail K. Poonawala. Tūnis: Dār al-Gharb al-Islāmi, 2011.

——. *Kitāb al-yanābiʿ*. Edited by Musṭafā Ghālib. Beirut: al-Maktab al-tijārī li-l-ṭibāʿa wa-l-tawzīʿ wa-l-nashr, 1965.

al-Siyāsa wa-l-ḥīla ʿind al-ʿarab. Edited by René Khawam. London: Dār al-sāqī, 1988. Translated by René Khawam as *The Subtle Ruse: The Book of Arabic Wisdom and Guile*. London: East-West Publications, 1980.

al-Suyūṭī, Jalāl al-Dīn. *Kitāb al-itqān fī ʿulūm al-Qurʾān*. Edited by Muṭafā al-Ḥalabī. Cairo: 1935.

al-Ṭabarī, Ibn Jarīr. *Jāmiʿ al-bayān ʿan taʾwīl al-Qurʾān*. Edited by Muḥammad Shākir. Cairo: Dār al-maʿārif, 1969.

——. *Tarʾīkh al-rusul wal-mulūk*. Edited by Michael Jan de Goeje. Leiden: E. J. Brill, 1879–1901.

Tāmir, ʿĀrif. *Khams rasāʾil Ismāʿīlīya*. Salamīya: Dār al-Anṣāf, 1956.

al-Ṭarafī, Ibn Muṭarrif. *The Stories of the Prophets*. Edited by Roberto Tottoli. Berlin: Klaus Schwarz, 2003.

al-Tawḥīdī, Abū Ḥayyān ʿAlī b. Muḥammad. *Akhlāq al-wazīrayn*. Edited by Muḥammad b. Tawīt al-Tanjī. Damascus: Arabic Academy of Damascus, 1965.

——. *Kitāb al-imtāʿ wa-l-muʾānasa*. Beirut: Dār al-kutub al-ʿilmīya, 1997.

——. *Muqābasāt*. Edited by Hasan al-Sandūbī. Kuwait: Dār suʿād al-ṣabāḥ, 1992.

al-Thaʿlabī, Abū Isḥāq Aḥmad ibn Muḥammad. *Qiṣaṣ al-anbiyāʾ al-musammā ʿAarāʾis al-majālis*. Cairo: Dār Iḥyāʾ al-Kutub al-ʿArabīyah, 1970.

al-Tirmidhī, Muḥammad ibn ʿĪsā. *al-Jāmiʿ al-ṣaḥīḥ*. Edited by Aḥmad Muḥammad Shākir, Muḥammad Fuʾād ʿAbd al-Bāqī, and Ibrāhīm ʿAṭwah ʿAwaḍ. Cairo: Musṭafá al-Bābī al-Ḥalabī, 1937.

al-Yamānī, Muḥammad b. Mālik. *Kashf asrār al-bāṭinīya*. Edited by M. Z. al-Kawtharī. Cairo: 1939.

Al-Yamānī, Muḥammad b. Mālik. *Kashf asrār al-bāṭinīya*. Edited by Muḥammad Zanahum Muḥammad ʿAzab. Cairo: Dār al-Ṣāhwah, 1986.

al-Yamānī, Muḥammad b. Muḥammad. *Sīrat al-ḥajīb Jaʿfar b. ʿAlī wa-khurūj al-Mahdī min Salamīya*. Edited by Wladimir Ivanow, in *Majallat Kullīyat al-Ādāb, al-Jāmiʿa al-Miṣrīya/Bulletin of the Faculty of Arts, University of Egypt* 4, part 2 (1936): 107–33.

Yefet ibn ʿAli. Arabic Translation of Genesis. British Library, Ms. OR 2462.

al-Zamakshari, Abū al-Qāsim Muḥammad. *al-Kashshāf ʿan ḥaqāʾiq ghawāmid al-tanzīl*. Vol. 2. Beirut: Dār al-kutab al-ʿarabī, 1407 h.

Secondary Sources

Abrahamov, Benyamin. *Anthropomorphism and Interpretation of the Qurʾān in the Theology of al-Qāsim ibn Ibrāhīm: Kitāb al-Mustarshid*. Leiden: E. J. Brill, 1996.

Adamson, Peter. *The Arabic Plotinus: A Philosophical Study of the Theology of Aristotle*. London: Gerald Duckworth, 2002.

Adang, Camilla. *Muslim Writers on Judaism and the Hebrew Bible: From Ibn Rabban to Ibn Hazm*. Vol. 22. Leiden: Brill, 1996.

Alon, Ilai. *Al-Farābī's Philosophical Lexicon*. Warminster: Trustees of the E. J. W. Gibb Memorial, 2002.

Altmann, Alexander, and S. M. Stern. *Isaac Israel: A Neoplatonic Philosopher of the Early Tenth Century: His Works Translated with Comments and an Outline of His Philosophy*. London: Oxford University Press, 1958.

Amir-Moezzi, Muhammad. *The Divine Guide in Early Shi'ism.* Translated by David Streight. Albany: State University of New York Press, 1994.

Anawati, Georges C. "Le Nom Suprême de Dieu (ism Allāh al-aʿẓam)." In *Atti del Terzo Congresso di Studi Arabi e Islamici*, 7–58. Naples: Instituto Universitario Orientale, 1966.

Anthony, Sean W. *The Caliph and the Heretic: Ibn Saba and the Origins of Shīʿsm.* Leiden: Brill, 2011.

Asatryan, Mushegh. "Heresy and Rationalism in Early Islam: The Origins and Evolution of the Mufaḍḍal-Tradition." Ph.D. diss., Yale University, 2012.

Babayan, Kathryn. *Mystics, Monarchs, and Messiahs: Cultural Landscapes of Early Modern Iran.* Cambridge, Mass.: Harvard University Press, 2002.

Bader, Chris. "When Prophecy Passes Unnoticed: New Perspectives on Failed Prophecy." *Journal for the Scientific Study of Religion* 38, no. 1 (March 1999): 119–31.

Bar-Asher, Meir. "Outlines of Early Ismaili-Fatimid Qurʾan Exegesis." *Journal Asiatique* 296, no. 2 (2008): 257–95.

——. *Scripture and Exegesis in Early Imāmī Shīʿism.* Jersualem: Magnes, 1999.

Barth, Fredrik. *Ethnic Groups and Boundaries: The Social Organization of Culture Difference.* Prospect Heights, Ill.: Waveland, 1998.

Bashir, Shahzad. *Messianic Hopes and Mystical Visions: The Nūrbakshiya between Medieval and Modern Islam.* Columbia: University of South Carolina Press, 2003.

Bauer, Karen. *Aims, Methods and Contexts of Qur'anic Exegesis (2nd/8th–9th/15th c.).* Oxford: Oxford University Press in association with the Institute of Ismaili Studies, 2013.

——. "Justifying the Genre: A Study of Introductions to Classical Works of Tafsīr." In *Aims, Methods, and Contexts of Qurʾanic Exegesis (2nd/8th–9th/15th c.),* ed. Karen Bauer, 39–66. Oxford: Oxford University Press in Association with the Institute of Ismaili Studies, 2013.

——. "Spiritual Hierarchy and Gender Hierarchy in Fātimid Ismāʾīlī Interpretations of the Qur'an." *Journal of Qur'anic Studies* 14, no. 2 (October 2006): 29–46.

Bayhom-Daou, Tamima. "The Imam's Knowledge and the Quran According to al-Faḍl b. Shādhān al-Nīsābūrī (d. 260/874)." *Bulletin of the School of Oriental and African Studies* 64, no. 2 (June 2001): 159–311.

——. "Hishām b. al-Ḥakīm (d. 179/795) and His Doctrine of the Imām's Knowledge." *Journal of Semitic Studies* 48, no. 1 (Spring 2003): 71–108.

——. "The Second-Century Šīʿite Ġulāt: Were They Really Gnostic?" *Journal of Arabic and Islamic Studies* 5, no. 2 (2003): 13–61.

Bierman, Rene. *Writing Signs: The Fatimid Public Text.* Berkeley: University of California Press, 1998.

Ben-Sasson, Menachem. "The Emergence of the Qayrawān Jewish Community and Its Importance as a Maghribi Community." In *Judaeo-Arabic Studies: Proceedings of the Founding Conference of the Society for Judaeo-Arabic Studies.* Edited by N. Golb, 1–13. Amsterdam: Harwood Academic Publishers, 1997.

Blair, Sheila S. "Floriated Kufic and the Fatimids." In *L'Égypte Fatimdie son art et son histoire,* ed. Marianne Barrucand, 107–16. Paris: Presses de l'Université de Paris-Sorbonne, 1999.

Bloom, Jonathan M. *Arts of the City Victorious: Islamic Art and Architecture in Fatimid*

North Africa and Egypt. New Haven, Conn.: Yale University Press in association with the Institute of Ismaili Studies, 2007.

Borrut, Antoine. *Entre mémoire et pouvoir: L'espace Syrien sous les derniers Omeyyades et les premiers Abbassides (v. 72–193/692–809).* Leiden: Brill, 2010.

Böwering, Gerhard. *The Mystical Vision of Existence in Classical Islam: The Qur'ānic Hermeneutics of the Ṣūfī Sahl At-Tustarī (d. 283/896).* Berlin: de Gruyter, 1980.

Brett, Michael. "The Mīm, the ʿAyn, and the Making of Ismāʿlism." *Bulletin of the School of African and Oriental Studies* 51, no. 1 (February 1994): 25–39.

——. *The Rise of the Fatimids: The World of the Mediterranean and the Middle East in the Fourth Century of the Hijra.* Leiden: E. J. Brill, 2001.

Brockelmann, Carl. *Geschichte der arabischen Litteratur* (*GAL*). Supplement 1. Leiden: E. J. Brill, 1943–49.

Burkert, Walter. *Lore and Science in Ancient Pythagoreanism.* Translated by Edwin L. Minar, Jr. Cambridge, Mass.: Harvard University Press, 1972.

Cabezón, Jose Ignacio. *Scholasticism: Cross-Cultural and Comparative Perspectives.* New York: State University of New York Press, 1998.

Cassirer, Ernst. *The Philosophy of Symbolic Forms.* Vol. 2, *Mythical Thought.* Translated by Ralph Manheim. New Haven, Conn.: Yale University Press, 1955.

Cave, Carolyn Backer. "Very Long-Lasting Priming in Picture Naming." *Psychological Science* 8, no. 4 (July 1997): 322–25.

Clarke, Emma C. *Iamblichus'* De mysteriis*: A Manifesto of the Miraculous.* Aldershot: Ashgate, 2001.

Cohen, M. *Mirka'ot Gedolot. Part 2. Based on the Aleppo Codex and Early Medieval MSS.* Tel Aviv: Bar Ilan University Press, 1999.

Cohen, Mark R. *Jewish Self-Government in Medieval Egypt: The Origins of the Office of Head of the Jews, ca. 1065–1126.* Princeton, N.J.: Princeton University Press, 1980.

Comerro, Viviane. *Les traditions sur la constitution du muṣḥaf de ʿUthmān.* Beriuter Texte und Studein 134. Beirut: Orient-Institute, 2012.

Conrad, Lawrence. Review of *The Making of the Last Prophet,* by Gordon Newby. *Journal of the American Oriental Society* 113 (1993): 258–63.

Cook, David. "An Early Muslim Daniel Apocalypse." *Arabica* 49, no. 1 (2002): 55–96.

Corbin, Henri. *Mundus Imaginalis; or, The Imaginary and the Imaginal.* Edited by Ruth Horine. Ipswich: Golgonooza, 1976.

——. *History of Islamic Philosophy.* London: Kegan Paul International, 1993.

——. *Temps cyclique et gnose Ismaélienne.* Paris: Berg International, 1982. Translated by Ralph Manheim and James W. Morris as *Cyclical Time and Ismaili Gnosis.* London: K. Paul in association with Islamic Publications, 1983.

Corriente, Federico. *A Dictionary of Andalusi Arabic.* Vol. 29. Leiden: Brill, 1997.

Cortese, Delia. *Arabic Ismaili Manuscripts: The Zāhid 'Alī Collection in the Library of the Institute of Ismaili Studies.* London: I. B. Tauris in association with the Institute of Ismaili Studies, 2003.

——. *Ismaili and Other Manuscripts: A Descriptive Catalogue of Manuscripts in the Library of the Institute of Ismaili Studies.* London: I. B. Tauris in association with the Institute of Ismaili Studies, 2000.

Craig, William Lane. *The Kalām Cosmological Argument.* London: Macmillan, 1979.

Crone, Patricia. "The First-Century Concept of *Hiğra.*" *Arabica* 41 (1994): 352–87.

——. *God's Rule: Government and Islam.* New York: Columbia University Press, 2004.

Crone, Patricia, and Martin Hinds. *God's Caliph.* Cambridge: Cambridge University Press, 1986.

Crone, Patricia, and Luke Treadwell. "A New Text on Ismailism at the Samanid Court." In *Texts, Documents and Artefacts: Islamic Studies in Honour of D. S. Richards,* ed. Chase F. Robinson, 37–67. Leiden: E. J. Brill, 2003.

Davidson, Herbert. *Proofs for Eternity, Creation, and the Existence of God in Medieval Islamic and Jewish Philosophy.* New York: Oxford University Press, 1987.

Daftary, Farhad. *The Assassin Legends: Myths of the Ismailis.* London: I. B. Tauris, 1994.

——. *Fifty Years in the East: The Memoirs of Wladimir Ivanow.* London: I. B. Tauris in association with the Institute of Ismaili Studies, 2015.

——. "Intellectual Life among the Ismailis: An Overview." In *Intellectual Traditions in Islam,* ed. Farhad Daftary, 87–111. London: I. B. Tauris in association with the Institute of Ismaili Studies, 2000.

——. *Ismaili Literature: A Bibliography of Sources and Studies.* London: I. B. Tauris in association with the Institute of Ismaili Studies, 2004.

——. *The Isma'ilis: Their History and Doctrines.* Cambridge: Cambridge University Press, 2011.

——. *Ismailis in Medieval Muslim Societies.* London: I.B. Tauris, 2005.

——. "The Medieval Ismāʿīlīs of the Iranian Lands." In *Studies in Honour of Clifford Edmund Bosworth.* Vol. 2, *The Sultan's Turret: Studies in Persian and Turkish Culture,* ed. C. Hillenbrand, 43–81. Leiden: E. J. Brill, 2000.

Daiber, Hans. "Abū Ḥātim al-Rāzī on the Unity and Diversity of Religions." In *Diaologue and Syncretism: An Interdisciplinary Approach,* ed. Jerald Gort, 241–49. Grand Rapids, Mich.: William B. Eerdmans, 1989.

D'Ancona, Cristina. "The *Timaeus*' Model for Creation and Providence: An Example of Continuity and Adaptation in Early Arabic Philosophical Literature." In *Plato's Timaeus as Cultural Icon,* ed. Gretchen J. Yeydams-Schils, 206–35. Notre Dame: University of Notre Dame Press, 2003.

de Blois, François. *Arabic, Persian and Gujarati Manuscripts the Hamdani Collection in the Library of the Institute of Ismaili Studies.* London: I. B. Tauris in association with the Institute of Ismaili Studies, 2011.

De Smet, Daniel. "Comment determiner le début et la fin du joûne de Ramadan? Un point de discorde entre sunnites et ismaéliens en Égypte fatimide." In *Egypt and Syria in the Fatimid, Ayyubid, and Mamluk eras: Proceedings of the 1st, 2nd, and 3rd International Colloquium Organized at the Katholieke Universiteit Leuven in May 1992, 1993, and 1994,* ed. Daniel De Smet and Urbain Vermeulen, 71–84. Leuven: Peeters, 1995.

——. *Empedocles Arabus: Une lecture néoplatonicienne tardive.* Brussels: Koninklijke Academie voor Wetenschappen, Letteren en Schone Kunsten van België, 1999.

——. "Les citations bibliques dan l'oeuvre du dāʿī Ismalién Ḥamīd ad-Dīn al-Kirmānī ." In *Law, Christianity and Modernism in Islamic Society,* ed. Urbain Vermeulen and J. M. F. Van Reeth, 147–60. Louvain: Peeters, 1998.

——. *La Quiétude de l'intellect: Néoplatonisme et gnose ismaélienne dans l'œuvre de Ḥamīd ad-Dīn al-Kirmānī.* Louvain: Peeters and Departement Oosterse Studies, 1995.

——. "La taqiyya et le jeûne du Ramadan: Quelques réflexions ismaéliennes sur le sens ésotérique de la charia." *Al-Qantara* 34, no. 2 (2013): 357–86.

——. "The *Risāla al-Mudhhiba* Attributed to al-Qāḍī al-Nuʿmān: Important Evidence for the Adoption of Neoplatonism by Fatimid Ismailism at the Time of al-Muʿizz?" In *Fortresses of the Intellect: Ismaili and Other Islamic Studies in Honour of Farhad Daftary*, ed. Omar Alí-de-Unzaga. London: I.B. Tauris, 2011.

Deutsch, Nathaniel. *The Gnostic Imagination: Gnosticism, Mandaeism, and Merkabah Mysticism.* New York: E. J. Brill, 1995.

Dozy, Reinhart. *Supplément aux dictionnaires arabes.* 2 vols. Beirut: Librairie du Liban, 1967.

Eberhart, Christian A. "A Neglected Feature of Sacrifice in the Hebrew Bible: Remarks on the Burning Rite on the Altar." *Harvard Theological Review* 97, no. 4 (October 2004): 485–93.

Ebstein, Michael. *Mysticism and Philosophy in Al-Andalus: Ibn Masarra, Ibn Al-ʾArabī and the Ismāʾīlī Tradition.* Leiden: Brill, 2014.

Encyclopædia of Islam. New Edition. Leiden: E. J. Brill, 1954–2003.

Endress, Gerhard. *The Works of Yaḥyā ibn ʿAdī: An Analytical Inventory.* Wiesbaden: Dr. Ludwig Reichert Verlag, 1977.

Endress, Gerhard, and Dimitri Gutas. *A Greek and Arabic Lexicon: Materials for a Dictionary of the Medieval Translations from Greek into Arabic.* Leiden: E. J. Brill, 1992–.

Erickson Bonnie H. "Secret Societies and Social Structure." *Social Forces* 60, no. 1 (1981): 188–210.

Ess, Josef van. *Theologie und Gesellschaft im 2. und 3. Jahrhundert Hidschra: Eine Geschichte des religiosen Denkens im frühen Islam.* 6 vols. Berlin: de Gruyter, 1991–97.

Faivre, Antoine. "Renaissance Hermeticism and Western Esotericism." In *Gnosis and Hermeticism from Antiquity to Modern Times*, ed. Roelof van den Broek and Wouter J. Hanegraaff, 109–24. Albany: State University of New York Press, 1998.

Faultless, Julian. *The Prologue to John in Ibn al-Ṭayyib's* Commentary on the Gospels. Ph.D. diss., Oxford University, 2001.

Feki, Habib. *Les idées religieuses et philosophiques de l'Ismaélisme Fatimide.* Tunis: L'Université de Tunis, 1978.

——. *Al-Taʾwīl.: Ususuhu wa-maʿnīhi fī al-madhhab al-Ismāʿīlī.* Tunis: al-Jāmiʿa al-tūnisīya, 1979.

Festinger, Leon, Henry W. Riecken, and Stanley Schachter. *When Prophecy Fails.* Minneapolis: University of Minnesota Press, 1956.

Fleisher, Cornell H. "The Lawgiver as Messiah: The Making of the Imperial Image in the Reign of Sülayman." In *Soliman la Magnifique et son temps: Actes du Colloque de Paris Galeries Nationales du Grand Palais, 7–10 mars 1990*, ed. Gilles Veinstein, 160–74. Paris: La documentation Français, 1992.

Fowden, Garth. "The Pagan Holy Man in Late Antique Society." *Journal of Hellenic Studies* 102 (November 1982): 33–59.

Frank, Richard. *Al-Ghazālī and the Ashʿarite School.* Durham, N.C.: Duke University Press, 1994.

Freidenreich, David M. "The Use of Islamic Sources in Saʿadiah Gaon's 'Tafsir' of the Torah." *Jewish Quarterly Review* 93, no. 4 (January–April 2003): 353–95.

Freudenthal, Gad. "The Medieval Astrologization of Aristotle's Biology: Averroes on the Role of the Celestial Bodies in the Generation of Animate Beings." *Arabic Sciences and Philosophy* 12, no. 1 (2002): 111–37.

Friedman, Yaron. "Kūfa Is Better." *Le Muséon* 126, no. 1–2 (2013): 203–37.

Fudge, Bruce. *Qurʾānic Hermeneutics: al-Ṭabarsī and the Craft of Commentary.* New York: Routledge, 2011.

Gacek, Adam. *Catalogue of Arabic Manuscripts in the Library of the Institute of Ismaili Studies.* London: Islamic Publications, 1984.

Gelder, Jan van. *God's Banquet: Food in Classical Arabic Literature.* New York: Columbia University Press, 2000.

Gil, Moshe. *Jews in Islamic Countries in the Middle Ages.* Leiden: Brill, 2004.

Gilliot, Claude. "The Beginnings of Qur'ānic Exegesis." In *The Qur'ān: Formative Interpretation,* ed. Andrew Rippin, 1–27. Brookfield, Vt.: Ashgate, 1999.

Gochenour, David Thomas. "The Penetration of Zaydi Islam into Early Medieval Yemen." Ph.D. diss., Harvard University, 1984.

Goldziher, Ignaz. *Introduction to Islamic Theology and Law.* Translated by Andras Hamori and Ruth Hamori. Princeton, N.J.: Princeton University Press, 1981.

——. *The Logic of Writing and the Organization of Society.* Cambridge: Cambridge University Press, 1986.

Goody, Jack. *The Interface Between the Written and the Oral.* Cambridge: Cambridge University Press, 1987.

Goriawala, Muʿizz. *A Descriptive Catalogue of the Fyzee Collection of Ismaili Manuscripts.* Bombay: University of Bombay Press, 1965.

Götz, Manfred. "Māturīdī and His *Kitāb ta'wīlāt al-Qur'ān.*" Translated by Michael Bonner. In *The Qur'ān: Formative Interpretation,* ed. Andrew Rippin, 181–214. Aldershot: Ashgate, 1999.

Green, Deborah. *The Aroma of Righteousness: Scent and Seduction in Rabbinic Life and Literature.* University Park: Pennsylvania State University Press, 2011.

Griffith, Sidney. *Yaḥya b. ʿAdī: The Reformation of Morals: A Parallel English-Arabic Text.* Translation and introduction by Sidney Griffith. Provo: Brigham Young University Press, 2002.

——. *The Bible in Arabic: The Scriptures of the "People of the Book" in the Language of Islam.* Princeton, N.J.: Princeton University Press, 2013.

Günthur, Sebastian. "Muhammad, an Illiterate Prophet: An Islamic Creed in the Qurʾan and Qur'anic Exegesis." *Journal of Qur'anic Studies* 4, no. 1 (April 2002): 1–26.

Gutas, Dimitri. *Avicenna and the Aristotelian Tradition.* Leiden: E. J. Brill, 1988.

Guyard, S. "Fragments relatifs á la doctrine des ismaélis." *Notices et Extraits* 22 (1874): 177–428.

Haider, Najam. *Shīʿī Islam: An Introduction.* New York: Cambridge University Press, 2014.

Hajnal, Istvan. "On the History of the Ismaili Hidden Imams as Reflected in the Kitāb at-tarātīb al-sabʿa." *Arabist: Budapest Studies in Arabic* 23 (2001): 101–16.

Hall, John R. *Apocalypse Observed: Religious Movements, Social Order, and Violence in North America, Europe, and Japan.* London: Routledge, 2000.

Halm, Heinz. "The Cosmology of the Pre-Fatimid Ismāʿīliyya." In *Mediaeval Ismaʿili*

History and Thought, ed. Farhad Daftary, 75–83. Cambridge: Cambridge University Press, 1996.

——. *The Empire of the Mahdī: The Rise of the Fatimids.* Translated by Michael Bonner. Leiden: E. J. Brill, 1996.

——. *The Fatimids and their traditions of learning.* London: I.B. Tauris in association with the Institute of Ismaili Studies, 1997.

——. "The Isma'ili Oath of Allegiance ('ahd) and the 'Sessions of Wisdom' (*majālis al-ḥikma*) in Fatimid Times." In *Medieval Isma'ili History and Thought*, ed. Farhad Daftary, 91–115. Cambridge: Cambridge University Press, 1996.

——. *Kosmologie und Heilslehre: Der frühen Ismāʿīlīya.* Wiesbaden: Deutsche Morgenländische Gesellschaft, 1978.

——. "Die *Sīrat Ibn Ḥaušab:* Die ismailitische da'wa im Jemen und die Fatimiden." *Die Welt des Orients* 12 (1981): 107–35.

——. "Zur Datierung des ismāʿīlitischen 'Buches der Zwischenzeiten und der zehn Konjunktionen' (*Kitāb al-fatarāt wa'l-qirānāt al-ʿaṣara*) Hs Tübingen Ma VI 297." *Die Welt des Orients* 8 (1975): 91–107.

Halperin, David. "Ibn Ṣayyād Traditions and the Legend of al-Dajjāl." *Journal of the American Oriental Society* 96 (1976): 213–25.

Hamdani, ʿAbbas. "An Early Fatimid Source on the Time and Authorship of the Rasā'il Ikhwān al-Ṣafā'." *Arabica* 26 (1979): 65.

——. "Evolution of the Organisational Structure of the Fāṭimī Daʿwah: The Yemeni and Persian Contribution." *Arabian Studies* 3 (1976): 85–125.

Hamdani, Abbas, and François de Blois. "A Re-examination of Al-Mahdī's Letter to the Yemenites on the Genealogy of the Fatimid Caliphs." *Journal of the Royal Asiatic Society of Great Britain and Ireland* 115, no. 2 (April 1983): 173–207.

Hamdani, Husayn F. *On the Genealogy of the Fatimid Caliphs: A Statement on Mahdī's Communication to the Yemen on the Real and Esoteric Names of his Hidden Predecessors.* Cairo: Publication of the American University of Cairo, School of Oriental Studies, 1958.

——. "Some Unknown Ismāʿīlī Authors and Their Works." *Journal of the Royal Asiatic Society* (1933): 359–78.

Haq, Syed Nomanul. *Names, Natures and Things: The Alchemist Jābir ibn Ḥayyān and His* Kitāb al-Aḥjār (*Book of Stones*). Dordrecht: Kluwer Academic Publishers, 1993.

Hava, J. G. *Arabic English Dictionary.* New Delhi: Goodword Books, 2001.

Heinen, Anton M. "The Notion of *Ta'wīl* in Abū Yaʿqūb al-Sijistānī's *Book of the Sources* (*Kitāb al-yanābīʿ*)." *Hamdard Islamicus* 2 (1979): 35–45.

Heinrichs, Wolfhart. "Contacts between Scriptural Hermeneutics and Literary Theory in Islam: The Case of Majaz." *Zeitschrift für Geschichte der arabisch-islamischen Wissenschaften* 7 (1991–92): 253–44.

Heller-Roazen, Daniel. *Dark Tongues: The Art of Rogues and Riddlers.* New York: Zone Books, 2013.

Herdt, Gilbert. "Secret Societies and Secret Collectives." *Oceania* 60 (1990): 360–81.

Hodgson, Marshall. "How Did the Early Shīʿa Become Sectarian?" *Journal of the American Oriental Society* 75, no. 1 (January–March 1955): 1–13.

——. *The Venture of Islam: Conscience and History in a World Civilization.* Chicago: University of Chicago Press, 1974.

Hollenberg, David. "Disrobing Judges with Veiled Truths: An Early Ismāʿīlī Torah Interpretation in Service of the Fāṭimid daʿwa." *Religion* 33 (2003): 127–45.

——. "The Empire Writes Back: Fāṭimid-Ismāʿīlī taʾwīl (Allegoresis) and the Mysteries of the Ancient Greeks." In *The Study of Shi ʿi Islam: History, Theology and Law*, ed. Farhad Daftary and Gurdofarid Miskinzoda, 135–47. London: I. B. Tauris, 2014.

——. "Interpretation after the End of Days: The Fatimid Ismaili ta'wil (Interpretation) of Jaʾfar b. Mansur al-Yaman (d. ca. 960)." Ph.D. diss., University of Pennsylvania, 2006.

——. "Neoplatonism in Pre-Kirmānīan Fāṭimid Doctrine: A Critical Edition and Translation of the Prologue of the Kitāb al-fatarāt wal-qirānāt." *Le Muséon* 122, no.1–2 (2009): 159–202.

Ivanow, Wladimir. *The Alleged Founder of Ismailism.* Bombay: Ismaili Society, 1946.

——. *Ismaili Tradition concerning the Rise of the Fatimids.* London: Oxford University Press, 1942.

Ivanow, Wladdimir. *A Guide to Ismaili Literature.* London: Royal Asiatic Society, 1933.

Ivry, Alfred L. "The Utilization of Allegory in Islamic Philosophy." In *Interpretation and Allegory: Antiquity to the Modern Period,* ed. Jon Whitman, 153–80. Leiden: Brill Academic Publishers, 2003.

Janowitz, Naomi, A. J. Droge, Carole A. Myscofski, Jorunn J. Buckley, and Helen Hardacre. "'Cults' and 'New Religious Movements.'" *History of Religions* 47, no. 3 (February 2008): 205–20.

The Jewish Encyclopedia. New York: Funk and Wagnalls, 1901–6.

Jiwa, Shainool. "The Initial Destination of the Fatimid Caliphate: The Yemen or the Maghrib?" *British Society for Middle Eastern Studies* 15 (1988): 50–63.

Johnston, Sarah Iles. *Hekate Soteira: A Study of Hekate's Role in the Chaldean Oracles and Related Literature.* Atlanta: Scholars Press, 1990.

Jokiranta, Jutta. *Social Identity and Sectarianism in the Qumran Movement.* Leiden: Brill, 2013.

Karamustafa, Ahmet T. *God's Unruly Friends: Dervish Groups in the Islamic Later Middle Period, 1200–1550.* Salt Lake City: University of Utah Press, 1994.

Kennedy, Edward S. "Ramifications of the World-Year Concept in Islamic Astrology." In *Proceedings of the Tenth International Congress of the History of Science.* Paris: Hermann, 1964.

Kennedy, Edward S., and David Pingree. *The Astrological History of Māshā'allāh.* Cambridge, Mass.: Harvard University Press, 1971.

Khalidi, Tarif. "The Role of Jesus in Intra-Muslim Polemics of the First Two Islamic Centuries." In *Christian Arabic Apologetics during the Abbasid Period (750–1258),* ed. Samir Khalil Samir and J. S. Nielsen, 146–56. Leiden: Brill, 1994.

Kilito, Abdelfattah. *The Author and His Double: Essays on Classical Arabic Culture.* Translated by Michael Cooperson. Foreward by Roger Allen. Syracuse, N.Y.: Syracuse University Press, 2001.

Kinberg, Naphtali. *A Lexicon of al-Farrāʾ's Terminology in His Qur'ān Commentary.* Leiden: E. J. Brill, 1996.

King, David A. "Architecture and Astronomy: The Ventilators of Medieval Cairo and Their Secrets." *Journal of the American Oriental Society* 104, no. 1 (January–March 1984): 97–133.

Kister, M. J. "Ḥaddithū 'an banī Isrā'īl wa-lā ḥaraja." *Israel Oriental Studies* 2 (1972): 215–39.

———. "Legends in Tafsir and Hadith Literature: The Creation of Adam and Related Stories." In *Approaches to the History of the Interpretation of the Qur'an*, ed. Andrew Rippin, 82–114. Oxford: Clarendon, 1988.

Kohlberg, Etan. *Belief and Law in Imāmī Shī'ism*. Hampshire: Variorum, 1991.

———. "Some Shi'i Views of the Antediluvian World." *Studia Islamica* 52 (1980): 41–66.

Kohlberg, Etan, and Mohammad Ali Amir-Moezzi. *Revelation and Falsification: The Kitāb al-qira'āt of Ahmad b. Muhammad al-Sayyarī*. Leiden: Brill, 2009.

Kraemer, Joel. *Humanism in the Renaissance of Islam: The Cultural Revival during the Buyid Age*. Leiden: E. J. Brill, 1986.

———. "The Jihād of the Falāsifa." *Jerusalem Studies in Arabic and Islam* 10 (1987): 288–324.

Kraus, Paul. *Galeni Compendium Timaei Platonis*. London: Aedibus Instituti Warburgiani, 1951.

———. "Hebräische und syrische Zitate in ismā'ilitischen Schriften." *Der Islam* 19 (1931): 243–63.

Lane, Edward William. *An Arabic-English Lexicon*. 8 vols. Beirut: Librairie du Liban, 1968.

Laoust, Henry. *La profession de foi d'ibn Batta d. 387/987*. Damascus: Institut Francais de Damas, 1978.

Larrain, Carlos J. *Galens Kommentar zu Platons Timaios*. Stuttgart: Teubner, 1992.

Layton, Bentley. *The Gnostic Scriptures*. New York: Doubleday, 1987.

Lazarus-Yafeh, Hava. *Intertwined Worlds: Medieval Islam and Bible Criticism* Princeton, N.J.: Princeton University Press, 1992.

Lewis, Bernard. "An Ismaili Interpretation of the Fall of Adam." *Bulletin of the School of Oriental Studies* 9, no. 3 (October 1938): 691–704.

———. *The Origins of Ismā'īlism: A Study of the Historical Background of the Fāṭimid Caliphate*. Cambridge, U.K.: W. Heffer, 1940.

———. "Palṭiel: A Note." *Bulletin of the School of Oriental and African Studies University of London* 30, no. 1 (February 1967): 177–81.

———. "The Regnal Titles of the First 'Abbāsid Caliphs." In *Dr. Zakir Husain Presentation Volume*. New Delhi: Dr. Zakir Husain Presentation Volume Committee, 1968.

Luhrmann, Tanya. "The Magic of Secrecy." *Ethos* 17, no. 2 (June 1989): 131–65.

———. *When God Talks Back: Understanding the American Evangelical Relationship with God* New York: Alfred A. Knopf, 2012.

Madelung, Wilferd. "Apocalyptic Prophecies in Hims in the Umayyad Age." *Journal of Semitic Studies* 31, no. 2 (Autumn 1986): 141–85.

———. "Ḥamdān Qarmāṭ and the Dā'ī Abū 'Alī." In *Proceedings of the 17th Congress of the UEAI [Union Européenne des Arabisants et Islamisants]*, ed. Wilferd Madelung et al., 115–24. St. Petersburg: Thesa, 1997.

———. "Das Imamat in der frühen ismailitischen Lehre." *Der Islam* 37 (1961): 43–135.

———. *Der Imam al-Qasim ibn Ibrahim und die Glaubenslehre der Zaiditen*. Vol. 1. Berlin: de Gruyter, 1965.

———. "The Religions Policy of the Fatimids toward Their Sunnī Subjects in the Mahgrib." In *L'Égypte Fatimide, son art et son histoire*, ed. M. Barrac, 97–104. Paris: Presses de l'Université de Paris-Sorbonne, 1999.

——. "The Sources of Ismāʿīlī Law." *Journal of Near Eastern Studies* 35 (1976): 29–40.

——. "A Treatise on the Imamate of the Fatimid Caliph al-Manṣūr bi-Allāh." *Texts, Documents and Artefacts in Islamic Studies in Honour of D. S. Richards,* ed. Chase F. Robinson,69–77. Leiden: Brill, 2003.

——. "A Treatise of the Sharīf al-Murtaḍā on the Legality of Working for the Government." *Bulletin of the School of Oriental and African Studies* 43, no. 1 (February 1980): 18–31.

Madelung, Wilferd, and Paul E. Walker. "The Kitāb al-rusūm wal-izdiwāj wal-tartīb Attributed to ʿAbdān (d. 289/899): Edition of the Arabic Text and Translation." In *Fortresses of the Intellect: Ismaili and Other Islamic Studies in Honour of Farhad Daftary,* ed. Omar Alí-de-Unzaga, 103–66. London: I. B. Tauris, 2011.

Madelung, Wilferd, and Paul Walker. *The Advent of the Fatimids: A Contemporary Shi'i Witness; An Edition and English Translation of Ibn al-Haythmam's Kitāb al-munāẓarāt.* London: I. B. Tauris in association with the Institute of Ismaili Studies, 2000.

al-Majdūʿ, Ismāʿīl ibn ʿAbd al-Rasūl. *Fihrist al-Majdūʿ.* In *Fahrasat al-kutub wal-rasāʾil,* ed. ʿAlī Naqī Munzavī. Tehran: Tehran University Press, 1344/1966.

Magdalino, Paul. "The History of the Future and Its Uses: Prophecy, Policy, and Propaganda." In *The Making of Byzantine History: Studies Dedicated to Donald M. Nicol,* ed. Roderick Beaton and Charlotte Roueche, 5–17. Aldershot, Hampshire: Variorum, 1993.

Makdisi, George. "The attitude of orthodox Islam toward the ancient sciences." In *Studies in Islam,* ed. Merlin L. Swartz, 185–215. Princeton: Princeton University Press, 1981.

——. *Ibn ʿAqīl: Religion and Culture in Classical Islam.* Edinburgh: Edinbrugh University Press, 1997.

——. "Nouveax details sur ʿaffaire d'Ibn ʿAqīl." In *Mélanges Louis Massignon,* 91–126. Paris: Institut français de damas, 1957.

Mann, Esther. *Judah and Tamar (Genesis 38) in Ancient Jewish Exegesis.* Leiden: Brill, 1997.

Mayer, Toby. *Keys to the Arcana: Shahrastānī's Esoteric Commentary on the Qur'an: A Translation of the Commentary on Sūrat Al Fātiḥa from Muḥammad b. ʿAbd Al-Karīm Al-Shahrastānī's Mafātīḥ Al-asrār Wa Maṣābīḥ Al-abrār.* Oxford: Oxford University Press in Association with the Institute of Ismaili Studies, 2009.

Mazzaoui, Michel M. *The Origins of the Ṣafawids: Šīʿism, Ṣūfism, and the Ġulāt.* Wiesbaden: F. Steiner, 1972.

McAuliffe, Jane Dammen, ed. *The Encyclopedia of the Quran.* Leiden: Brill Academic Publishers, 2004.

McGinn, Bernard. *Visions of the End: Apocalyptic Traditions in the Middle Ages.* New York: Columbia University Press, 1979.

Meier, F. "Der ʿUrknall': Eine Idee des Abū Bakr ar-Rāzī." *Oriens* 33 (1992): 1–21.

Melchert, Christoph. *The Formation of the Sunni Schools of Law, 9th–10th Centuries* C.E. Leiden: Brill, 1997.

Melton, Gordon. "Perspective: Toward a Definition of 'New Religion.'" *Nova Religio* 8, no. 1 (July 2004): 73–87.

Merchant, Alnoor Jehangir. "'And the Word of Your Lords Has Been Fulfilled in Truthfulness and Righteousness': Qur'anic Instructions on Fatimid Coinage, AH 296–488/AD 909–1095." In *Word of God, Art of Man: The Qur'an and Its Creative Expressions: Selected Proceedings from the International Colloquium, London, 18–21 October 2003*, ed. Fahmida Suleman, 105–22. Oxford: Oxford University Press in association with the Institute of Ismaili Studies, 2007.

Michot, Jean. *La destinée de l'homme selon Avicenne: Le retour à Dieu (maʿād) et l'imagination.* Louvain-la-Neuve: Peeters, 1986.

Mir-Kasimov, Orkhan. *Words of Power: Ḥurūfī Teachings between Shīʿism and Sufism in Medieval Islam.* London: I. B. Tauris, 2014.

Mitha, Farouk. *Al-Ghazālī and the Ismailis: A Debate on Reason and Authority in Medieval Islam.* London: I. B. Tauris in association with the Institute of Ismaili Studies, 2001.

Morris, James W. *The Master and the Disciple: An Early Islamic Spiritual Dialogue; Arabic Edition and English Translation of Jaʿfar b. Manṣūr al-Yaman's* Kitāb al-ʿĀlim wa'l-ghulām. London: I. B. Tauris in association with the Institute of Ismaili Studies, 2001.

Morrison, Robert G. "The Portrayal of Nature in a Medieval Qur'an Commentary." *Studia Islamica* 93 (2002): 115–37.

Nagel, Tilman. "Die Qiṣaṣ al-anbiyāʾ-ein Beitrag zur arabischen Literaturgeschichte." Ph.D. diss., Rheinische Friedrich Wilhelms Univerität zu Bonn, 1967.

Nasr, Seyyed Hossein. *An Introduction to Islamic Cosmological Doctrines: Conceptions of Nature and Methods Used for Its Study by the Ikhwān al-Ṣafā,' al-Bīrūnī, and Ibn Sīnā.* Cambridge, Mass.: Belknap Press of Harvard University Press, 1964.

Netton, Ian. *Muslim Neoplatonists: An Introduction to the Thought of the Brethren of Purity.* London: G. Allen and Unwin, 1982.

Newby, Gordon. *The Making of the Last Prophet: A Reconstruction of the Earliest Biography of Muhammad.* Columbia: University of South Carolina Press, 1989.

The New Princeton Encyclopedia of Poetry and Poetics. Princeton, N.J.: Princeton University Press, 1993.

Nomoto, Shin. "Early Ismāʿīlī Thought on Prophecy According to the Kitāb al-Iṣlāḥ by Abū Ḥātim al-Rāzī (d. ca. 322/934–5)." Ph.D. diss., McGill University, Institute of Islamic Studies, 1999.

Nora, Pierre. "Between Memory and History: Les lieux de mémoire." *Representations* (1989): 7–24.

Nuckolls, Charles W. "Cognitive Anthropology." In *A Companion to Cognitive Science*, ed. William Bechtel and George Graham, 140–46. Malden, Mass.: Blackwell Publishers, 1998.

Pauliny, Ján. "Some Remarks on the *Qiṣaṣ al-'anbīyā'* Works in Arabic literature." In *The Qur'ān: Formative Interpretation*, ed. Andrew Rippin, 313–27. Brookfield, Vt.: Ashgate, 1999.

Pellitteri, Antonino. "The Historical-Ideological Framework of Islamic Fāṭimid Sicily (4th–10th c.) with Reference to the Works of the Qāḍī l-Nuʿmān." *Al-Masāq: Studia Arabo-Islamica Mediterranea* 7, no. 1 (1994): 111–63.

Pickthall, Marmaduke. *The Glorious Koran: A Bi-lingual Edition with English Translation, Introduction, and Notes.* Albany: State University of New York Press, 1976.

Pines, Shlomo. "The Spiritual Force Permeating the Cosmos According to a Passage in the Treatise *On the Principles of the All* Ascribed to Alexander of Aphrodisas." In *Studies in Arabic Version of Greek Texts and in Medieval Science,* edited by Shlomo Pines, 252–355. Jerusalem: Magnes Press; Leiden: E. J. Brill, 1986.

Poonawala, Ismail K. *Biobibliography of Ismāʿīlī Literature.* Malibu, Calif.: Undena Publications, 1977.

——. "Ismāʿīlī Manuscripts from Yemen." *Journal of Islamic Manuscripts* 5, no. 2 (2014): 220–45.

——. "Isma'li *ta'wīl* of the Qur'ān." In *Approaches to the History of the Interpretation of the Qur'an,* ed. Andrew Rippin, 199–205. Oxford: Oxford University Press, 1988.

——. "Al-Qāḍī Al-Nu'mān and Ismāʿīlī Jurisprudence." In *Ismaili History and Thought,* Farhad Daftary, 117–43. Cambridge: Cambridge University Press, 1996.

Poor, Daryoush Mohammad. *Authority without Territory: The Aga Khan Development Network and the Ismaili Imamate.* New York: Palgrave Macmillan, 2014.

Pyysiäinen, Ilkka. "Holy Book—a Treasury of the Incomprehensible: The Invention of Writing and Religious Cognition." *Numen* 46, no. 3 (1999): 269–90.

Qutbuddin, Saifiyah. "History of the Da'udi Bohra Tayyibis in Modern Times: The da'is, the Da'wat and the Community." In A *Modern History of the Ismailis: Continuity and Change in a Muslim Community,* ed. Farhard Daftary, 297–330. London: I. B. Tauris, 2011.

Redfield, Robert, Friedrich Georg Friedmann, and David Rees. *The Ethnographic Moment.* New Brunswick, N.J.: Transaction Publishers, 2006.

Reynolds, Gabriel Said. *The Qur'an and its biblical subtext.* Vol. 10. New York: Routledge, 2010.

Robbins, Vernon K. "Conceptual Blending and Early Christianity." In *Explaining Christian Origins and Early Judaism: Contributions from Cognitive and Social Science,* ed. Petri Luomanen, 161–98. Leiden: Brill, 2007.

Roggema, Barbara. *The Legend of Sergius Baḥīrā: Eastern Christian Apologetics and Apocalyptic in Response to Islam.* Leiden: Brill, 2013.

Rosenthal, Franz. *The History of al-Ṭabarī.* Vol 1. *General Introduction.* Albany: State University of New York Press, 1989.

Rowson, Everett. "Cant and Argot in Cairo Colloquial Arabic." *Newsletter of the American Research Center in Egypt* 122 (1983): 13–24.

——. "The Theology of Aristotle and Some Other Pseudo-Aristotelian Texts Reconsidered." *Journal of the American Oriental Society* 112 (1992): 478–84.

——. "An Unpublished Work by al-ʿĀmirī and the Date of the Arabic *De Causis.*" *Journal of the American Oriental Society* 104 (1984): 193–99.

Rubin, Uri. "Apocalypse and Authority in Islamic Tradition: The Emergence of the Twelve Leaders." *Al-Qantara* 18, no. 1 (1997): 11–42.

——. *Between Bible and Qur'ān: The Children of Israel and the Islamic Self-Image.* Princeton, NJ: Darwin, 1999.

——. "Prophets and Progenitors in the Early Shi'a Tradition." *Jerusalem Studies in Arabic and Islam* 1 (1979): 41–65.

Rudolph, Kurt. *Die Gnosis.* Götingen: Vandenhoeck and Ruprecht, 1977.

Rustow, Marina. *Heresy and the Politics of Community: The Jews of the Fatimid Caliphate.* Ithaca, N.Y.: Cornell University Press, 2008.

Saleh, Walid A. *The Formation of the Classical Tafsīr Tradition: The Qur'ān Commentary of al-Thaʿlabī (d. 427/1035).* Leiden: Brill, 2004.

———. *In Defense of the Bible: A Critical Edition and an Introduction to al-Biqāʿī's Bible Treatise.* Leiden: Brill, 2008.

Sambursky, S. *The Physical World of Late Antiquity.* Princeton, N.J.: Princeton University Press, 1962.

Sanders, Paula. *Ritual, Politics, and the City in Fatimid Egypt.* Albany: State University of New York Press, 1994.

Schacter, Daniel L., and Randy L. Buckner. "Priming and the brain." *Neuron* 20, no. 2 (1998): 185–95.

Schmidtke, Sabine. "The Muslim Reception of Biblical Materials: Ibn Qutayba and His Aʿlām al-nubuwwa." *Islam and Christian-Muslim Relations* 22, no. 3 (2011): 249–74.

Scholem, Gershom. *Jewish Gnosticism, Merkabah Mysticism, and Talmudic Tradition.* New York: Jewish Theological Society of America, 1960.

Sezgin, Fuat. *Geschichte des arabischen Schriftums.* Leiden: E. J. Brill, 1967–.

El-Shamsy, Ahmed. "The Social Construction of Orthodoxy." In *The Cambridge Companion to Classical Islamic Theology,* ed. Timothy J. Winter, 97–117. Cambridge: Cambridge University Press, 2008.

Shoemaker, Stephen J. "'The Reign of God Has Come': Eschatology and Empire in Late Antiquity and Early Islam." *Arabica* 61 (2014): 514–58.

Simmel, Georg. *The Sociology of Georg Simmel.* Edited and translated by K. H. Wolff. Glencoe, Ill.: Free Press, 1950.

Sindawi, Khalid. "Noah and Noah's Ark as the Primordial Model of Shīʿism in Shīʿite Literature." *Quaderni di Studi Arabi,* new ser., 1 (2006): 29–48.

Stark, Rodney, and W. S. Bainbridge. *The Future of Religion: Secularization, Revival, and Cult Formation.* Berkeley: University of California Press, 1985.

Steigerwald, Diana. "Ismāʿīlī ta'wīl." In *The Blackwell Companion to the Qur'ān,* ed. Andrew Rippin, 386–400. Malden, Mass.: John Wiley and Sons, 2006.

Stern, S. M. "Abu'l-Qasim al-Bustī and His Refutation of Ismāʿīlism." *Journal of the Royal Asiatic Society* (April 1961): 14–35. Reprinted in *Studies in Early Ismāʿīlism.* Jerusalem: Magnes Press, 1983.

———. "Cairo as the Center of the Ismaili Movement." In *Studies in Early Ismāʿīlism,* 234–56. Jerusalem: Magnes Press, 1983.

———. "The Earliest Cosmological Doctrines of Ismāʿīlism." In *Studies in Early Ismāʿīlism,* 3–29. Jerusalem: Magnes Press, 1983.

———. "The Early Ismāʿīlī Missionaries in North-West Persia and in Khurāsān and Transoxania." *Bulletin of the School of Oriental and African Studies* 23, no. 1 (February 1960): 56–90.

———. "Heteredox Ismāʿīlism at the Time of al-Muʿizz." *Bulletin of the School of Oriental and African Studies* 17, no. 1 (February 1955): 10–33.

———. "Ismāʿīlī propaganda and Fāṭimid rule in Sind," *Islamic Culture* 23, (1949): 298–307.

———. "Ja'far b. Manṣūr al-Yaman's Poems on the Rebellion of Abū Yazīd." *Studies in Early Ismāʿīlism,* edited by S. M. Stern, 146–62. Jerusalem: Magnes Press, 1983.

Stewart, Devin. *Islamic Legal Orthodoxy: Twelver Shiite Responses to the Sunni legal System.* Salt Lake City: University of Utah Press, 1998.

Stroumsa, Guy, and Hans G. Kippenberg. *Secrecy and Concealment: Studies in the History of Mediterranean and Near Eastern Religions.* Leiden: Brill, 2005.

Taylor, Richard C. "The *Kalām fī maḥd al-khair* (*Liber de causis*) in the Islamic Philosophical Milieu." In *Pseudo-Aristotle in the Middle Ages: The Theology and Other Texts,* ed. Jill Kraye, W. F. Ryan, and C. B. Schmitt, 37–52. London: Warburg Institute, 1986.

Thomas, Samuel. *The "Mysteries" of Qumran: Mystery, Secrecy and Esotericism in the Dead Sea Scrolls.* Atlanta: Society of Biblical Literature, 2009.

Toorawa, Shawkat M. *Ibn Abī Ṭāhir Ṭayfūr and Arabic Writerly Culture: A Ninth-Century Bookman in Baghdad.* London: Routledge Curzon 2005.

Tottoli, Roberto. *Biblical Prophets in the Qur'ān and Muslim Literature.* Richmond, Surrey: Curzon, 2001.

——. "Origin and Use of the Term *isrā'īlīyāt* in Muslim Literature." *Arabica* 46, no. 2 (1999): 193–210.

Traboulsi, Samer F. "The Ṭayyibī Ismāʿīlīs in Medieval Yemen." Ph.D. diss., Princeton University, 2005.

Treadwell, W. Luke. "The Political History of the Samanid State." D. Phil., Oxford University, 1991.

Tucker, William. *Mahdis and Millenarians: Shi'ite Extremists in Early Muslim Iraq.* Cambridge: Cambridge University Press, 2008.

——. "Rebels and Gnostics: al-Mughīrīya ibn Saʿīd and the Mughīriyya." *Arabica* 12 (1975): 33–47.

Tulving, Endel, and Daniel L. Schacter. "Priming and Human Memory Systems." *Science* 247 (1990): 301–6.

Urban, Hugh B. "The Torment of Secrecy: Ethical and Epistemological Problems in the Study of Esoteric Traditions." *History of Religions* (1998): 209–48.

Virani, Shafique N. *The Ismāʿīlīs in the Middle Ages: A History of Survival, a Search for Salvation.* Oxford: Oxford University Press, 2007.

Wagner, Richard K., Christopher Schatschneider and Caroline Phythian-Sence, eds. *Beyond Decoding: the Behavioral and Biological Foundations of Reading Comprehension.* New York. The Guilford Press, 2009.

Walker, Paul. *Abū Yaʿqūb al-Sijistānī: Intellectual Missionary.* London: I. B. Tauris in association with the Institute of Ismaili Studies, 1996.

——. *Early Philosophical Shīʿism: The Ismāʿīlī Neoplatonism of Abū Yaʿqūb al-Sijistānī.* Cambridge: Cambridge University Press, 1993.

——. *Exploring an Islamic Empire: Fāṭimid History and Its Sources.* London: I. B. Tauris, 2002.

——. *Ḥamīd al-Dīn al-Kirmānī: Ismaili Thought in the Age of al-Ḥākim.* London: I. B. Tauris in association with the Institute of Ismaili Studies, 1999.

——. *Master of the Age: An Islamic Treatise on the Necessity of Government.* London: I. B. Tauris in association with the Institute of Ismaili Studies, 2008.

——. *The Wellsprings of Wisdom: A Study of Abū Yaʿqūb al-Sijistānī's Kitāb al-yanābiʿ.* Salt Lake City: University of Utah Press, 1994.

Wasserstrom, Steven. *Between Muslim and Jew: The Problem of Symbiosis under Early Islam.* Princeton, N.J.: Princeton University Press, 1995.

———. "The Moving Finger Writes: Mughira B. Said's Islamic Gnosis and the Myths of Its Rejection." *History of Religions* 25 (1985): 1–29.

———. *Religion after Religion: Gershom Scholem, Mircea Eliade, Henry Corbin at Eranus.* Princeton, N.J.: Princeton University Press, 1999.

Wensinck, A. J. *A Handbook of Early Muhammadan Tradition, Alphabetically Arranged.* Leiden: E. J. Brill, 1927.

Williams, Michael A. *Rethinking "Gnosticism": An Argument for Dismantling a Dubious Category.* Princeton, N.J.: Princeton University Press, 1996.

Wilson, Bryan R. *The Social Dimensions of Sectarianism: Sects and New Religious Movements in Contemporary Society.* Oxford: Clarendon, 1990.

Yamamoto, Keiji, and Charles Burnett. *Abu Maʿshar on Historical Astrology: The Book of Religions and Dynasties.* Leiden: E. J. Brill, 2000.

Yücesoy, Hayrettin. *Messianic Beliefs and Imperial Politics in Medieval Islam: The ʿAbbāsid Caliphate in the Early Ninth Century.* Columbia: University of South Carolina Press, 2009.

Zaman, Muhammad Qasim. *Religion and Politics under the Early ʿAbbāsids: The Emergence of the Proto-Sunnī Elite.* Leiden: Brill, 1997.

Zimmermann, Fritz W. "The Origins of the So-Called *Theology of Aristotle.*" In *Pseudo-Aristotle in the Middle Ages: The Theology and Other Texts,* ed. Jill Kraye, W. F. Ryan, and C. B. Schmitt, 110–240. London: Warburg Institute, 1986.

INDEX